dustrial-
sities in
manent
enth
ver-
er

MOCRATIC LAW

The Berkeley Tanner Lectures

The Tanner Lectures on Human Values were established by the American scholar, ist, and philanthropist Obert Clark Tanner; they are presented annually at nine unive the United States and England. The University of California, Berkeley became a perm host of annual Tanner Lectures in the academic year 2000–2001. This work is the fourt in a series of books based on the Berkeley Tanner Lectures. The volume includes a revised sion of the lectures that Seana Valentine Shiffrin presented at Berkeley in April 2017, togeth with commentaries by Niko Kolodny, Richard R. W. Brooks, and Anna Stilz, as well as a fina rejoinder by Professor Shiffrin. The volume is edited by Hannah Ginsborg, who also contributes an introduction. The Berkeley Tanner Lecture Series was established in the belief that these distinguished lectures, together with the lively debates stimulated by their presentation in Berkeley, deserve to be made available to a wider audience. Additional volumes are in preparation.

Kinch Hoekstra
R. Jay Wallace
Series Editors

RECENT VOLUMES IN THE SERIES

Derek Parfit, *On What Matters: Volumes 1& 2*
Edited by Samuel Scheffler
With T. M. Scanlon, Susan Wolf, Allen Wood, and Barbara Herman

Jeremy Waldron, *Dignity, Rank, and Rights*
Edited by Meir Dan-Cohen
With Wai Chee Dimock, Don Herzog, and Michael Rosen

Samuel Scheffler, *Death and the Afterlife*
Edited by Niko Kolodny
With Susan Wolf, Harry G. Frankfurt, Seana Valentine Shiffrin, and Niko Kolodny

F. M. Kamm, *The Trolley Problem Mysteries*
Edited by Eric Rakowski
With Judith Jarvis Thomson, Thomas Hurka, and Shelly Kagan

Eric Santner, *The Weight of All Flesh: On the Subject Matter of Political Economy*
Edited by Kevis Goodman
With Bonnie Honig, Peter E. Gordon, and Hent de Vries

Didier Fassin, *The Will to Punish*
Edited by Christopher Kutz
With Bruce Western, Rebecca M. McLennan, and David W. Garland

Philip Pettit, *The Birth of Ethics*
Edited by Kinch Hoekstra
With Michael Tomasello

Arthur Ripstein, *Rules for Wrongdoers*
Edited by Saira Mohamed
With Oona A. Hathaway, Christopher Kutz, and Jeff McMahan

DEMOCRATIC LAW

Seana Valentine Shiffrin

With Commentaries by

Niko Kolodny, Richard R. W. Brooks, and Anna Stilz

Edited and introduced by

Hannah Ginsborg

OXFORD
UNIVERSITY PRESS

OXFORD
UNIVERSITY PRESS

Oxford University Press is a department of the University of Oxford. It furthers the University's objective of excellence in research, scholarship, and education by publishing worldwide. Oxford is a registered trade mark of Oxford University Press in the UK and certain other countries.

Published in the United States of America by Oxford University Press
198 Madison Avenue, New York, NY 10016, United States of America.

Library of Congress Cataloging-in-Publication Data
Names: Shiffrin, Seana Valentine, author. | Kolodny, Niko, contributor. |
Brooks, Richard Rexford Wayne, contributor. | Stilz, Anna, 1976–
contributor. | Ginsborg, Hannah, editor, writer of introduction.
Title: Democratic law / Seana Valentine Shiffrin, with commentaries by Niko Kolodny,
Richard R. W. Brooks, Anna Stilz ; edited and introduced by Hannah Ginsborg.
Description: New York, NY : Oxford University Press, [2021] |
Series: Berkeley Tanner lectures | Includes index.
Identifiers: LCCN 2021016416 (print) | LCCN 2021016417 (ebook) |
ISBN 9780190084486 (hardback) | ISBN 9780190084509 (epub)
Subjects: LCSH: Law—Philosophy. | Democracy.
Classification: LCC K240 .S55 2021 (print) |
LCC K240 (ebook) | DDC 340/.1—dc23
LC record available at https://lccn.loc.gov/2021016416
LC ebook record available at https://lccn.loc.gov/2021016417

DOI: 10.1093/oso/9780190084486.001.0001

1 3 5 7 9 8 6 4 2

Printed by Sheridan Books, Inc., United States of America

CONTENTS

COMMENTS

ACKNOWLEDGMENTS

I am grateful to the Tanner Foundation and the University of California, Berkeley for the occasion to create these lectures and to the three Tanner commentators, Richard R. W. Brooks, Niko Kolodny, and Anna Stilz, for our dialogue and its attendant criticism, advice, and warm support. I originally delivered two lectures in April 2017. Our conversations on that occasion prompted me to expand the second lecture into two separate chapters, as presented here.

In addition to the stimulating feedback from the commentators and the audience at UC Berkeley, I also benefited from help and criticism about these ideas in one venue or another from other friends and colleagues, especially Devon Carbado, Joshua Cohen, Christopher Essert, Stephen Gardbaum, Mark Greenberg, Barbara Herman, A. J. Julius, Liam Murphy, Richard Re, William Rubenstein, Larry Sager, Samuel Scheffler, Steve Shiffrin, Mary Valentine, Jeremy Waldron, R. Jay Wallace, and Jennifer Whiting. Hannah Ginsborg was generous both as a critical interlocutor and as a sympathetic and encouraging editor.

I also received insightful feedback from audiences at UC Berkeley at the lectures and from audiences at New York University Law

School; University of California, Los Angeles (UCLA) School of Law; University of Michigan Law School; University of Pittsburgh; University of Southern California; and the University of Sydney Law School, who heard versions of these ideas at different, sometimes partial, stages. I have been thinking about these themes and issues for some time. Over the years, Alexander Cooper, Jenna Donohue, Sarah Fisher, Erin Hallagan, Haruka Hatori, Gabbrielle Johnson, Nicole Miller, Matthew Strawbridge, and Jordan Wallace-Wolf provided excellent research assistance, funded through the generosity of the Hugh & Hazel Darling Law Library at UCLA School of Law and the UCLA Academic Senate.

Seana Valentine Shiffrin
January 2020

CONTRIBUTORS

Richard R. W. Brooks is the Emilie M. Bullowa Professor of Law at New York University. His scholarly approach combines economic and historical methods with juris-analytic modes of reasoning and doctrine common to private law fields such as property, contract, and fiduciary and corporate law. An exemplar of this approach is found in *Saving the Neighborhood: Racially Restrictive Covenants, Law, and Social Norms* (Harvard University Press, 2013) (with Carol M. Rose).

Hannah Ginsborg is Willis S. and Marion Slusser Professor of Philosophy at the University of California, Berkeley. She is the author of *The Normativity of Nature: Essays on Kant's Critique of Judgement* (Oxford University Press, 2015) and has published articles in a range of areas including Kant, Wittgenstein, philosophy of mind, and theory of meaning.

Niko Kolodny is Professor of Philosophy at the University of California, Berkeley. He works in moral and political philosophy and has written papers on love, rationality, promises, and democracy, among other subjects.

SEANA VALENTINE SHIFFRIN is Professor of Philosophy and Pete Kameron Professor of Law and Social Justice at the University of California, Los Angeles. Shiffrin's work in both law and philosophy focuses on the social conditions and communicative ethical structures that support individual autonomy and egalitarian relationships. Her research has addressed issues concerning contracts, promises, misrepresentation and deception, freedom of speech, intellectual property, distributive justice, anti-discrimination, procreation, and abortion. She is the author of *Speech Matters: On Lying, Morality, and the Law* (Princeton University Press, 2014). She serves as an advisory editor of *Philosophy and Public Affairs* and is a member of the American Academy of Arts and Sciences.

ANNA STILZ is Laurance S. Rockefeller Professor of Politics and Human Values at Princeton University. She is the author of *Liberal Loyalty: Freedom, Obligation, and the State* (Princeton University Press, 2009) and *Territorial Sovereignty: A Philosophical Exploration* (Oxford University Press, 2019), as well as many articles on various topics in political philosophy. She is Editor-in-Chief of *Philosophy and Public Affairs.*

DEMOCRATIC LAW

Introduction

HANNAH GINSBORG

Democracy is widely recognized to be in serious trouble. Around the world, an increasing number of formerly democratic countries, or countries which had realistic aspirations toward democracy, have come under autocratic rule. Populism has been on the rise, fueled by rapidly increasing economic inequality, the power of social media to spread misinformation and demagoguery, and a weakening of trust in traditional news media. In the United States in particular, we have witnessed, over the past four years, an alarming series of attempts by an elected leader to undermine or subvert democratic institutions for corrupt ends, along with a shocking level of acquiescence by other elected officials in his self-serving actions and statements. In a number of countries, increased political polarization, exacerbated by the willingness of elected leaders to fan the flames of racism, xenophobia, anti-gay sentiment, and other forms of prejudice, has made it increasingly harder for democratic legislatures to function effectively and in a way which inspires trust in citizens. All of this raises questions about whether democratic forms of government can survive. Can we resist the current trend toward authoritarian rule, both worldwide, and (going by the past four years) in the United States? But

Hannah Ginsborg, *Introduction* In: *Democratic Law*. Edited by: Hannah Ginsborg, Oxford University Press.
 DOI: 10.1093/oso/9780190084486.003.0001

it also—and perhaps more fundamentally—gives a new urgency to questions about what democracy is and why it is of value. What makes a form of government qualify as genuinely democratic in the first place? And why, given all the problems besetting current democratic regimes, including their vulnerability to manipulation and destabilization by self-serving demagogues and other hostile forces, should we continue to see democratic rule as a positive thing, something which societies should aspire to and seek to preserve?

The text which forms the core of this book—a reworking of the Tanner Lectures that Seana Shiffrin presented at Berkeley in April 2017—speaks in part to this last set of questions. Although its ostensible focus is not democracy as such, but rather the nature of law in a democratic society, Shiffrin's views about law are inseparable from her conception of the nature and function of democracy. Stated very briefly, the thesis of *Democratic Law* is that law in a democracy has a communicative function. As Shiffrin explains in the first chapter (constituting Part I of her main text), law is the primary means by which we, as participants in a democratic society, fulfill our obligation of conveying to one another a message of equal respect, a message which affirms each person's inclusion as an equal in the society to which we belong. However, Shiffrin makes clear that it is not just law within a democracy, but also democracy itself, which has this communicative function. It is part of the value of democracy that it allows us, both through the generation, articulation, and implementation of law, and through other means intrinsic to a democratic society (e.g., participation in elections, involvement in community groups, educational activities, conversations about politically relevant issues), to realize the conditions of justice by communicating respect to our fellow citizens. Law plays a uniquely important role in allowing us to fulfill the communicative function of democracy, and the second and third chapters of *Democratic Law* (constituting Part II) explore some of the implications of this point for specific legal issues regarding the preemption of common law by statutory law and the balancing of state interests and constitutional rights. But Shiffrin's detailed discussion of these legal issues in these chapters is at the same time a deepening of her account of the distinctive value of democracy. Indeed, it is part of the overarching aim of Shiffrin's work to show that law and democracy need to be considered together. For Shiffrin, we cannot arrive at a complete understanding of the nature of either law or democracy without understanding both the essential role played by law within a democracy and the dependence of law, for its essence, on a democratic context. Her exploration of the interconnection of law and democracy yields a powerful, ambitious, and wide-ranging set of ideas that—as I will indicate further at the end of this introduction—speak clearly and inspiringly to the currently prevailing sense that democracy is in crisis.

To understand Shiffrin's argument, we need to be clear about the conception of democracy that serves as her pretheoretical starting point. It is often thought that the defining characteristic of democracy is that social policy is determined on something like a "one person, one vote" principle, either through referenda on specific policies or, more typically, through the election of representatives. If this is our starting conception of democracy, then we are likely, in trying to understand the value of democracy, to focus on the value of elections and referenda as a means of determining policy, and to ask why a system in which we elect our leaders should be thought to serve the general interest better than, say, a system where leadership roles are inherited or assigned on the basis of supposed merit or fitness to rule.[1] But Shiffrin starts out with a very different understanding of democracy. Her initial "rough characterization"

1. This represents, at least in part, the kind of approach taken by Niko Kolodny. See his "Rule over None I: What Justifies Democracy?" *Philosophy & Public Affairs* 42, no. 3 (2014): 195–229.

describes it as a system that "treats all its members with equal concern, regards their lives as of equal importance, and treats all competent members of the community . . . as, by right and by conception, the equal and exclusive co-authors of and co-contributors to the system, its rules, its actions, its directives, its communications, and its other outputs" (p. 20). In requiring that citizens in a democracy be treated as "co-authors" of laws and other products of government, this conception of democracy goes substantially beyond one characterized in terms of elections. It requires in particular a culture of free speech, in which citizens regularly exercise their right not only to engage with one another in reasoned discussion about substantive policy issues, but also to express their views (and the reasons for them) to those in positions of authority and to have those views considered seriously and afforded an appropriately reasoned response.[2] It is thus intrinsic to a genuine democracy that the laws that govern it are not produced, top-down, by elected officials, judges, and administrators, but rather emerge, bottom-up, from citizens' reasoned exchange of views with one another and with those in authority.

Another aspect of Shiffrin's starting point that deserves emphasis is the idea that democracy and law need to be considered from a moral perspective. More specifically, democracy is a means for us to fulfill our moral obligations, in particular those required by justice in a political context. Drawing on Rawls' conception of the basis of equality among persons, Shiffrin takes us to be equal in respect of two higher order moral capacities, the first (roughly) to pursue a life structured by our conception of the good and the second (again, roughly)

2. Proponents of a voting-focused conception of democracy are also likely to view free speech as essential to democracy since (for example) restrictions on free speech deprive citizens of the information they need to vote in a way that reflects their interests. But this is a different rationale for free speech than that offered by Shiffrin.

to understand and pursue justice.[3] What is relevant in this context is the second of these capacities, which can also be glossed as the capacity to "act morally and justly by treating others' lives as valuable, and, politically, as equally important to our own."[4] Such a capacity, according to Shiffrin, can be adequately exercised only in a democracy, since it is only as members of a democracy that we can actively contribute to a system which "treats all its members with equal concern [and] regards their lives as of equal importance" (p. 20, quoted earlier). The reasoned exchange of views from which democratic law emerges is not, then, a matter of our expressing personal preferences and attempting to give reasons as to why they should prevail over the personal preferences of others. Rather, it is a way of articulating and making specific our collective moral commitments and, in particular, how we think the demands of justice should be implemented. The significance of democracy for Shiffrin lies, then, not only in what it does for us, but also in what it allows us to do for others: namely, fulfill our duties toward them. The question of why democracy should be preferred over other systems of government is not (or at least not only) a matter of the supposedly greater benefits conferred on us in our role as recipients of what government provides. It is primarily a matter of the unique character of democracy in enabling us, as contributors to government, to exercise our capacity for the pursuit of justice in a political context.

With these general considerations in mind, we can turn to Shiffrin's specific argument, in Part I of *Democratic Law*, for the communicative role of democracy in general and of democratic law in particular. The argument invokes another idea from Rawls, that of

3. This is made clear in the Replies, at p. 191; see also Seana Valentine Shiffrin, *Speech Matters: On Lying, Morality, and the Law* (Princeton: Princeton University Press, 2014), 168–69.

4. Shiffrin, *Speech Matters*, at 169.

self-respect as a 'primary good'—indeed, the most important primary good—and its dependence on the awareness that one is respected by others.[5] For Rawls, this latter consideration gives rise to what he calls a "natural duty of mutual respect," a duty which we owe to all human beings as our moral equals and which includes, among other things, civil treatment and willingness to provide reasons for our actions, especially those that affect others' interests.[6] But Shiffrin draws from it a more specific duty that we, as citizens of a state, owe to our fellow citizens in particular.[7] We must communicate to others our recognition of them not just as moral but also as political equals: that is, as having an equal status and equal claim to full inclusion in the political community we share with them. Moreover, this communication cannot be a mere verbal affirmation, but must involve a commitment to action appropriate to the status we recognize one another to have. If we fail to communicate with one another in this way, then we fail to fulfill a requirement of justice, that of supplying the social conditions necessary for all citizens to enjoy the essential primary good of self-respect.

The distinctive value of democracy as compared to other political systems is that it allows us to fulfill that communicative duty.[8] It does so primarily, although not exclusively, by making us co-authors of law. Because law in a properly democratic society expresses and articulates the moral commitments of that society's members, and

5. Primary goods are goods which every rational person is presumed to want; see John Rawls, *A Theory of Justice* (Cambridge: Harvard University Press, 1971), 62). Rawls' theory of justice is constructed around the idea of their fair distribution. Shiffrin quotes Rawls' "understatement" that self-respect is "perhaps" the most important primary good (*id.* at 396 and 440), but some other passages (*id.* at 422 and 525) are unequivocal about its preeminence.
6. See Rawls, *Theory of Justice*, at 179 and at 337–38.
7. "Citizen" here should be understood in a broad sense, potentially including residents who, under current law, do not qualify for legal citizenship. See p. 181.
8. For an especially clear statement, see Ch. 1, fn. 38 (p. 52), where Shiffrin contrasts her view of democracy with Kolodny's.

because the pursuit of justice, including the mutual recognition of equality and inclusion, is among those moral commitments, our co-authorship of law is a way of communicating the required message. To the extent that I contribute to the process that yields a just statute or a just judicial or administrative decision, the message conveyed by that statute or decision is mine. And whatever the specific content of the law or decision—whether, for example, it guarantees same-sex couples the right to marry across the United States or fixes the per-hour fee at parking meters in a particular locality—it will, in conveying that content, also convey recognition of all citizens as deserving of equal respect. Although the free speech ethos of democracy offers other ways of communicating this recognition, it is only through law that our communication can incorporate a systematic commitment to the kind of action needed to ensure its effectiveness, by publicly binding us to policies aimed at the concrete realization of justice and to an implementation of those policies that is sensitive to the needs and rights of particular individuals.[9] So democracy needs law in order to fulfill the function that constitutes its distinctive value.

What does this tell us about the nature of law? One point which emerges from Part I is that, as indicated earlier, law and democracy are interdependent: not only does democracy need law, but law depends for its essence on a democratic context. We can now see more clearly the significance of the second direction of dependence. If we see the essential task of law as articulating our moral commitments and, more specifically, as communicating those commitments to one another, then law is, strictly speaking, possible only in a democracy. This conclusion may seem surprising given that, for example,

9. The structure of this aspect of Shiffrin's view might be captured by saying that communication of equal recognition is required to secure one very important component of political justice, that is, provision for all citizens of the social bases of self-respect, but that this communication is empty ("cheap talk," as Richard R.W. Brooks puts it in his commentary in this volume) if it fails to manifest commitment to securing the other components of justice.

theocratic oligarchies and dictatorships are commonly thought of as governed by laws. But unless we see the essence of law as determined by its coercive function—a view firmly rejected by Shiffrin—we will regard the edicts of undemocratic regimes as, at the most, degenerate cases of law.[10] The law which is Shiffrin's topic, and which she regards, along with democracy, as a "morally powerful and inspiring human achievement" (p. 18), is law which has evolved in a democratic context or as a result of democratic impulses (which she allows can exist outside of full-fledged democracies; see p. 210).

Part II explores some of the more specific consequences for law of the communicative conception developed in Part I. In Chapter 2, Shiffrin focuses on a specific legal case, *Northwest v. Ginsberg,* where the issue at stake was whether a statutory federal law, the Airline Deregulation Act, could preempt the state rule of common law that parties to a contract must act in good faith when they exercise the duties stipulated by the contract. The Supreme Court ruled unanimously that the statutory law preempted the duty of good faith. Shiffrin argues that this decision was mistaken and, more specifically, that it relied on a reductionist view of law as nothing more than a means of resolving disputes, ignoring its role—central to the communicative conception of democratic law—as publicly articulating our collective moral commitments. (Another important manifestation of this reductionist view, which she mentions in passing, is the encouragement of mandatory private arbitration to resolve disputes which might otherwise go to court, thus inhibiting the bottom-up generation of publicly articulated law.) One of several morals emerging from her discussion of the case bears on the political significance

10. This is perhaps a stronger statement of the second direction of dependence than Shiffrin herself makes, but I believe that it is implicit in her conception of democratic law as the paradigm of law and of its democratic character as the source of its value as a human institution.

of common as opposed to statutory law. If we regard elections as the defining feature of democracy, then we will be inclined to privilege statutory law, since it is made by elected legislatures. But on Shiffrin's communicative view of democracy, common law is no less democratic, and indeed plays an essential democratic role that statutory law cannot play, in that it articulates reasons for decisions about the content of the law. This role is democratic because judges' reasoning in common law is influenced in multiple ways by the contributions of citizens, not only through citizens' more or less direct involvement in court cases (e.g., as litigants, defendants, *amici curiae,* or expert witnesses), but also through the tendency of courts to be responsive to the moral expectations embodied in our customary practices.[11] The duty of good faith articulates an important expectation of this kind, which is part of the reason why Shiffrin finds the Supreme Court decision in *Northwest v. Ginsberg* particularly inimical to a democratic conception of law.

Chapter 3 turns to a different consequence for law of the communicative conception: namely, that legal decisions must be suitably responsive to the role of law in articulating a coherent set of moral commitments. Here Shiffrin considers the issue of "constitutional balancing," an issue that arises when a discretionary state interest appears to be in conflict with a constitutionally guaranteed right. One of the examples she considers is *Washington v. Glucksberg,* a 1997 case in which the Supreme Court upheld as constitutional the state of Washington's prohibition on assisted suicide, citing Washington's "unqualified interest in the preservation of human life" (citation at Ch. 3, fn. 18 (p. 102)). Shiffrin criticizes the reasoning behind the decision for multiple reasons, in particular that the Court took at face value Washington's assertion of its interest in preserving human life, without considering whether other aspects of state law, for example

11. This is brought out especially in the Replies, pp. 211–213.

regarding the death penalty or medical support for the disabled, were consistent with its genuinely having that interest. Part of her aim in the chapter is to make a normative claim about constitutional balancing: it is permissible only when, as she puts it, "the state demonstrates an actual commitment to that interest beyond its mere articulation" (p. 121). But the chapter also illustrates a broader point about the communicative conception of law, in contrast to more outcome-oriented approaches. Because of law's role in articulating and communicating moral commitments, it must be held to a corresponding standard of coherence, one which makes it possible to read the law as expressing a unified moral vision. The Court's reasoning in *Washington v. Glucksberg* was flawed because it failed to recognize, let alone uphold, this standard.

The present volume includes reworkings of three commentaries that were presented on the occasion of Shiffrin's lectures at Berkeley, followed by a reply from Shiffrin. The commentaries are immensely valuable, not only for the light they themselves shed on Shiffrin's initial text, but also for their role in prompting Shiffrin to a deeper and more expansive articulation of her views in the replies. Niko Kolodny's commentary raises a series of probing questions centered primarily on the first chapter. Given that our compliance with law has multiple motivations, including fear of sanctions, how can it be effective in sending the morally required message of equal respect? Why do we have to be authors of the message as opposed to merely affirming a message authored by someone else? Why does the message have to be sent from the collective, rather than from each of us individually? Why, assuming that we do have to be authors and not just signatories of the message, do we have to play an equal role in authoring the message? Why does the function of democratic law as communicating this message give each of us a reason for participating in a democratic system? These questions give rise to two challenges of a more general kind. The first is that Shiffrin's view embodies a tension between the demand that I, as an individual citizen, convey a message of equal respect to my fellow citizens and the idea, presupposed in the thought that this message is conveyed by law, that it is the collective which conveys the message. The second questions the connection Shiffrin draws between the communicative character of law and its dependence on a democratic context. Couldn't law, say in an aristocracy or theocracy, have the role of communicating public commitments without those commitments being democratic?

Richard R. W. Brooks' commentary offers an illuminating restatement and elaboration of key points from each of Shiffrin's three chapters, developing and examining several detailed examples which help make vivid some of the more abstract aspects of her account. He underscores the importance of law as a means for the public communication of moral commitments—in particular commitments to treat one another with equal respect—by invoking the game-theoretic idea of common knowledge. It is not enough for equal respect to be implicit in our interpersonal practices, or even for each of us individually to know that we are respected as equal by our fellow citizens. What is required for the social bases of self-respect is that our commitments be known to be shared, and that that knowledge in turn be known to be shared, and so on ad infinitum. This offers a perspective on the importance of common law from a democratic framework: common law, he suggests, can be seen as a "mechanism for generating common knowledge" about disputes and their resolution (p. 155). Brooks invokes another game-theoretic notion, that of the contrast between "cheap talk" and "costly signaling", in connection with Shiffrin's discussion of constitutional balancing. Where the interests of speaker and addressee are not aligned, cheap talk lacks credibility, and this is something to which courts need to be sensitive in balancing state and constitutional interests.

Anna Stilz's commentary provides a substantive and detailed discussion of four critical questions, two of them reflecting concerns shared also by Kolodny. Like Kolodny, she is concerned about a potential tension between the fact that the requirement to communicate applies to me as an individual citizen and the fact that the messages conveyed by law come from a collective body, the state. For the tension to be resolved, the messages of the collective have to be attributable to each of us individually, but, she suggests, it is unclear how that can be if the attitudes and intentions expressed in the law differ from those which we have as individuals. A second question she shares with Kolodny is that of why the communicative conception of democracy requires that we participate equally in the process through which law is created. In connection with this question, she challenges Shiffrin's defense of the democratic character of common law: since common law is produced by judges, in what sense can we be regarded as its co-authors? Two further questions concern, respectively, the scope of our duty to communicate respect to others and the permissibility and value of discretionary state ends. Regarding the former, Stilz notes that we are morally obliged to communicate respect not just to fellow citizens, but also to human agents generally, and she suggests that more needs to be said about the relations which constitute us as fellow members of a democratic state. Regarding the latter, she takes issue with Shiffrin's suggestion, in her discussion of constitutional balancing, that discretionary state ends are not only permissible, but also valuable in promoting a state's distinctive identity. As she points out, many discretionary ends that might be adopted by states—for example, the promotion of the national culture of a subgroup within the state, or the preservation of fetal life—might appear to be incompatible with equal respect for all of the state's citizens.

I will not here attempt to summarize the rich and detailed replies that Shiffrin offers to these commentaries. I will, however, mention her replies to the two concerns that are shared by Kolodny and Stilz, since I think that these bring out aspects of her view that deserve special emphasis. Shiffrin's reply to the question about equal participation draws on her central thought that democracy is a means not only of serving our interests, but of enabling us to fulfill our moral obligations. As moral equals, we have an equal responsibility for justice, and it is because of this responsibility that we must have an equal say in the process through which democratic law is constructed. This distinguishes our participation in democracies and democratically structured voluntary associations from the relationship citizens typically have to the organizations which employ them, although, invoking points made by Brooks, Shiffrin offers reasons for promoting increased democratic structure in corporations as well. On the question about the tension between the individual and the collective, her reply again draws on her conception of democracy as a way of fulfilling our moral commitments and of democratic law as an expression of those commitments. In a well-functioning democracy—one in which democratic processes and the workings of government are not impeded by such social pathologies as extreme economic inequality, the wilful spread of misinformation, racial discrimination, and corruption—the laws generated will all express the fundamental commitment to justice which, following Rawls, Shiffrin assumes that we share. As an individual I may dissent from a particular law or decision on the grounds that it fails to serve justice as effectively as the competing proposal which I prefer. But I can still endorse the commitment to justice incorporated in the law, and, to that extent, I can think of the law as speaking for me, even if I view it as falling short in its realization of the shared commitment.

This brings us back to our starting theme, that democracy is in trouble. The United States, to take a salient example, is far from being a well-functioning democracy, and many of the decisions made by its government, especially under the administration of Donald Trump, are not merely inadequate implementations of ideals of justice, but antithetical to justice. That makes it especially difficult, for citizens of the United States and of other states where democracy is on shaky ground, to regard our government and the laws to which we are subject as speaking for us. But this is not a reason for skepticism about Shiffrin's communicative account of democracy and law. On the contrary, it is a reason to welcome her account as offering both an explanation of why the decline of democracy in the United States and elsewhere is so dismaying and a model of what we should aspire to in our attempts to reform our flawed or damaged democratic institutions. Shiffrin at times expresses concerns that her account is somehow out of place at a time when democracy faces such obvious and serious threats. Commenting on her criticisms of current approaches to common law and constitutional balancing in Part II, she refers to the "oddity of dwelling on a slow-acting disease afflicting some trees while a fire threatens the forest" (p. 63), and, at the conclusion of her replies, after noting some egregious recent abuses of the US political system, she says that it can "feel precious" to persist in articulating abstract ideals whose realization "seems more than distant" (p. 222). Although Shiffrin goes on to address these concerns, she is not emphatic enough, it seems to me, in dismissing them as misplaced. Her theoretical elaboration of the aims of democracy, combined with her demonstrations of how law might better approximate to the democratic ideal, add up to a powerful and coherent account of why democracy is valuable and why we have compelling reason to resist its decline. It is precisely at a time when democracy is under threat that an account of this kind is most needed.

PART I

THEORETICAL UNDERPINNINGS

Chapter 1

Democratic Law

SEANA VALENTINE SHIFFRIN

INTRODUCTION

Law and democracy seem oddly estranged in much academic philosophical discourse. Aside from some controversies about constitutionalism, there is, at best, only passing mention of democracy in most contemporary analytical jurisprudential treatments.[1] Likewise, one can leaf through extensive discussions of democracy that do not elaborate any distinctive, essential role that law plays in achieving democratic aims. Law tends to be treated as an instrumental afterthought.

This self-imposed relegation of law and democracy to different intellectual compartments of inquiry does us a disservice. It encourages simplistic instrumental views of law and democracy as institutional devices that control untrustworthy agents and manage

1. Two important exceptions are Jeremy Waldron, "Can There Be a Democratic Jurisprudence?" *Emory Law Journal* 58 (2009): 675–712 (exploring some distinctive features of law in a democracy within a positivist framework) and Jean Hampton, "Democracy and the Rule of Law," *Nomos* 36 (1994): 13–44 (enumerating a special sort of tertiary rule of recognition characteristic of democracies that plays an important role in managing conflict and disagreement without resorting to political coercion to expunge opposition).

Seana Valentine Shiffrin, *Democratic Law* In: *Democratic Law.* Edited by: Hannah Ginsborg, Oxford University Press. © Regents of the University of California 2021. DOI: 10.1093/oso/9780190084486.003.0002

suboptimal circumstances, whether by managing conflict and temptation on the one hand or by refereeing between warring interest groups on the other. Certainly, law and democracy perform these functions, but the blinkered emphasis on them deprives us of much articulate insight about why law and democracy are morally powerful and inspiring human achievements. When we lose sight of our aspirations for these institutions, we begin to ask and expect them to do less than they can. There lies a path to apathy, cynicism, and decline.

I suspect that this academic estrangement bears a complex relation to positivist temptations to think that the most significant features of law must hold true within decidedly non-democratic states like Saudi Arabia[2]; a latent mistrust for law contained within some (often nonpositivist) conceptions of law as essentially coercive; outcome-oriented conceptions of morality that denigrate the significance of motive; and malaise about whether democracy's intrinsic value can be convincingly defended.[3] My mission here is more constructive than diagnostic or critical, however. It is to sketch a distinctive account of democracy's intrinsic value that, non-accidentally, highlights the virtues that law may uniquely display within democratic circumstances. To vindicate my claim that law and democracy enjoy an intimate relationship, I will offer an account of democracy's intrinsic communicative value and law's special constitutive role in that communicative endeavor through which we represent our institutional, collective expression of justice and other forms of collective morality.

2. Cf. Liam Murphy, *What Makes Law: An Introduction to the Philosophy of Law* (New York: Cambridge University Press, 2014), at 118 ("Most discussions of the obligation to obey the law . . . take for granted that law can have any content and be created by all kinds of regimes, democratic or despotic").

3. See, e.g., Niko Kolodny, "Rule over None I: What Justifies Democracy?" *Philosophy & Public Affairs* 42, no. 3 (2014): 195–229, at 196; Niko Kolodny, "Democracy for Idealists," (unpublished manuscript, 2016) (on file with author).

The view I will defend stresses that we must execute some of our collective moral duties through democratic laws generally as well as through the democratic generation of some *particular* laws. Neither democracy nor law is well-conceived primarily as a fungible, if highly effective, means of installing the proper egalitarian institutions which themselves are required by justice and that may be specified independently from their mode of generation. To the contrary, the generation of democratic law is an element of what justice requires and a constituent condition of other requirements of justice. If law's function is, in part, to execute our collective moral duties through collective, communicative means, then a full and proper legal system must be democratic.

My enterprise may be framed as a discussion about the content and value of law and democracy in ideal theory, motivated by my disappointment that many current jurisprudential discussions seem, perhaps unconsciously, to be squarely situated in the non-ideal theoretical capital of Riyadh. Some important democratic theories also seem to locate themselves squarely in non-ideal territory, portraying democracy's role as exclusively one in assisting or partly constituting the struggles to install material and intellectual forms of justice, temper injustice, or provide some "at least we all had a say" style legitimacy to how we bumble along given inevitable failures in achieving just conditions.[4] These are partly insightful accounts but they are also

4. Here, I signal some disagreement with the approach taken by Thomas Christiano, *The Constitution of Equality: Democratic Authority and Its Limits* (New York: Oxford University Press, 2008). Christiano's theory is perhaps one of the more celebratory accounts, seeing democracy as a way to manifest publicly our recognition of each person's equal claim to advance her interests. But his celebration often takes an indirect, non-ideal cast. First, Christiano's emphasis is on the importance of implementing a just scheme of equality, understood as ensuring our equal well-being; because, he notes, no mechanism of direct implementation is at hand, we must construct a just scheme ourselves in a climate of disagreement. Second, a combination of factors of difference and distrust drive his commitment to publicity and democracy. Because we have such different judgments, fairness to each of us demands a system in which no one's biased judgment may exert unequal influence. Thus, he

incomplete—assembled midway, so to speak. They fail to capture the full aspirations of both law and democracy, aspirations that are part of the constitutive conditions of realized justice, not only the fair conditions of approximating justice in non-ideal conditions. Important progress can be made in understanding moral and political values by concentrating on what we may aspire to under favorable conditions, rather than tailoring our regulative ideals to a wide range of possible conditions of strife, division, hierarchy, apathy, and non-compliance.[5] So, I will investigate what role democracy and law would play in a state whose institutions otherwise manifest features of material and intellectual forms of justice and whose citizens largely endorse the principles of justice and their instantiation.

TERMS

By 'democracy,' I mean, roughly, a political system that treats all its members with equal concern, regards their lives as of equal importance, and treats all competent members of the community (by which I mean those having reached the age of majority and without profound intellectual disabilities) as, by right and by conception, the equal and exclusive co-authors of and co-contributors to the system, its rules, its actions, its directives, its communications, and its other outputs. A healthy democracy is one in which the members have

frames the need for democracy as responsive to non-ideality and not as, also, part of an ideal system of mutual constitution and mutual regard (Christiano 2008, 95–96). See also David M. Estlund, *Democratic Authority: A Philosophical Framework* (Princeton, NJ: Princeton University Press, 2009), at 6.

5. Think, for example, of the intellectual strides made by concentrating on the specific interrelations of the two principles of Rawls' special conception of justice as fairness, rather than on the broader general conception of justice—even though, arguably, many extant societies only enjoy the conditions suited to the general conception. John Rawls, *A Theory of Justice* (Cambridge, MA: Harvard University Press, 1971), at 62–63, 151–52, and 541–42.

regular opportunities to exercise these rights and do so with some frequency.

It is worth highlighting two preliminary points about the institutions that constitute a democratic system. First, my rough characterization of democracy lends little support to the view that elections, in particular, are *the* defining characteristic of democracy. A free speech regime including the legal right to petition government (and to expect consideration and a reasoned response) and a robust, vibrant free speech culture are equally essential components. Without the ability to discuss, debate, and understand issues and characters with others, elections have little purpose, whether as exercises of deliberate communication, self-determination, or efforts at meaningful preference satisfaction. Indeed, because elections are framed with determinate boundaries, whereas a free speech culture is free-ranging with indeterminate boundaries, a free speech culture is arguably more foundational to democracy than any particular mechanism of decision formation, including elections. Moreover, elections of people as representatives inevitably consolidate many disparate issues into one decision at a particular time, whereas, a free speech culture enables reasoned but focused discussion and feedback about singular issues but at no time in particular. This temporal and substantive dispersal permits more targeted forms of discussion on specific issues as they arise and progress. Among other virtues, this disaggregation facilitates the provision of information and advice to elected representatives about the specific issues and about constituents' convictions concerning them. I mention these points only as a corrective to the fixation on elections as the *sine qua non* of democracy. To be sure, there is no need to rank them; a free speech regime without elections and other methods for citizens to contribute to deliberations would also be severely impoverished.

Second, I will say more about non-legislative democratic institutions in Part II. Briefly, although elections and referenda may serve as important anchoring mechanisms of influence and political formation by co-contributors, they are not the exclusive means by which a political system may make decisions compatible with a democratic structure. There is also little reason reflexively to regard other elements of a political system, including judicial, administrative, or custom-based authority, as, ipso facto, anti-democratic or, at least, 'lesser' from a democratic point of view. I will elaborate in due course. For now, I will register the point that a group of authors may reasonably divide labor and delegate one or more of their members to speak for them in certain fora without sacrificing or compromising their equal status. As many of us know from happy experience, an egalitarian co-author relation usually involves a division of labor in which each party brings her special talents and insights to bear on producing a joint message.[6] One co-author may take the

6. The allusion to academic co-authorship may be misleading in some respects, however, because academic co-authorship has some distinctive constraints that do not hold for all egalitarian co-authorships. Academic co-authors writing an academic article represent their research findings as true, or, at least, they warrant it as representing their expert conclusions. The academic article usually represents the joint and unanimous consensus about a subject. (At least with egalitarian co-authorship. I leave aside hierarchical practices of co-authorship in the sciences.) The standards of accuracy are quite high, and hence disagreement between co-authors may be a sufficient reason to suspend joint communication about that subject or to narrow the scope of the claims made about it to the areas of consensus. The special standards of academic co-authorship are, in part, tied to the other special norms and obligations of expertise and the distinctive role of the academic enterprise. In part, they are also apt because what academics publish about and with whom they publish is importantly discretionary. There may be some professional urgency for academics to write *something*, but an important aspect of academic freedom is that there is no requirement to speak about particular topics at a particular time; hence, there is reduced pressure for co-authors to compromise or forge a pragmatic consensus about a particular topic by a deadline.

These features render academic co-authorship somewhat unusual. Consider, by contrast, the co-authored invitation, condolence cards, and many committee reports. The aim of these communications is not primarily to warrant a detailed account of the truth but to convey an offer, a message, or a jointly acceptable version of events, recommendations, and commitments. In this way, they more closely resemble the aims of law. They often involve topics on which there is some time sensitivity to communicate and by parties who have some obligations to communicate and act collectively. No reasonable recipient of such communications would take each co-author to endorse fully each contribution of every other co-author. The same condolence card may be

lead and speak for the group. The relation may remain egalitarian so long as each co-author retains the ability at some fundamental level to contribute and exercise decision-making authority, each

signed by an observant Jew and a devout evangelical, the latter of whom words her sympathies with a reference to Christ's grace and the afterlife. The recipient of such a card would have no reason to think this was also a conversion notice of the Jewish colleague. More important, the Jewish colleague does not have reason to withdraw her signature in light of the evangelical's sentiments. I think even the agnostic may not have reason to withdraw if the card's printed text itself, and not only the individual signatures, adverts to God. Where the communicative aim is not something akin to an affidavit, the standards for unanimity relax, given the temporal and moral pressures to communicate something as a group. Participants attempting to craft a joint message should understand that the production of a joint message by a group of distinctive individuals with distinctive points of view may defy efforts to craft an unanimously endorsed message endorsed by each member for shared reasons. So long as they have the right to contribute their thoughts on the matter and their contributions are considered in good faith, co-authors of missives like cards, invitations, and reports have reason to accept compromises and other decisions they do not individually endorse as theirs by virtue of the nature of their shared enterprise and by virtue of the nature of their diverse collective perspectives. Recipients of such messages have reason to interpret accordingly: the collective message is not necessarily the individual message of each co-author.

Still, each co-author has a reason to assume responsibility *as a member of the collective* for the joint message that was sent even while she may disagree with it as an individual. Sometimes that responsibility may take the form of collective pride (e.g., for having participated in the process that led to successful communication even if one was a dissenting voice about its exact contents). And, sometimes, that form of responsibility may take the form of collective regret. If the religious card offended the mourner, the agnostic may owe an apology qua member of the collective even if the agnostic pointed out at the time that the mourner might be offended by the card.

Why are there these patterns of responsibility even when a co-author does not endorse the message and did not fully control the process? Suppose we start with the idea that there are some projects that we must pursue but that we cannot pursue alone—they require a joint effort, whether because they are too cumbersome or difficult for people to perform individually, because their successful pursuit is incompatible with parallel and conflicting individual efforts, or because their meaning demands that they emanate from a collective and not a pool of individuals. When group action or group communication is imperative and group members have diverse perspectives, then expectations of and interpretations presupposing unanimity or complete control by each member seem unreasonable. Plentiful deliberative occasions, arguments, and time will contribute to the formation of a joint decision and will leave open the possibility of achieving worthy aspirations of unanimity. But, taking unanimity to represent a requirement on communication seems unwarranted. It seems either to reflect one or more of the following flawed ideas: that unanimity is more important than timely, if suboptimal, action or communication; that the correct view will emerge in time and be sufficiently evident to everyone; or, that a fair compromise will be identified and evidently acceptable to all parties in a timely way. One worries that insistence on unanimity will risk paralysis or, in the alternative, that it will operate as an implicit demand that some parties insincerely represent their substantive agreement with the majority position.

co-author retains equal responsibility for the collective endeavor, and those co-authors who take the lead still attempt to speak for and reflect the contributions of all authors, not only or predominantly themselves.[7]

If, as I will urge, democracy is a system for the joint specification, communication, and implementation of mandatory and discretionary values, then whether we are communicating to deliberate, report, or commit, the appropriate mode of communication may vary, depending on what value is at issue, to whom we are communicating, and the requisite level of specificity. Hence, the 'co-author' characterization harbors no explicit or latent attitude of hostility or resignation to mechanisms of representation, including forms of administrative and judicial authority. Indeed, I'll signal some of the democratic shortcomings of ideals of direct democracy shortly.

7. This conception of egalitarian power-sharing and division of labor has much in common with Dworkin's democracy-as-partnership conception articulated in Ronald Dworkin, *Justice for Hedgehogs* (Cambridge, MA: Harvard University Press, 2011), at 384, and Ronald Dworkin, *Is Democracy Possible Here?: Principles for a New Political Debate* (Princeton, NJ: Princeton University Press, 2006), at 131, but Dworkin did not emphasize the *communicative* core of democracy. There are also significant affinities between this conception and deliberative models of democracy, especially as developed by Joshua Cohen. See, e.g., Joshua Cohen, "Reflections on Deliberative Democracy," in Joshua Cohen, *Philosophy, Politics, Democracy* (Cambridge, MA: Harvard University Press, 2009), 326–47; Joshua Cohen, "Procedure and Substance in Deliberative Democracy," in Seyla Benhabib ed., *Democracy and Difference: Changing Boundaries of the Political* (Princeton, NJ: Princeton University Press, 1996), 95–116. Along with deliberative democrats, I understand democracy as the egalitarian and free way we have to think together and thereby to justify to ourselves the actions we undertake together, especially those pursued under the rubric of justice. Through our mutual, deliberative participation, we pursue mutual understanding and a collective self-understanding—that we are doing something together and why. This idea represents a piece of the view that I affirm, but sometimes—and perhaps it is only a matter of emphasis—the ideal celebrated by many deliberative democrats hits more notes of reflection and insight about the procedures of respectful co-authorship than it does of the *communicative* value to each other of our generating commitments together and the special significance of democratically generated *law* as the way we generate such commitments. (Many of the deliberative democrats' points have no essential place for law but could be satisfied, were there time enough, through robust discussion about each discrete action we undertake.)

Having indicated what I mean by 'democracy,' parallelism would recommend that I do the same for 'law.' For the sake of getting on with the argument, though, I will allow my use of 'law' to emerge through discussing its democratic virtues and functions. Two brief points, though: (1) although I conceive of law as public—as having a publicly accessible, even if incomplete and partly inchoate, account of its contents—and as having temporal duration, I do not privilege statutes over judicial or administrative decisions nor the textual ingredients of law over its other ingredients.[8] (2) I sometimes use 'law' to refer to discrete legal principles, doctrines, or decisions that have general application and, where applicable, have precedential effect or another form of presumptive duration (whether those decisions are judicial, executive, or legislative). At other points, I refer to 'law' as a legal system composed of such public principles, doctrines, or decisions that aims for (and substantially achieves) some justificatory cohesion. By 'democratic law,' I mean a legal system the content and generation of which justifies its characterization as democratic.

Let me now turn to my thesis: Some of our mandatory moral ends require democratic law, generally, for their realization as well as the democratic generation of some *particular* laws. The democratic generation of law is not, as many prominent theories would have it, a mere means to achieve just conditions that can be identified without reference to their provenance; nor is it merely the

8. Here, I agree with my colleague Mark Greenberg. See, e.g., Mark Greenberg, "The Moral Impact Theory of Law," *Yale Law Journal* 123 (2014): 1288–342; Mark Greenberg, "Legislation as Communication? Legal Interpretation and the Study of Linguistic Communication," in Andrei Marmor and Scott Soames eds., *Philosophical Foundations of Language in the Law* (New York: Oxford University Press, 2011), 217–56; Mark Greenberg, "How Facts Make Law," *Legal Theory* 10, no. 3 (2008): 157–98. Although Greenberg targets the so-called "communicative-content theory of law," his attack is aimed at a theory of legal *meaning* on which legal interpretation hinges entirely on *linguistic considerations*. Such a theory is distinct from, indeed antithetical to, the theory I defend here.

fairest method of resolving conflict. Democratic law, as I will defend it, is an element of what justice requires even within ideal theory. Moreover, it is not simply one item on a general list of necessities or desiderata. Democratic law is not merely a means to or a complement of just material, social, and intellectual conditions that are independently specifiable. Democratic law is a constituent condition of the full realization of such conditions and hence of the full realization of justice.

THE COMMUNICATIVE SIGNIFICANCE OF DEMOCRATIC LAW

My defense starts with a problem for which democratic law is the solution. The problem that I am interested in is not the familiar problem of how to justify coercion, a problem that unduly fascinates many democratic theorists. The problem that I am interested in arises prior to disagreement, dissension, threats, and the prospect of disobedience. Even in a largely just society full of citizens of good will, each of us, in communal living, would face significant communicative challenges of a moral nature. Democracy may uniquely address these challenges, often, importantly, through democratic law. Understanding these challenges and democratic law's ability to meet them forms a basis for claiming that democracy is intrinsically valuable as a necessary endeavor of collective moral agency and that, at least in ideal theory, the moral functions of law and democracy are closely intertwined.

What sort of challenges? One concerns our status as equals, which I take to be exemplary of the problems we face. The forthcoming argument that describes the challenge and the ingredients for a solution has four major steps, positing (1) some moral requirements for citizens to communicate with and to each other, (2) the importance of direct and at least partially articulate communication for certain sorts of messages, (3) the role that actions and commitments play in effective and sincere communication of some morally important messages, and (4) the unique role democratic law serves in communicating those messages. My path through these steps will be circuitous, departing for a stretch from a political beeline to take an interpersonal detour.

I'll begin with the moral imperative of communication among citizens. Start with the assumptions that, first, we are all moral equals and, second, that our status, our perception of our status, and our mutual recognition of our status (and the needs and interests that accompany it) influence our sense of self-respect. That is, I assume that Rawls is roughly correct that the social bases of self-respect are a crucial component of the conditions for maintaining one's self-respect. This maintenance, in turn, is an essential component of our mutual flourishing. As Rawls may have understated it, self-respect is, "perhaps the most important primary good."[9] As a just citizen living in community with others, I should be interested in contributing to the social bases of self-respect.[10]

As an individual, I confront the difficulty that the social bases of self-respect are not merely material in nature but are communicative. It matters that we manifest our respect for one another and not merely that we co-exist in circumstances that give everyone access

9. Rawls, *Theory of Justice*, at 396 and 440. In what follows, I attempt to offer a particular specification of Rawls' claim that "self-respect is secured by the public affirmation of the status of equal citizenship for all" by drawing a tight connection between *law* and democratic law, in particular, and the sort of public affirmation that could achieve this morally imperative end. See *id.* at 545.

10. By starting with the issue of how democratic law serves as a necessary mechanism through which moral agents may fulfill their duties, my approach dovetails with Anna Stilz's observation that a beneficiary-oriented perspective on the state's value and on democracy's value is objectionably partial, viewing citizens only as "takers" and not crucially as "makers." Anna Stilz, "The Value of Self-Determination," *Oxford Studies in Political Philosophy* 2 (2016): 98–127, at 100–101 and 119–20.

to the basic minimum, that no one sets fire to the central distribution depot, and that we pay our taxes. A just allocation of material resources is compatible with mutual indifference, grudging accommodation, or even mutual contempt should the penalties for destructive behavior be severe enough to induce patterns of compliance from even Justice Holmes' bad apple.

Why, it might be asked, should this matter so long as the conditions of material (and intellectual) justice obtain, whether through coercion, grudging compliance, or barely registered automation? How would such motivations diminish the social bases of self-respect? Is it simply a psychological liability that I care what you all think? Perhaps I ought to steel myself against this vulnerability rather than expect you to make ingratiating gestures. Another critic might worry that the need for demonstrations of respect may signal latent distrust of one's peers, showing that this need is a symptom of political non-ideality. This latter objection is thematically related to a cluster of positions claiming that, as Daniel Markovits puts it, "perfectly rational and reasonable creatures would not require politics or any political agreement" or, for that matter, promises or contracts.[11]

I resist these ideas. In hostile circumstances, our mutual sensitivity to each other's attitudes can certainly represent a vulnerability (and an asset). Generally, however, mutual sensitivity is not accurately understood as a mere psychological vulnerability or a symptom of otherwise defective relations or irrationality. It flows from a proper sort of moral sensitivity. If I see you as a distinct individual, as

11. See, e.g., Daniel Markovits, "Good Faith as Contract's Core Value," in Gregory Klass, George Letsas, and Prince Saprai eds., *Philosophical Foundations of Contract Law* (Oxford: Oxford University Press, 2014), 272–94, at 286 and 289; see also Daniel Markovits, "Promise as an Arm's-length Relation," in Hanoch Sheinman ed., *Promises and Agreements: Philosophical Essays* (New York: Oxford University Press, 2011), 295–326, at 309–10. For a rebuttal with respect to promises, see Seana Valentine Shiffrin, "Promising, Intimate Relationships, and Conventionalism," *Philosophical Review* 117, no. 4 (2008): 481–524, at 498–508.

a moral agent and as a moral equal capable of moral judgment whose life and thoughts matter, how could I not reasonably care what *you think* about all sorts of matters, including about me? (It is difficult for me not to view as gendered and hierarchical the critics' equation of having interests in recognition and in the alleviation of potential feelings of vulnerability with signs of failure, weakness, imperfection, and a lack of rationality.)

Furthermore, it is not sufficient that we live in materially just relations with each other and know indirectly, however incontestably, of each other's good will. It is an aspect of our respect for each other as *individuals* that we afford special significance to agents' efforts to make their thoughts public and thereby to affirm and endorse those thoughts. Our important capacity to control what we reveal about our thoughts renders normatively meaningful the distinction between what we intentionally convey, what we conceal, and what we leave to be indirectly inferred about our wills. Because I do not leave it to you to puzzle out my attitudes from my actions and omissions, when I make an intentional effort to convey my respect, other things equal, my action is more meaningful than my leaving my respect to be assumed or inferred by you. Rather, I assume responsibility as an individual to affiliate myself with that respectful content, and I aim to ensure you know it matters enough to me that I exert my agency to convey it.[12]

Although we may reasonably care what we think of each other and whether and how we make it known, one may object that it doesn't follow that my sense of *self-respect* should hinge on others' explicit regard. Consider Justice Thomas's related objection in *Obergefell v. Hodges*, the US same-sex marriage case, against the majority's

12. There are hazards here, including that my conveyance should not raise the possibility that my respect is morally discretionary. How it is conveyed and with what spirit should dispel this risk.

argument sounding in dignity.[13] Thomas argued that dignity may be recognized or ignored by the government, but it couldn't be bestowed or deprived by the government. One either has the qualities that confer dignity or one does not. So, too, one either has the qualities that make one a moral equal or one does not. If one does not, then their proclamations of one's equality could not make it so. If one does, then one merits self-respect as an equal and that merit cannot be diminished by one's fellows' errors in judgment or ignorance.

Of course, the qualities that qualify one as a moral equal among others are ones that cannot be bestowed or deprived through their recognition or denial. Their unjust denial by other intelligent agents, however, may make it difficult to sustain one's confidence in oneself, given our general and important practices of epistemic interdependence and affiliative identification. Even those who are able to maintain their self-confidence may still, unfairly, have to exert extra effort to do so and may have to develop a degree of costly emotional fortitude, reserve, and even distance from others to substitute for the social support and affirmation that others enjoy.

It matters politically not only that I receive the reinforcing regard I am due as a moral equal for that regard is also due to visitors. It matters also that I am respected as an equal *member* of the community—as one among her peers whose belonging is secure. When my peers do not acknowledge my standing as one of them, they successfully, if wrongfully, diminish my security as a member. My need for membership somewhere is inherent in my status as a human being, but my status *here, in this community* is not; it is conferred, even if, for the lucky some of us, our place of birth makes that conferral feel automatic.

So it is important that we underwrite the social bases of self-respect both through what I am calling the material and intellectual

13. Obergefell v. Hodges, 135 S. Ct. 2584, 2639 (2015) (Thomas, J., dissenting).

forms of justice—ensuring that people are afforded the opportunities, goods, rights, and services they are due—and also through communicative means—conveying that these provisions stem from our non-grudging recognition of each other as equal co-members of our political society. As I have just argued, the communicative component is not conveyed convincingly simply by forbearing from resisting the material components.

Our communicative challenge is compounded by the fact that, in our daily lives, it is nearly inevitable that we will send mixed signals about our commitments. As just agents, we may be committed to the equal moral value of our lives and our equal entitlement to secure membership in a society of equals, irrespective of our distinctive individual features—including our race, gender, ethnicity, orientation, beliefs, and affiliations. Nevertheless, these commitments cannot regularly be read off of the patterns of our daily behaviors, the content of which is often driven by partial commitments—to family, to smaller communities and affiliations, and to associations with strong substantive commitments. The personal value of each of our lives in large part derives from our immersion in and dedication to these particular and partial activities. This immersion may create the understandable impression, however hazy, that affiliations do matter for our social and political status. Moreover, our immersion in them may create the hazard that we will start, however unconsciously, to associate substantive commonalities with the indices of moral status. To counteract these hazards, we need to convey our mutual recognition of each other's moral status—and our intentional, deliberate implementation of the commitments that flow from it—to ensure that recognition is communicated, to counteract any inadvertent suggestions to the contrary, and, to remind ourselves of the limits of the significance of our substantive affiliations.

Insofar as we act as lone individuals, communicating respect to every other citizen is difficult. Time constraints alone prevent us from reading the essays, ads, or tweets of all fellow citizens.[14] Moreover, my words as a lone individual, absent a collective method of representation, will represent me as a private individual but not the collective. Nonetheless, part of my imperative is to belong to a collective that communicates to its members their inclusion as equal members. I need to communicate as a *citizen*, not only as a private individual.

Moreover, a merely discursive affirmation that one's fellows are moral equals deserving of just treatment would not suffice to convey this commitment convincingly. It is not simply that words alone may be received as rationalizing bromides given our more partial patterns of action. The reason why our partial actions may overshadow our discursive affirmations, rendering them mere platitudes, is that some moral beliefs, attitudes, and stances, if they are fully appreciated by those who hold them, dictate appropriately motivated action. Hence, to an observer and particularly to the putative object of those beliefs, attitudes, and stances, the absence of the relevant action *by me* (and *by us*) may reasonably suggest a failure of full and sincere affirmation. It's not enough that I endorse the pattern of installed justice for discursive affirmation or endorsement of a system may be issued from a posture of remove that will not succeed as a communication of *respect*, an interpersonal relationship requiring more substantive participation by its members than mere approval of one party's circumstances or another's action toward him. For example, I (a US citizen) may endorse the general approach Sweden takes to economic production and distribution as a rough approximation of

14. Orchestrating a nationwide, daily, digital affirmation would, to be feasible and digestible by its recipients, have to take the sort of bite-sized, standardized form that quickly devolves into empty words; this, arguably, is one of the defects of the Pledge of Allegiance. This and other issues with the Pledge of Allegiance are discussed in Vincent Blasi and Seana Shiffrin, "The Story of *West Virginia v. Barnette*: The Pledge of Allegiance and the Freedom of Thought," in Michael Dorf ed., *Constitutional Law Stories*, 2nd ed. (New York: Foundation Press, 2009), 433–76, at 437–38.

what economic justice demands. Yet, in doing so, I do not convey my part in a relation of mutual respect toward the denizens of Sweden because I am not a Swede and my endorsement plays no internal role in generating these relations.[15]

In other words, discursive affirmation of a moral proposition and appropriate, conforming action, when considered or rendered separately, may each be insufficient to communicate the appropriate level of commitment to that proposition. They must be rendered together as a legibly interconnected pair for either component to realize fully its role in the communicative expression of the moral proposition's endorsement. This idea is not unfamiliar to moral life. Action with a particular content and structure, motivated in a particular and transparent way, may be necessary for some moral beliefs and attitudes to be successfully communicated and to be received as sincere.[16] Let's dwell on an illustrative, quotidian case before returning to politics.

AN INTERPERSONAL INTERLUDE: GRATITUDE

Consider a case of gratitude for neighborly concern. Suppose, for two years worth of Tuesdays, you (my neighbor) have regularly knocked on my door to remind me that my car is, yet again, in danger of

15. See also Stilz, *supra* note 10, at 123. My position on democracy has commonalities with Stilz's associative view, although I contest her division of a democratic view and an associative view, along with her related suggestion that the associative view's aspirations could be achieved in a non-democratic state with sufficient opportunities for dissent (*id.*, at 125). Although citizens in such a state could affirm their membership in it, their lack of opportunity to exert agency in jointly crafting the state's actions and commitments would strain the communicative meaning of the state's actions as communicative measures by the citizenry to itself.

16. Similar points about apology are made in Jeffrey Helmreich, "The Apologetic Stance," *Philosophy & Public Affairs* 43, no. 2 (2015): 75–108.

ticketing due to street cleaning. Occasionally, I succeed at remembering for myself, but I haven't entirely changed my behavior to make your help superfluous. Nor have I gently rebuffed your efforts to help. For me, morally speaking, you are no officious intermeddler;[17] rather, I regularly, if implicitly, rely on you, relieved that you have my back. I could just voice my gratitude for your generosity. Sometimes a card suffices. It may depend on what the gratitude is for—whether a trivial one-off or whether something ongoing or more substantial. It also depends on what I am positioned to do and whether you have a roughly comparable need. Where you have no roughly comparable needs, gratitude may effectively take a purely discursive form.

But, where the circumstances of reciprocity present themselves, action may be required to communicate gratitude successfully. Suppose you plan to travel this summer, but you care about your garden. It is a fitting expression of gratitude that, when I come to know of your need, I promise to water your plants while you are away and then that I keep the promise. Other things being equal, where you have a need that I could fulfill without unreasonable effort, but I do not, my gratitude could be called into question even as I drop off my ornately lettered card. My ability and failure to reciprocate in the face of your apparent need would signal that I do not completely appreciate your efforts or that I somehow take them for granted as my entitlement.

My promise and my practice of watering, by contrast, convey my gratitude. In the circumstances, these behaviors may be what are communicatively required. The entire episode of gratitude here involves a promise with a particular content, an explanation behind

17. Compare Restatement (Third) of Restitution & Unjust Enrichment § 2 (Am. Law Inst. 2011) (evincing a legal preference for contracting and denying restitutionary compensation to officious intermeddlers, that is, to parties who voluntarily confer unrequested benefits).

the proffer, a performance of the promise, the underlying motives that give rise to the promise and the performance, and their expression through the promise and the performance. All these elements, intertwined, play an important role in the gesture's operation as a communication of gratitude. My watering would fail as gratitude if I did it *because* I was paid by a reality show to do so. Were I just to water your plants secretly, your needs might be met but even if your informant identified me as the waterer, the watering would not read, between us, as an intentional communication of gratitude from me to you. My offer must be substantially and transparently motivated by a deliberatively grounded sense of gratitude, and a similar motivation must propel my ongoing performance (here, nestled within and buttressed by a sense of promissory duty). Furthermore, it matters that these motives have recognizable deliberative roots—that they arose from my recognition of the magnanimousness of your efforts and not from some delusional story or gratitude-adducing pill—and that I convey them to you. Certainly, interpersonal delicacy may often require an indirect approach to returning a favor, yet whatever indirect methods are deployed must be sufficiently transparent that the observant recipient can infer the actions were intended as a gesture of thanks. Subtle maneuvers may be suited to fragile relations or very well-established ones; still, explicit articulation is often an important way to convey gratitude and disambiguate it from other motives and objects of gratitude.[18]

Not only do the behavior, the motive, and its communication matter. So does the form the gratitude takes. Suppose you left town without a promise, but I sent a weekly email reporting that it so

18. My interest in gratitude owes a great deal to Barbara Herman and Collin O'Neil. Other important moral dimensions of gratitude are discussed in Herman's "Being Helped and Being Grateful: Imperfect Duties, the Ethics of Possession, and the Unity of Morality," *The Journal of Philosophy* 109, no. 5/6 (2012): 391–411 and O'Neil's "Lying, Trust, and Gratitude," *Philosophy & Public Affairs* 40, no. 4 (2012): 301–33.

happened this week that I watered your plants. In so doing, I would convey some gratitude but my method of expression would also convey its limits, namely that I regard fulfillment of your ongoing need as a matter of my discretion that I may elect not to fulfill, subject to my own interests and weekly whims.[19] It would not convey that I acknowledged an obligation to respond appropriately to your reciprocal need.[20] Even where the recipient has reason to trust in my abiding gratitude or can infer it through observation, by communicating my gratitude, I thereby take responsibility for ensuring my attitudes are known and for contributing to the content and health of the relationship. My articulate communication relieves the recipient of the burden of performing inferential and charitable work on my behalf.

In addition to its assurance value, the promise plays an important communicative role. Offering the promise expresses gratitude through the concrete action of altering my degrees of moral freedom. Performing on the promise not only delivers you a service responding to your need, but also conveys the strength and constancy of my gratitude, which serves as an appropriate, fitting response to your constancy in alerting me each time I was at risk. The promise coupled with the performances are not only especially clear methods of expression. Other things being equal, they approach being uniquely

19. Even were I to set an automatic timer that indefinitely guaranteed the watering, if I did not disclose it to you, I would not enact adequate gratitude because I would not convey the guarantee I put into action.

20. Doesn't it matter that your assistance to me is sporadic, prompted by your happening to be at home and to notice that my car is in danger? You've made me no promise. Doesn't that make my sporadic response appropriate in return? One major difference here is that I am capable, at any time, of changing the facts that put me in need by parking more prudently. More importantly, you repeatedly see my need, arising again and again, and have apparently resolved to address it when you see it. Once you embark on a trip, you have an ongoing need; to address it satisfactorily requires an explicit commitment in response. There may be further things to be said here about whether expressions of gratitude may appropriately be expected to exceed the magnitude of the original beneficence, but they would take us further afield than necessary.

appropriate methods of communication; doing less or only "saying" something discursively may convey something limply that is lesser. Other things may be unequal. If I have a lethal touch with plants, a better concretization of my gratitude might be to clean your gutters before the winter rains if delaying roof work is your weakness. Still, at some juncture, a failure to act beyond only *voicing* gratitude signals an incomplete or insincere gratitude.

More generally, in some cases, the circumstances and content of a significant moral attitude demand action on that attitude and not merely its discursive expression. Similar points have been made about punishment and the idea that an appropriate educative condemnation of a criminal act may require a (rehabilitation-motivated) sanction or intervention, not simply a critical telegram.[21] For those inclined to contest either example, my quarry is neither neighborly relations nor moral education, but the more philosophical points embedded in the example: namely, that an action may perform communicative work, in conjunction with speech and speech acts, and that a combination of circumstances—both my neighbor's need and my ability to fulfill it—could work to render inadequate exclusively discursive efforts at communication, exclusively behavioral efforts at repayment, and also disconnected discursive and behavioral gestures.[22]

21. See e.g., Jean Hampton, "The Moral Education Theory of Punishment," *Philosophy & Public Affairs* 13, no. 3 (1984): 208–38; Robert Nozick, *Philosophical Explanations* (Cambridge, MA: Harvard University Press, 1981), at 370–74. See also Joshua Kleinfeld, "Reconstructivism: The Place of Criminal Law in Ethical Life," *Harvard Law Review* 129, no. 6 (2016): 1485–565 (portraying criminal law as well as criminal punishment as a partly expressive enterprise that aims to reconstruct a shared, concretized moral code that is threatened by criminal activity and its communicative content).

22. There are, of course, other familiar examples of the further point that a promise may serve an essential communicative and performative function, as with efforts to convey concern in a way consistent with conveying recognition of the recipient's dignity and independence. A promise may be necessary, not only ongoing beneficent deeds. See also Shiffrin, *supra* note 11, at 498–508.

My analogous claim is that the communication of our respect for others as moral equals within a political community may be imperative in the way that conveyance of gratitude may be imperative in the interpersonal case. The gravity of the moral needs and values at stake, coupled with our circumstances, require a form of communicative action with, but not limited to, discursive content.

TURNING BACK TO POLITICS: THE ROLE OF DEMOCRATIC LAW

Before our foray into gratitude, I described four structural problems in satisfying this political imperative that might be summarized as follows:

1. We cannot convey our mutual respect to one another as equal members on an individual basis given what, in this context, sincere and effective communication of a collective commitment would require.
2. Much of our behavior is communicatively ambiguous. Our valuable relations of partiality are often open to interpretations that are in tension with a stance of mutual respect. Furthermore, mere compliance with just institutions is compatible with an absence of mutual respect and recognition.
3. Mere endorsement, whether vocal or mental, of a just distribution and of other elements of a just basic structure is insufficient to discharge this communicative obligation.
4. There is the risk that our valuable relations of partiality may become overly dominant and transgress their normative limits if they are not tempered by activities that generate, convey, and reinforce our commitments to impartiality.

Democracy and democratic law play unique roles in addressing these problems. My argument follows fairly closely from the statement of the problem. Each of us needs to perform (and receive) a form of communicative action that enacts and thereby expresses our commitment to the respectful treatment that each of us merits as a moral equal and joint member of our social cooperative venture. Even if endorsed by each of us individually, in our hearts and in our editorials, a system of civil and economic rights that satisfied the substantive requirements of justice with respect to each member's just entitlements, claims, or needs, would fail to satisfy this communicative need. The system, therefore, must not only be endorsed by us but also must be *our* product. Its production must have a communicative component to it, one that could be publicly grasped. So, other things equal, each of us must be involved in the generation and maintenance of this (otherwise) just system for its creation to be *our* product and for each of us to fulfill our communicative duties through it. The involvement must take a democratic form because each of us must have the opportunity to participate for the communication to be ours and publicly so. The terms of that participation must themselves be equal, under some salient description, or else the message will not be *each* of ours and the participatory structure will belie at least part of the message of our mutual equality.[23]

Law plays a special role in fulfilling this communicative mission. Recall how the promise played an important role in accomplishing what gratitude required. First, by limiting my degrees of moral freedom, the promise committed me to a course of action that justified normative expectations by the recipient and thereby facilitated

23. See also Joshua Cohen, "For a Democratic Society," in Samuel Freeman ed., *The Cambridge Companion to Rawls*, (Cambridge: Cambridge University Press, 2003) 86-138 at 96–97 ("a democratic political arrangement expresses, in the design of the highest level of political authority, the idea that the members of the society are equal persons").

reliance that made my actions of gratitude more valuable. Second, the intertemporal nature of the promise underscored the expression of gratitude. Finally, the promise itself created those expectations through communicative means and thereby transmitted both my recognition that I owed gratitude and that my actions were intended to be taken as such by the recipient. The promise was itself communicative and substantive at once. Likewise, law also has the capacity to communicate our collective stance and at least one embodiment of our motive while also achieving substantive normative results. Although the analogy is imperfect, the articulate generation[24] of a law with specific content is analogous to the promise, its implementation and enforcement are akin to the performance of the commitment, and its democratic provenance is what makes the law and its implementation an expression of our voice.

Were we just to perform what justice (otherwise) requires of us without declaring our commitment through law, in a sense, we would perform the right actions and we might act from respect, but we would fail to do so clearly, under the banner of a self-assumed, joint public commitment. Some actions, especially those implicating fundamental status, require deliberately communicated motivation of a particular kind from the proper recognition of the relevant reasons.[25] Of course, it can be better for the conforming action to be taken without an accompanying clear message of recognition and commitment than for no action to be taken at all. Take the familiar friend who always denies error and who does you a wrong. When confronted,

24. I use the phrase "articulate generation" to underscore that my thesis encompasses not only legislatively generated law, but also other forms of the generation and articulation of law, including through the development of common law, judicial interpretation, and executive interpretation.

25. At the same time, other moral actions embroider their motives on their sleeves but may achieve greater subtlety and value when unaccompanied by further commentary. See the related point in Seana Valentine Shiffrin, *Speech Matters: On Lying, Morality, and the Law* (Princeton, NJ: Princeton University Press, 2014), at 180–81.

she may resist recognition of the error but subtly begin to alter her conduct and engage in small kindnesses that work some compensatory repair. Sometimes such gestures are a sufficient form of communication themselves, but in other cases, something more articulate may be required—such as when the transgression is substantial or a repeat offense, the denial was outrageous, or the principle at stake is fundamental. The behavioral change matters, as do the material offerings, but the friendship may not be fully repaired without the more articulate recognition of the relevant principle, the shortcoming, and their articulation as part of a commonly understood history and commitment going forward.

Similarly, even if we were to vote, day by day, to endorse and enable these performances in a thorough exercise of direct democracy, we would not be undertaking a commitment to which its recipients could point as publicly common ground. It would be akin to my repeated but still spontaneous decisions to water my neighbor's plants. True, certain overtures and some deliberate patterns of behavior directed at others may themselves generate reasonable forms of reliance that exert normative force akin to the force of a promise.[26] But, at best, such overtures only indirectly and ambiguously convey a commitment to a substantive expression of respect with longevity. They ambiguate between a commitment and a more temporary grant supplemented by a perpetual reauthorization process. Patterns of beneficence without the backing of a commitment render awkward—to put it mildly—appeals and references to the prospect of continued performance by their beneficiaries.

Even back in what now seem like the halcyon days of the Obama Administration, the lack of presumptive longevity was the shortcoming of Deferred Action for Childhood Arrivals (DACA) and Deferred

26. This principle is encapsulated legally in the doctrine of promissory reliance. RESTATEMENT (SECOND) OF CONTRACTS, § 90 (AM. LAW INST. 1981).

Action for Parents of Americans and Lawful Permanent Residents (DAPA), the executive orders that refrained from enforcing immigration controls against undocumented residents who arrived here as children and their families. Even assuming their contested constitutional validity and, counterfactually, their perpetual and predictable renewal by successive presidents,[27] an ongoing discretionary refusal to enforce an extant law authorizing deportation, rather than a long-term commitment to inclusion, conveys only a partial recognition of belonging and deprives such residents of security as well as the ability to demand recognition and the rights of members.

By contrast, by generating public commitments through law, we give evidence that the system of justice is endorsed by us, so much so that we choose it and we choose to commit to it in a public way that

27. Under President Obama, the US Department of Homeland Security (DHS) implemented a policy known as Deferred Action for Childhood Arrivals (DACA) in 2012, allowing certain undocumented immigrants who entered the United States as minors to apply for temporary relief from removal, and employment authorization. See Memorandum from Janet Napolitano, Sec'y of Homeland Sec., to David V. Aguilar, Acting Comm'r, U.S. Customs & Border Prot., et al., Exercising Prosecutorial Discretion with Respect to Individuals Who Came to the United States as Children (June 15, 2012), https://www.dhs.gov/xlibrary/assets/s1-exercising-prosecutorial-discretion-individuals-who-came-to-us-as-children.pdf. In 2014, DHS expanded eligibility for DACA and also implemented Deferred Action for Parents of Americans and Lawful Permanent Residents (DAPA), allowing certain undocumented parents of US citizens and lawful permanent residents to apply for the same benefits of the DACA program. See Memorandum from Jeh Charles Johnson, Sec'y of Homeland Sec., to León Rodriguez, Dir., US Citizenship & Immigration Servs., et al., Exercising Prosecutorial Discretion with Respect to Individuals Who Came to the United States as Children and with Respect to Certain Individuals Who Are the Parents of U.S. Citizens or Permanent Residents (Nov. 20, 2014), https://www.dhs.gov/sites/default/files/publications/14_1120_memo_deferred_action_2.pdf. Subsequently, some states challenged the 2014 DAPA program, and a preliminary injunction went into effect soon after the program's creation. See Texas v. United States, 86 F. Supp. 3d 591, 677–78 (S.D. Tex. 2015), aff'd, 809 F.3d 134 (5th Cir. 2015), aff'd by an equally divided Court, 136 S. Ct. 2271 (2016). Before litigation about the program concluded, the Trump Administration rescinded the program (as of this writing). See Memorandum from John F. Kelly, Sec'y of Homeland Sec., to Kevin K. McAleenan, Acting Comm'r, US Customs and Border Prot., et. al., Rescission of Memorandum Providing for Deferred Action for Parents of Americans and Lawful Permanent Residents (June 15, 2017), https://www.dhs.gov/news/2017/06/15/rescission-memorandum-providing-deferred-action-parents-americans-and-lawful.

typically carries a substantial degree of longevity. As with promises, public commitments through law deliberately alter the normative status of recipients to provide them with a common reference point on which to base expectations and to form entitlements to call on our adherence. Analogous to promises, by virtue of our collective, evinced willingness to enact the associated normative changes, they partly achieve their normative communicative aims simply through their generation and public declaration.

As I earlier observed, the analogy between promise and law is inexact. The *form* of law provides two important points of contrast with the form of promise. First, in addition to grounding legitimate expectations *in* the recipient, laws often also empower the declarer to form substantial normative expectations *of* the recipient, such as that residents will file taxes by April 15, notify the state of a car accident causing substantial damage within ten days, and refrain from deceptive commercial advertising. By contrast, not all promises generate reasonable expectations *about* the promisee. Reciprocal promises where both parties make entangled commitments conditional on each other do so, of course. Arguably, at least some promises create normative expectations that the promisee will, where reasonable, waive the promissory commitment, but expectations of waiver are fairly dilute requirements compared to the more robust expectations law generates. Notably, when we are both co-authors and co-recipients of law's address, this idea that a communicative declaration could empower declarers to expect something substantial of their audience makes more sense than it does in non-democratic authority relations.

Second, absent conditions of excuse, a promise, being irrevocable, is normatively resilient to the promisor's change of mind. A law has greater normative resilience than a mere stated intention (which can be revoked on the spot) because a change of law requires following procedures that usually take time. Especially with respect to democratic law, these procedures include the ability of the audience (and authors) of the law to comment on and deliberate together about the change of law. But, with the exception of some entrenched constitutional provisions, most laws are revocable through collective expressions of will, making laws less normatively resilient than promises. This feature is not a shortcoming but fits the requirements of a communicative agent whose composition alters over generations. With that compositional change, its deliberations and its message may alter, too. Hence, the commitments made through law have normative force and for some duration, but, normatively, the duration is more discretionary and subject to change than with a promise.[28] Still, these notable differences do not threaten my use of the analogy. Both types of commitment, law and promise, fulfill the need to communicate through public, normative achievements that have duration.[29] Making such commitments reinforces the social bases of self-respect by creating and communicating publicly common normative ground.

Other expressive theories of law have focused predominately on the negative expressive potential of law—to oppress, marginalize, disparage, or discriminate through expressive means[30]—and neglect

28. Depending on your theory of excuse, non-performance of a promise may be excused by a wider range of circumstances than failures to comply with or enforce the law.

29. Unlike mere custom, for example, democratic law, as a system, involves public, official commitments whose alteration and interpretation themselves involve public procedures; custom does not involve a *commitment* between citizens to honor their mutual equality. Furthermore, the methods by which customs may change permit non-deliberate drift and change propelled by some without the input or agency of others.

30. See, e.g., Christopher Eisgruber and Lawrence Sager, *Religious Freedom and the Constitution* (Cambridge, MA: Harvard University Press, 2007), at 124–28; Deborah Hellman, *When Is Discrimination Wrong?* (Cambridge, MA: Harvard University Press, 2008), at 38–41; Deborah Hellman, "The Expressive Dimension of Equal Protection," *Minnesota Law Review* 85, no. 1 (2000): 1–70, at 2; Elizabeth S. Anderson and Richard H. Pildes, "Expressive Theories of Law: A General Restatement," *University of Pennsylvania Law Review* 148, no. 5 (2000): 1503–75, at 1527. Some other accounts are also focused on what the government expresses and may be understood to mean, whereas I use the term "communicative" to emphasize that what matters is not only what is said, but also successful conveyance and uptake by the audience. This marks a substantial departure from Anderson

what I have been emphasizing, namely, the positive communicative capacity of law.[31] I think this difference in emphasis may trace to the fact that many expressive theories work, often implicitly, with a nondemocratic model in which the government or state as speaker is treated as distinct and separate from its audience.[32] By contrast, a democratic legal approach understands government speech as, ultimately, ours. If law embodies our speech to ourselves, then when its communicative content subordinates or disparages a portion of our community, we are implicated and not only entitled to a horrified reaction from the sidelines. At the same time, because democratic law is ours, we are enabled to perform our communicative duties through it.

As with other forms of communication, the appropriate mode may vary depending on the subject matter. In some cases, any old sort of democratic provenance may not be enough, given the myriad forms of democratic action and the levels of commitment that the law may enact. The particular mode of democratic conveyance may matter. Consider, for example, the legal status of women vis-à-vis the US government and our fellow citizens. Achieved through a hodgepodge of statutes and constitutional decisions, roughly speaking,

and Pildes, who are interested predominantly in speaker meaning (*id.* at 1508; but see 1571–72).

31. But see Richard Brooks' fascinating forthcoming work on titles and addresses, "The First Law of Address" (unpublished manuscript), which explores both the positive and the negative expressive power of titles and addresses, whether privately or legally conferred. Another important exception is Marianne Constable, who explores a range of specific ways that legal activities, through their use of language, function as forms of mutual communication and dialogue that invoke conceptions of justice and, as speech acts, contribute to the characterization and constitution of our political community. Marianne Constable, *Our Word Is Our Bond: How Legal Speech Acts* (Stanford, CA: Stanford University Press, 2014).

32. This implicit assumption also operates in the literature on criminal punishment. In that literature, expressive theories have also highlighted the constructive communicative function of punishment but have not imagined the communication as bi- or multidirectional, but rather unidirectional, from state to criminal. See also *supra* note 21.

women enjoy an equal legal status with men in the sense that *governmental* gender discrimination is putatively illegal. (Some major forms of private discrimination against women are illegal but, notably, although private racial discrimination in all forms of contracting is recognized as illegal in theory, the same is not true in theory or in practice about gender discrimination in contracting.)[33] Putting aside the substantial shortcomings in enforcement, as a pure method of recognition, the achievement of this status seems wanting primarily because the more straightforward and direct methods of acknowledging our equal status have been rebuffed. We were excluded in the original Constitutional declaration of equality; the most straightforward, direct acknowledgment of our equal status, the Equal Rights Amendment, was rebuffed; and the constitutional enshrinement of our equality affords intermediate but not strict scrutiny of gender discrimination. Our claim to equality is cobbled together, does not take a direct and straightforward form, and must be reargued at every turn; we may win many of the intermediate scrutiny battles, but they have to be fought. Our equality is not a definite right we can claim and demand accountability for, but is in the continual process of being forged. The outcome may resemble equality, it's a lot better than the practice preceding it, but, in historical context, the message feels ambivalent.

33. See Ian Ayres, *Pervasive Prejudice: Unconventional Evidence of Race and Gender Discrimination* (Chicago: University of Chicago Press, 2001). While Ayres draws important attention to the problem and its financial ramifications with respect to car sales, he is mistakenly sanguine about California's efforts to address this discrimination (*id.* at 3 and 136). California's Gender Tax Repeal Act of 1995 prohibits gender discrimination in *service* contracts but not contracts for the sales of goods. Cal. Civ. Code § 51.6 (1999); see also Harold E. Kahn & Robert D. Links, California Civil Practice: Civil Rights Litigation § 10.4 (2016); Amy J. Schmitz, "Sex Matters: Considering Gender in Consumer Contracting," *Cardozo Journal of Law & Gender* 19, no. 2 (2013): 437–510; Whitney Brown, "The Illegality of Sex Discrimination in Contracting," *Berkeley Journal of Gender Law & Justice* 32 (2017): 137–76 (arguing that, *contra* common interpretations, private gender discrimination in contracting violates the Civil Rights Act of 1866).

I mention this example not to pursue the specific complaint but to underscore two themes of my discussion: first, the installation of the "pattern" that justice requires is significant but often insufficient as an adequate communicative manifestation of mutual recognition. Second, what is insufficient about the governmental action qua recognition is neither that the entire country isn't vocally supporting inclusion or equality nor that some citizens harbor ambivalence in their hearts. Rather, the expression is inadequate because the moral message, to be communicated properly, requires a communicative commitment of the right form and content. Democratic law embodies commitments on behalf of an entire collective. Furthermore, where fundamental principles of equality and inclusion are at stake, an explicit, direct, foundational, and unequivocal commitment is required, advanced for the right reasons, from a collective that is correctly constituted and empowered.

WHAT DOES LAW ADD TO A WELL-ORDERED CULTURE?

Of course, even absent public, official commitments, citizens can and must call on each other to fulfill their duties of justice in extra-legal contexts. In part, we must do this to persuade each other; to draw attention to our needs, failures, and aspirations; and to ensure that we generate more explicit and official forms of legal recognition where appropriate. Still, even in ideal circumstances, the ability to refer to democratic law has some special moral force even when its content is co-extensive with what justice already demands and what citizens already privately say to one another.[34] In myriad cases, democratic

34. See Seana Valentine Shiffrin, "Immoral, Conflicting and Redundant Promises," in R. Jay Wallace, Rahul Kumar, and Samuel Freeman eds., *Reasons and Recognition: Essays on the Philosophy of T.M. Scanlon* (New York: Oxford University Press, 2011), 155–78.

law renders determinate how principles of justice are to apply in the instant context. Justice may clearly demand, for instance, fair equality of opportunity. Citizens may mutually affirm that demand to each other in their daily lives, in classroom discussions, and in the halls of the workplace and do their best, as individuals, to conform to that ideal's requirements. But, the law may, in response to the specific needs and threats encountered in the relevant environment, render significantly more concrete how that requirement will be understood and implemented. Thereby, the law gives specific shape and coordination to the direction of our actions and the content of our expectations. Concretizing a partly indeterminate obligation figures among the standard functions of a democratic law and is crucial to the generation of a particular polity's distinctive identity.

Still, it would be worth considering the (possibly hypothetical) case where the law is fully redundant of the requirement of justice, adding no detail or specific content. For instance, some (though not I) might think this characterization holds of the First Amendment's commitment that the state "shall make no law respecting an establishment of religion, or prohibiting the free exercise thereof." Even if redundant, its *articulation* has distinctive communicative moral resonance because it conveys to everyone that we, as a community, know we have this duty, we know it is relevant to our situation, and we aim to convey our knowledge of this duty to each other as fellow duty-holders and claimants. Putting it into words—and putting it into our own words—conveys sincerity and a sense that this moral commitment is sufficiently important to make salient. This acknowledgment is a central moral good for the recipient and may also assure the recipients and induce reliance. This point is a familiar one in criminal procedure circles. Officers should recite the Miranda warnings to their arrested peers, lawyers, and repeat offenders even when their recipients obviously already know their rights. Recitation of the warnings to the knowledgeable conveys that the reciting officer knows the applicable rights, acknowledges them to the party those rights protect, and therefore conveys a commitment to respect them.[35] Articulation is not only important to the recipient but to the duty-holder who articulates it. Public articulation forges a personal connection to the duty in a way that silent acknowledgment does not, reinforcing the duty's role as an organizing principle for the speaker.

Finally, articulation alters the moral dynamics between speaker and listener. When a duty-holder conveys her acknowledgment and affirmation to the person to whom it is owed, she also acknowledges that the beneficiary has a stake in her performance and in being assured. By establishing the duty as common ground between them, she invites the beneficiary's perspective on the performance.[36] This invitation enhances the meaningfulness of the communication and alters the moral posture of the claimant. When I ask you to perform your unacknowledged duty, the dynamic is likely to be one of demand or moral education. Our mutual posture structurally tends toward the hierarchical or the adversarial. By contrast, when I ask you to perform a duty you have publicly affirmed, the dynamic is more one in which I supply a reminder. Because of your public acknowledgment of the duty and my stake in it, my reminder could fit more into a cooperative model. I am reminding you of something you have affiliated yourself with and that, to some extent, is publicly connected to your identity and your integrity. We could understand my

35. See Welsh S. White, "Defending Miranda: A Reply to Professor Caplan," *Vanderbilt Law Review* 39, no. 1 (1986): 1–22, at 6–7. Of course, mere recitation of rights (even when sincere) may fall short of effective communication and, in some circumstances, may induce a false complacency by suspects that the police protect and respect their other rights and interests. Adequate communication in many circumstances may require ensuring accurate understanding (as well as good faith implementation of the voiced commitment).

36. See also Shiffrin, "Immoral Promises," *supra* note 33, at 156; Jorah Dannenberg, "Promising Ourselves, Promising Others," *The Journal of Ethics* 19, no. 2 (2015):159–83, at 178.

reminder as a partial effort at joint collaboration in working out how and when to advance something of mutual, shared concern.

Of course, that's the ideal case. If you are recalcitrant, things may take a turn for the testy. But, in simpler cases where I need to call on you to plan your own performance so I can coordinate and plan, or where you forget or procrastinate, your acknowledgment of your duty facilitates, more naturally, a cooperative dynamic given the voiced mutual understanding. Even when we have conflicting interpretations, our discussion will tend to center more on what we mean and value about dis-establishmentarianism, for example, rather than whether religion or atheism are bunk. I suggest the same thing is true in politics. To take just one example, this may sometimes characterize the posture of parties in litigation about cases of first impression. Both sides have a strong view about what justice requires, but they also regard the process as a necessary one of working out, with greater articulation, the implications of our prior voiced commitments. That we need to work it out does not always reveal the other side as evil or recalcitrant. Even in an adversarial context, there can be an underlying cooperative spirit.

I began by arguing that even were the material and intellectual components of justice already in place, each individual would have a need for an organized social forum that affords each person the opportunity to participate in a communicative endeavor, alongside others, directed at all her fellow citizens. Equally, she has a need to receive that forum's communicative output. The assumption of realized justice was not meant to be a plausible approximation of our circumstances. Rather, it was meant to highlight that the value of democratic law is not fully captured by its role in obtaining the results of material and intellectual justice, whether in circumstances amenable to social consensus or social conflict. But, of course, the material and intellectual components of justice do not come to us prepackaged and preinstalled. Consequently, our individual obligations of justice are not confined merely to taking ownership of an otherwise extant system of justice in a communicatively resonant way, but also to ensuring that the material and intellectual components of justice are crafted and realized in a communicatively resonant way as *ours*.

As with the communicative burdens with which I began, our individual obligations of material and intellectual justice could not be discharged through individual, uncoordinated action. But they can be achieved collectively through an organization to which we all belong and contribute that manifests equality in its explicit structure, its processes of creation and implementation, and the consequences of its output. While each of us cannot *show* our recognition of each other's mutual equal status and belonging through our everyday interpersonal conduct, our legal system can do this. It can adopt explicit laws that declare and support our equal status and needs. Its laws can aim to create environments in which individuals interact with one another on an equal basis, including the avenues of access to power. Furthermore, its own internal procedures of generation, implementation, and enforcement can reflect this fundamental recognition. These processes and outputs themselves may serve as our collective expression to ourselves when their generation arises from processes that pay tribute to our mutual equality.

The state is the crucial organizational structure to achieve these communicative aims. Families and voluntary associations cannot achieve their values while paying full tribute to the value of inclusion. Families cannot achieve intimacy while embracing a stance of terrific inclusiveness. To achieve the substantive affiliative values and purposes of voluntary associations, they must have the ability to exclude on the basis of perceived fit and congeniality as well as on the basis of substantive dissonance.[37] They cannot even be achieved by a

37. See Seana Valentine Shiffrin, "What Is Really Wrong with Compelled Association?" *Northwestern University Law Review* 99, no. 2 (2005): 839–88.

group that includes everyone in virtue of some common substantive feature or aim, such as our each being a child of God. For while the all-inclusive association may insist on our common possession of the feature, the individual may disavow its possession or importance. The association will thus fail to convey the appropriate message of inclusion, one that must be capable of being received and endorsed by the included. To convey our endorsement of the value of belonging, we need an organization that has the qualities and resources necessary to be a site of unselective inclusion—namely, one that has some control over a geographical space and sufficient resources to ensure that its members can be afforded access to them that will allow them to function effectively within its space as an equal member.

The democratic state has a unique ability to convey this mutual recognition that is connected to its unique ability to respect and address a related, fundamental moral fact: namely, that we each, as social beings, have a legitimate need to have a home among others—a place to which we belong and in which our other needs have standing, just in light of our status as human beings. (This legitimate need places pressure on us to resist qualification-based citizenship and immigration policies and to favor those policies using automatic, random, or need-based criteria.) Fulfilling these two interconnected missions—most importantly, expressing through action the recognition of our mutual equality as free persons and the complementary recognition of our legitimate claim of inclusion and membership in a collective moral body—is the fundamental charge of the state, achieved in their most meaningful form through laws crafted within a democratic setting in which we each have participatory powers in the construction of law and the mode and direction of its implementation.[38] Those

38. Contrast Kolodny, "Rule over None I," *supra* note 3, at 221–22, who highlights the insulting message conveyed by an unequal distribution of power but identifies nothing positive about democratic schemes to recommend them. Thus, his theory, as he concedes, lacks the resources to object to a system of universal, disempowered, but equal subjection

participatory powers allow the state's expressive actions to be reasonably attributed to its citizens. Two features of democratic law do work here: (1) law effects a persistent institutional commitment applicable to all, and (2), in a democratic structure, law has a communicative dimension whose content may be attributed to all of us together, even if not to each of us as individuals.

PARTICIPATION AND INTERPRETATION

This account offers answers to puzzles that dog other democratic theories: it offers reasons why one has reason to participate in democratic processes even when, predictably, one's preferred position would win without one's support or lose even with one's support; it offers reasons to follow and respect laws; and it supplies a connection between the two endeavors. My reason to vote is not exhausted by my interest in influencing the election's outcome but is provided by the imperatives that I should express my affiliation with the joint collective body that has the function of embodying our commitment to our equal status and that I, as a co-author, should contribute to the joint deliberation about and determination of the particular

imposed by a benevolent dictator from afar who imposed a basic structure (otherwise) compliant with justice. On Kolodny's view, a commitment to democracy only clearly yields a commitment to substantive levels of power equally shared because no benevolent distant dictator happens to be on the far horizon as an equally palatable alternative. By contrast, my view identifies the positive contribution of democratic schemes that the schemes of equal subordination lack: democratic schemes enable us to meet our communicative duties to one another. Daniel Viehoff's account of political authority, which emphasizes the importance of "coordination without subjection" or of avoiding political authority emanating from unequal relations of power, is also vulnerable to a similar complaint; as he acknowledges, his argument for the special connection between political authority and democracy does not rest on any special positive feature of *democracy* but only the absence of subordination—an omission that holds just as well for decision-making by coin-flipping. See Daniel Viehoff, "Democratic Equality and Political Authority," *Philosophy & Public Affairs* 42, no. 4 (2014): 337–75, at 374–75.

form that commitment should take (whether directly, as with a referendum, or indirectly, when we elect agents who themselves offer a concrete vision of how to make our joint commitment more determinate).[39] Even when I believe that my substantive policy positions or representative choices are doomed or overdetermined, there are independent grounds to contribute my voice to the public communicative affirmation of the democratic legal process as itself part of the substantive embodiment of our commitment to equality.

Adherence to law may be given a similar treatment.[40] My reasons to adhere include the communicative recognition that democratic law is an ongoing effort to express our joint mutual respect.[41]

39. To be sure, elections are not the sole or sufficient sites of such contributions. Such contributions should occur at many stages of the political process and may take many forms, including through informal political conversations, commentary and advice, participation in voluntary associations and political groups, and other ways of becoming informed and working jointly to develop and express sound positions.

40. This argument is not intended to be exclusive, but it is compatible with other accounts of the reasons to vote and of reasons to respect the law. With respect to the latter, my argument may be a version or specification of Scheffler's recent argument in which he argues that when membership in a group is non-instrumentally valuable, there are prima facie obligations to abide by its norms. See Samuel Scheffler, "Membership and Political Obligation," *Journal of Political Philosophy* (2017), doi:10.1111/jopp.12125. I find his argument intriguing, but I am more confident that it is persuasive when there is a close substantive connection between the group's system of norms (or conformance with them) and the reasons why membership in the group is non-instrumentally valuable. That connection need not always hold, but it does in the case of democratic law where the norms themselves, the system of their generation, and the effort to abide by them aim in conception to express respect for our mutual equality and the achievement of a concrete realization of our equality is, partly, why membership is valuable.

41. An account of this kind may evade the criticisms Liam Murphy lodges against other efforts to connect democratic law with reasons to respect the law; these criticisms note a gap between arguments for democracy *as an institution* and arguments for *individual* compliance. See Murphy, *supra* note 2, at 123–26. The argument I have pursued for democratic law foundationally connects the institution of democratic law to individual duties to show respect for others and so avoids the gap. Moreover, the communicative grounds for respecting democratic law does not appeal to the disrespect that disobedience may show to others who comply or vote, whether because of concerns about free-riding or unfairly substituting one's own will for the general will. Rather, the reason to vote and to respect democratic law that I identify is grounded in the *positive* communicative respect such actions distinctively

By adhering to it, I express my affiliation with and ongoing effort in that joint affirmation, even when I might have urged us to express our joint mutual respect in quite different terms.[42] Protest and other visible, vocal means of dissent work alongside voting and compliance. Separate from any hope of sparking repeal or future reform, these activities add nuance and complexity to the message conveyed by an election or the passage of a law. They render vivid, where necessary, that a particular law's claim to represent *us* may be especially precarious (and not only dis-preferred by a large minority) and that it certainly does not represent the convictions of many of us as individuals. These activities may even ambiguate, in a normatively meaningful way, the message these political events convey; for example, large-scale protests may cast doubt on the meaning of a landslide vote. For example, at first, the vote might have seemed to provide a "mandate" for a party's platform, but the protests may instead suggest that the asymmetrical vote was the product of social division, voter exclusion or suppression, fraud, and/or boycotts. This symbiotic complementarity of participations in elections following the law *and* vocal protest underscores a point I made at the outset that a free speech culture is as essential to democracy as elections and other representative devices.

A communicative account also offers reasons of a different kind for a Dworkinian, morally tethered approach to legal interpretation.

convey because they are distinctive ways of endorsing a system whose structure and content is designed to embody respect for others as equals.

42. See also Meir Dan-Cohen, *Normative Subjects: Self and Collectivity in Morality and Law* (New York: Oxford University Press, 2016), at 221–24. Dan-Cohen argues that because "communal communication expresses an aspect of the members' identity defined by their collective affiliation," communal speech may represent community members, even when there is internal disagreement between members about the content of the appropriate message. When an authorized member speaks for the collective, even if other members would have said something different had they been called upon to speak, all the members may bear responsibility for what is said.

Very roughly speaking, the aim to legitimize law's intrinsic coercive power drives Dworkin's argument for a morally infused justificatory element of interpretation.[43] A conception of law as coercive, however, evokes some of the estrangement and resignation toward law and democracy I gestured toward at the outset—starting with the idea that law fundamentally envisions reluctant compliers toward whom we must imagine how, morally, we could threaten them. When one keeps foremost the idea that law is *ours*, coercion might not figure among the ur-qualities to recite about law unless one conceived of oneself as weak-willed or perhaps into bondage. For these and other reasons, I have never been persuaded that coercion is an essential feature of law.

But, on a communicative view, moral readings do not arise from a need to legitimate otherwise suspect or regrettable threats.[44] For two reasons other than the justification of coercion, legal materials should be interpreted, insofar as possible, to be sensitive to the demands of justice: first, if an essential function of democracy is to convey jointly to each other our respect for our mutual equality as well as our commitment to justice and our other moral aims, then the principle of interpretative charity recommends that democratic legal materials should be interpreted in light of this aim. Second, a judge herself, as a citizen representing the collective, has reason to contribute to the moral communicative process of which law is a

43. See, e.g., Ronald Dworkin, *Law's Empire* (Cambridge, MA: Harvard University Press,1986), at 108–12. The emphasis on legitimating state coercion also drives David Estlund's defense of democracy and elections. Estlund, *supra* note 4, at 65–66 and 99. See also Hans Kelsen, *The Essence and Value of Democracy*, translated by Brian Graf, edited by Nadia Urbinati and Carlos Invernizzi Accetti (Lanham, MD: Rowman & Littlefield, 2013), at 27–34.

44. Thus, a communicative view of democracy is also better positioned to explain why democratic structure and a morally tethered interpretative approach is also apt for the governing rules of voluntary associations—even those that forswear coercive methods of enforcement.

component by infusing its legal decisions with appropriate moral content. A judge would be sensitive to precedent and continuity with the past (what Dworkin labels "fit") in order to realize our interest in expressing ourselves, when called for, with the constancy that contributes to the depth and steadiness of our commitments. Attending to fit also preserves and extends the coherence of our distinctive voice as a community over time. Finally, to the extent that fit roughly serves the values of horizontal equity, albeit intertemporally, sensitivity to fit also institutionally manifests our commitment to equality.

BREAD-AND-BUTTER LAWS

Suppose laws forged and maintained in democratic circumstances do play a role in the articulation of our moral status and our joint moral values. Why not view this communicative function as an important anomaly true only of a handful of legal materials dedicated to high values, such as the Constitution and quasi-constitutional statutes like the Civil Rights Acts and the Affordable Care Act? My theory may seem a poor characterization of bread-and-butter laws, by which I mean not only agricultural laws like those that regulate the purity of the food supply but also the laws and regulations enforced by the departments of weights and measures or the regulation establishing the fee per hour at a parking meter. Most laws do not sport the high values of a constitution. Most laws are crafted by officials rather than a gathering and simultaneous expression of the electorate. In other words, what significant value and relation do *we* convey to one another when the Department of Motor Vehicles sets a $2 per hour parking rate?

In response, I deny the premise that there is a substantial qualitative distinction between everyday law and high constitutional and statutory law. First, bread-and-butter laws, when justified, serve to promote our moral ends together. Often, they enable us to pursue our own robust ends as individuals, allowing for meaningfully autonomous lives compatible with our simultaneous participation in collective life. Bread-and-butter laws often do so at a material level, aiming to ensure that food production is done safely, that transport routes and other elements of infrastructure are maintained, etc. When they operate well, everyday laws support a structure that frees us from addressing daily and directly the safe provision of each of our material needs; the legal structure supports a social division of labor that we may rely on as safe, fair, and adequate to the task. Everyday law also preserves public spaces, which in turn serve public values, including that of free social interchange, which, itself, is a constituent of democratic culture. Even parking regulations serve an important moral end by enabling a variety of people to flow through public space rather than permitting access points to be monopolized by a few. When it operates well, private law likewise shoulders some burdens to facilitate individuals' concentration on their own projects, permitting strangers and intimates alike to arrange their lives together on just terms with some security and direction for the range of unforeseen or suboptimal circumstances that may arise. Furthermore, private law, like public law, encodes other commitments and facilitates other forms of healthy moral relationships. Contract law, for instance, may be considered as a legal structure dedicated to upholding the public values of promissory honesty and fidelity and to supporting a culture of trust. Once we consider the underlying moral purposes of quotidian law, it seems difficult to sustain a sharp contrast between its normative communicative functions and the more explicit moral aims of the Constitution.

CONCLUSION

I have been arguing that a system of democratic law is an essential mechanism through which the community's members express to each other their joint recognition of each other's membership—their belonging by right and their equal status, substantively understood. This argument might serve as a counterpoint to the widespread sense of many that democracy has no intrinsic value or that it serves mainly as a mechanism of fair conflict management among disputants. It might also revive some interest in the law by democratic theorists and perhaps encourage the idea that the role and function of law (or legal materials) in a democracy differs substantially from its role in unjust systems.

Such a theory lends itself to a more positive, inspirational view of law, democracy, and their aspirations than many extant views that cast law and democracy as methods of controlled skirmish between opposed interest groups. There is a puzzling mismatch between the dedication and zeal people have for democracy and the resigned air of many desultory accounts of democracy. Having the resources to describe democratic law as aspirational would have the virtue of befitting the urgency of democratic movements worldwide and the courage and sacrifices made by their members. Effective communication of a deliberate and sincere motive of inclusion in a society of equals through articulate and practical means is a cause; its achievement is a moral accomplishment.

On some views, successful efforts at moral agency represent the realization or at least the pinnacle of freedom. Certainly, the public affirmation, in discourse and action, has substantial meaning to its recipients that goes beyond the pattern of action it produces. One lives in a substantially superior community when one knows that one is equal because the community recognizes and values one's equality and has gone to the effort to make this palpable, rather than because the community will suffer economic sanctions if international observers perceive a pattern of discrimination. Successful communication of a deliberate motive of inclusion is a rather substantial achievement. Its great importance and its personal, expressive dimension make it a worthy end—a deliberate destination of one's activity—rather than merely the site on which one is deposited if one has avoided important dangers and catastrophes. Moreover, given the palpable challenges of moral understanding and communication and the elements of creativity and expression in moral performance, the process of articulating our moral commitments together may contribute to a climate of trust and cohesion and the pursuit of a collective political identity. These accomplishments in turn may allow us to proceed to embark on modes of moral expression that represent us as a distinctive moral community. The moral and expressive collective opportunities that democracies afford, not their status and function as lesser evils, are what make sense of the passion for democracy.

PART II

LEGAL APPLICATIONS

Introduction to Part II

SEANA VALENTINE SHIFFRIN

In Chapter 1, I argued that citizens have a moral need to convey and receive certain moral messages from each other that affirm their mutual equality, basic rights, and their belonging in a moral community. Those particular messages must take the form of collective commitments. Democratic law plays a unique and inspiring role in satisfying that need by constituting a community of equal membership that can pursue collective moral ends for and in the name of the community by producing articulate, public commitments to mandatory and discretionary ends.

The following two chapters aim to illustrate that this conception of democratic law is not a mere overlay, so abstract as to be divorced from the considerations that shape law's content. Rather, a communicative conception of democratic law can and should make a difference to concrete legal issues. If mutual, ongoing communication and affirmation of our values and commitments is a foundational organizing end of democratic law, then we must *generate* coherent, morally legible law as an articulate representation of our values.

By contrast, reductionist conceptions of democratic law that understand law merely as a procedurally fair method of managing discrete disputes between contesting interests will view the generation of articulate law as more dispensable. Should disputes be managed another way, the absence of law represents no loss. Moreover, reductionist views regard incoherence within law as the unremarkable byproduct of compromises reached by conflicting forces whose identity and power shift over time and circumstance. On such views, incoherence and inconsistency may be undesirable when they impede predictions of legal outcomes, but they do not otherwise represent intrinsic normative shortcomings, whereas a communicative conception regards incoherence and moral illegibility as substantial self-defeating defects of a democratic legal system.

In this Part, I will pursue two examples to illustrate how greater consciousness of a communicative conception of democratic law could influence the generation and content of law. Chapter 2 explores the communicative moral significance of generating law and, in particular the common law, by investigating a specific case involving federal preemption and the common law of contract. Chapter 3 addresses issues of incoherence and incompletely realized commitments in the context of constitutional balancing by asking how we should understand the composition and sincere articulation of state interests within a balancing framework.

In both chapters, I focus on American examples because they are what I know and because our system has *some* of the background architecture of democratic law. Although the United States is a deeply flawed and endangered exemplar of an aspiring democratic legal system, our Constitution expresses firm commitments about the equality of all persons, however imperfectly those commitments are understood or attained. It also expresses firm commitments to protect some of our essential rights and interests, however incomplete its lists and strained its realized protections. Furthermore, our precedential, adversarial judiciary entertains arguments by the parties' own representatives, typically offers reasons for its decisions that guide future cases, and engages in an ongoing dialogue of reasons with the public and other reason-giving officials. Indeed, the examples I will pursue highlight the judiciary's special role in a system of democratic law, a role that is neither secondary nor subordinate to the legislature's.

In concentrating on some shortcomings in the contemporary approach to common law and constitutional methodology, I leave aside extensive criticism of the more obvious defects of our aspirant democracy, both persistent and fresh. I appreciate the oddity of dwelling on a slow-acting disease afflicting some trees while a fire threatens the forest. I bracket some pressing issues not to diminish them, but because it is so clear that our democratic aspirations compel us to resist contemporary initiatives to renege on these (already imperfectly fulfilled) commitments and impel us better to realize them—by eradicating social oppression, economic and status inequalities, discriminatory policing, pointless and excessive incarceration, and private campaign financing (to name only a few priorities). Pragmatically, while we must counter attacks on our core principles and address shortfalls in their realization, we must also protect our still operative democratic institutions from decay. Conversations about their best functioning are part of their maintenance. We may teeter on the precipice of some cataclysmic changes, but some institutions and practices remain downstream from the earliest line of fire; their operation, on well-considered principles, may help to preserve some of the skeletal architecture of the republic or at least slow the destructive momentum.

The examples I will discuss are, moreover, theoretically interesting because their departures from a communicative model of democratic law are subtler than the blunt and shameless contemporary threats that now dominate our agenda of daily anxieties. They do not involve egregious violations of human rights and the flirtation with dictatorship. Yet, in both cases, an implicit, if partial, reliance on reductionist impulses leaves our legal approach wanting. Our contemporary approach to federal preemption exemplifies insufficient moral sensitivity to democratic interests in articulating common law. With respect to constitutional balancing, our methodology seems indifferent to coherence in ways that render the methodology empty. By contrast, a communicative approach would take the methodology seriously. In doing so, it would elicit coherence and a more deliberative perspective on the interests advanced by state actors.

Chapter 2

Democratic Law and the Erosion of Common Law

SEANA VALENTINE SHIFFRIN

INTRODUCTION

The conception of democratic law that I outlined in Chapter 1 should ignite a concern about a growing indifference to the democratic importance of the generation of common law. My allusion to the "democratic importance of the generation of the common law" may startle some readers given the alleged tension between judicially articulated law and democracy. In Chapter 1, I gave some reasons to question that tension. In this chapter, I will elaborate on my conviction that the common law has a central place in a communicative conception of democratic law by focusing on the recent case of *Northwest v. Ginsberg*, a unanimously decided Supreme Court preemption case that displaced the state common law about contractual good faith in the air travel context.[1] It is a somewhat obscure case, but it is not an isolated example of the troubling undervaluation of the common law

1. Nw., Inc. v. Ginsberg, 134 S. Ct. 1422 (2014).

Seana Valentine Shiffrin, *Democratic Law and the Erosion of Common Law* In: *Democratic Law*.
Edited by: Hannah Ginsborg, Oxford University Press.
DOI: 10.1093/oso/9780190084486.003.0003

that partly propels its disposition. Indeed, its perceived unremarkability is itself telling, signaling an internalization and normalization of substantial defects in the Court's implicit view of the value of law and its relation to markets as well as of the common law in particular.

SOME BACKGROUND

To make one's way into the case and the issues that concern me, it may help to introduce some preliminary background on federal preemption and common law. (I will also say more, in a bit, about the duty of good faith.) *Federal preemption* is one of many legal doctrines that enforce the supremacy of the federal government over state governments. The basic notions, with which I have no quarrel, are simple: within the range of its enumerated powers, the federal government may decide to occupy a field of legislation and displace state law, whether or not the state law substantively conflicts with federal legislation and whether or not the federal legislation contains counterpart provisions that address the same questions or problems as the state law. This power to occupy complements the supremacy of federal law over state law, which resolves conflicts between valid federal legislation and state law in favor of federal law.[2] Interesting *legal* issues arise in these domains about what counts as a conflict beyond explicit contradiction, which fields the federal government may occupy exclusively, whether the federal intent to displace state law

2. Stephen Gardbaum distinguishes between *supremacy* (conflicts are to be resolved in favor of the federal government), an automatic federal power, and *preemption*, a discretionary federal power through which the federal government elects to displace state power. Stephen Gardbaum, "Congress's Power to Preempt the States," *Pepperdine Law Review* 33, no. 1 (2006): 39–68, at 40–41. Although his distinction is sound and important, I use "preemption" to refer to both for convenience.

must be clearly articulated, and how far the occupied field's boundaries extend.

Interesting *political* issues arise concerning *when* the federal government should exercise its preemption power to displace concurrent state law. Resolving these issues requires considering when tensions between diverse state and federal means and purposes become untenable, whether we want dual sovereigns pursuing the same aims or prefer a single agent of implementation, and how to interpret provisions and purposes that are not explicitly articulated. Should we interpret federal statutory provisions and preemptive intent narrowly to preserve a robust arena in which states may develop a distinctive form of law, or should we interpret federal provisions broadly to ensure the more successful pursuit of federal aims and a unified national approach?

From a communicative perspective on democratic law, these are important questions for two reasons. First, local and state governments may have a special significance for communicative approaches. Some democratic legal aims are better realized when the community is powerful enough to develop a distinctive voice yet small enough to generate a distinctive identity and camaraderie between citizens. An overly expansive preemption regime may foreclose some of the opportunities for developing distinctive communities that elicit strong affiliations.

Second, the balance struck between federal and state power will also affect the scope of common law. Judicially articulated common law is the primary source of general property, contract, and tort law. When courts act as common law courts, rather than interpreting and applying a statutory text, they apply and expand on previously judicially articulated law to articulate the law further as cases present themselves. With some exceptions,[3] since the landmark case of

3. See Nat'l Soc'y of Prof'l Eng'rs v. United States, 435 U.S. 679, 688 (1978) (finding that Congress "expected the courts to give shape to the [the Sherman Antitrust Act's] broad

Erie Railroad Company v. Tompkins,[4] common law jurisprudence has been largely a state law matter, given definitive articulation by state courts.[5] So, when a federal statute preempts state law, it may hinder the development and articulation of common law; in tandem, it may weaken or constrain the reach and depth of the local social-moral culture. These ramifications should trouble us from a democratic, communicative perspective.

Although it officially espouses a doctrine of narrow construction to preserve state autonomy,[6] the Supreme Court has increasingly expanded the scope of federal preemption in recent years. For example, the Court has preempted states' common law unconscionability jurisprudence through its finding that the Federal Arbitration Act evinces strong support for clauses in standard employment and consumer contracts that mandate individual arbitration.[7] I share critics' reservations about the Act's interpretation and the hazards of facilitating corporate preferences for

mandate by drawing on common-law tradition"); Ernest A. Young, "Preemption and Federal Common Law," *Notre Dame Law Review* 83, no. 4 (2008): 1639–80, at 1639–46 (discussing the forms federal common law has taken, as well as its origins).

4. 304 U.S. 64 (1938).
5. For example, there is no general federal common law of contracts, although there is federal common law for some specific situations, such as cases involving federal government contracts or those contracts governed by Employee Retirement Income Security Act of 1974 (ERISA). See 14D Charles Alan Wright et al., Federal Practice & Procedure § 3803.1 (4th ed.) (2017) & 19 Charles Alan Wright et al., Federal Practice & Procedure § 4514 (3d ed.) (2017). And, of course, federal courts may rule on state common law issues appropriately presented to them (as when they have diversity jurisdiction), but they are bound to follow the relevant state's interpretation of its common law (or, where it is unsettled, to predict the state's highest court's interpretation). 19 Charles Alan Wright et al., Federal Practice & Procedure § 4507 (3d ed.) (2017).
6. See, e.g., Medtronic, Inc. v. Lohr, 518 U.S. 470, 485 (1996) (presuming that an act of Congress does not preempt state action without Congress's express intent to the contrary and directing that Congress's express intent to preempt state law should be interpreted narrowly).
7. See, e.g., AT&T Mobility LLC v. Concepcion, 563 U.S. 333 (2011); Am. Express Co. v. Italian Colors Rest., 133 S. Ct. 2304 (2013).

mandatory individual arbitration. Such reservations are reasonably intensified when the arbitration process is too cumbersome, time-consuming, and expensive for individuals to navigate just for themselves; when repeat arbitrators tilt corporate; and when a rigid, asymmetric bargaining dynamic precludes individual bargaining around these clauses.[8]

As enforceable arbitration clauses proliferate, in addition to depriving individual litigants of due process, the common law may languish because substantive, important disputes over commonplace contracts may never reach court.[9] Similarly, the growing trend of permissiveness toward enforcing remedial clauses (commonly known as *liquidated* or *stipulated damages* clauses) may likewise suppress the development of common law remedial principles.[10] Enabling these private agreements thus deprives us of the opportunities to resolve important disputes publicly through the articulation of legal principles and thereby contribute to our evolving public understanding of our mutual commitments.

8. See, e.g., Judith Resnik, "Fairness in Numbers: A Comment on *AT&T v. Concepcion, Wal-mart v. Dukes,* and *Turner v. Rogers,*" *Harvard Law Review* 125, no. 1 (2011): 78–170, at 114; David S. Schwartz, "Mandatory Arbitration and Fairness," *Notre Dame Law Review* 84, no. 3 (2009): at 1247; David S. Schwartz, "The Federal Arbitration Act and the Power of Congress over State Courts," *Oregon Law Review* 83, no. 2 (2004): 541–630. See also William B. Rubenstein, "Procedure and Society: An Essay for Steve Yeazell," *UCLA Law Review Discourse* 61 (2013): 136–48, at 142–43 (decrying the inconsistency between corporate insistence on individual arbitration and its conveyance through standard-form contracts of adhesion).

9. See Myriam Gilles, "The Day Doctrine Died: Private Arbitration and the End of Law," *University of Illinois Law Review* 2016, no. 2 (2016): 371–424, at 409–13; Resnik, *supra* note 8, at 114.

10. See Seana Valentine Shiffrin, "Remedial Clauses: The Overprivatization of Private Law," *Hastings Law Journal* 67 (2016): 407–42 (discussing how enforceable remedial clauses may suppress the development and refinement of common law remedial principles).

NORTHWEST V. GINSBERG AND THE DUTY OF GOOD FAITH

Triggering a common law vacuum is not only a potential side effect of the Court's arbitration decisions and the proliferation of remedial clauses. It is also the direct, unacknowledged product of another, unanimously decided preemption case, *Northwest v. Ginsberg,* that flew under the nation's radar. Three years ago, *Ginsberg* held that the Airline Deregulation Act (ADA) preempts state common law with respect to the implied covenant of good faith and fair dealing in contractual relations involving frequent flyer programs.

Rabbi Ginsberg was a platinum-level frequent flyer with Northwest Airlines who regularly lodged complaints. Northwest Airlines abruptly terminated his membership in the program, citing this contractual provision: "[a]buse of the . . . program (including . . . improper conduct as determined by [Northwest] in its sole judgment[)] . . . may result in cancellation of the member's account."[11] Northwest provided neither a description of Ginsberg's alleged improper conduct nor any compensation for his accumulated miles. Ginsberg sued, claiming inter alia, that Northwest violated an implicit, common law covenant of good faith and fair dealing by failing to give reasons for his termination.

The implied duty of good faith invoked by Ginsberg is a theoretically noteworthy doctrine. It requires that contractual parties exhibit "faithfulness to an agreed common purpose and consistency with the justified expectations of the other party."[12] Contractual parties need not serve as each other's advocates or fiduciaries just by virtue of their having formed a contract. They are, however, expected to avoid "[s]ubterfuges and evasions . . . of the spirit of the bargain . . . [and]

11. *Ginsberg,* 134 S. Ct. at 1426–27.
12. Restatement (Second) of Contracts § 205 cmt. a (Am. Law Inst. 1981).

abuse of a power to specify terms. . . ."[13] As one court put it, the duty of good faith demands that "neither party shall do anything which will have the effect of destroying or injuring the right of the other party to receive the fruits of the contract."[14] While contracts may allocate degrees of discretion to parties in how they assess and execute their agreed-upon duties, they are constrained to exercise that discretion with good faith.

One manifestation of good faith is that one's exercise of discretion is guided by non-arbitrary reasons, the contents of which respect the point of the agreement and could be understood, publicly, to do so.[15] Described in this way, the duty of good faith naturally commands the interest and approbation of the sort of motive-attentive democratic legal theory I defended in Chapter 1. Incorporating a duty of good faith into its contract law is a way a democratic legal system concretizes our expectation that citizens should keep their commitments and that they should do so in a deliberate way that reflects an understanding of the purpose of the agreement. This latter expectation resonates with the moral conviction that while respectful action involves some actions that may be specified in advance, respectful action also depends on animating motives that, among other things, provide meaning and guidance when parties enter interstitial territory.

So, although under the contract Northwest had substantial discretion to assess 'improper conduct,' Ginsberg alleged that Northwest had to have a reason related to improper conduct to terminate Ginsberg. That reason, as well as Northwest's conception of what constitutes improper conduct would have to be consistent with

13. *Id.* at cmt. d.

14. Dalton v. Educ. Testing Serv., 663 N.E.2d 289, 291 (N.Y. Sup. Ct. 1995) (quoting Kirke La Shelle Co. v. Paul Armstrong Co., 263 N.Y. 79, 85 (1933)).

15. Nickerson v. Fleet Nat'l Bank, 924 N.E.2d 696, 704 (Mass. 2000) (explaining that focus of a good faith inquiry is not on the action but the reason or motive for its performance and whether it showed an absence of good faith).

the spirit of their bargain. It could not simply terminate him for reasons of convenience or profit. In turn, Northwest countered that the ADA preempted the duty of good faith through its provision that "a State . . . may not enact or enforce a law, regulation, or other provision having the force and effect of law related to a price, route, or service of an air carrier . . . ."[16] The ADA did not explicitly articulate any intent to displace common law, in general, or the implied duty of good faith, in particular, so the dispute was over whether the ADA's preemptive provision implicitly extended that far.

In addressing this dispute, the Court operated under some pressure to remain true to an earlier preemption decision, *American Airlines, Inc. v. Wolens*,[17] in which plaintiffs challenged retroactive changes to American Airlines' frequent flyer program. The *Wolens* Court held that the ADA preempted a state statute regulating fraud but not breach of contract claims, including claims of improper modification of terms, because contracts represent voluntary undertakings by the parties.[18] If preemption did not reach breach of contract

16. 49 U.S.C. § 41713(b)(1) (1994).
17. 513 U.S. 219 (1995).
18. *Id.* at 222. How *Wolens* understood the division between state-imposed regulation and contract law is questionable. In what follows, I advocate a distinction between statutory law and common law based on their different normative contributions to a legal system, but I do not think that division is well understood by checking to see if there is a statutory text. Some statutory texts, after all, are simply codifications of common law principles. See, e.g., Lewis Grossman, "Codification and the California Mentality," *Hastings Law Journal* 45, no. 3 (1994): 617–39, at 621; Cal. Civ. Code §5; Gunther A. Weiss, "The Enchantment of Codification in the Common-Law World," *Yale Journal of International Law* 25, no. 2 (2000): 435–532 (analyzing the codification movement in common law societies, including the United States); see also *Wolens*, 513 U.S. at 236 (Stevens, J., concurring in part and dissenting in part) (analogizing state's fraud statute to "a codification of common-law negligence rules"). Moreover, looking for a text only makes sense if you think the issue turns on whether the state has exerted extra effort or zeal as a marker of its agency in imposing an obligation. I think the issue is less the degree of state activity and more one of substance. Among the factors one might investigate include whether the statute attempted to move beyond or to reverse common law principles and whether the duty in question is part of an agreement elected by the parties, incident to one, or independent of one.

claims, then breach of the implied covenant of good faith would seem to fall under *Wolens'* protective umbrella. After all, the default interpretative rule of good faith is both a constitutive portion of the parties' 'voluntary undertaking' and a rule of interpretation that makes sense of specific terms. Furthermore, state court oversight of whether airlines administer frequent flyer programs in good faith is not a back-door way for states to reintroduce price controls into the airline market, so the covenant of good faith need not conflict with those federal aims.

Nonetheless, Northwest prevailed for reasons that flirt with the sort of reductionism about law that I contrasted with a democratic conception at the outset of this Part. Justice Alito reasoned that the frequent flyer program related to price because Ginsberg used his miles for flights and upgrades.[19] Furthermore, the opinion offered the assurance that the free market and the Department of Transportation would adequately police bad faith.[20] The decision stressed that the implied covenant of good faith cannot be contracted around in Minnesota and so that duty was deemed not a 'voluntary undertaking,' but instead a 'state-imposed' obligation.[21] The Court considered whether it should matter that the federal law would preempt a common law doctrine rather than a state statutory provision.[22] It batted off this concern rather brusquely, reasoning that both statutory and common law have the force of law and declaring that "[w]hat is important . . . is the effect of a state law, regulation, or provision, but

19. *Ginsberg,* 134 S. Ct. at 1430–31. This rationale is rather strained, for surely the plaintiffs in *Wolens* who objected to an airline's retroactive change of frequent flyer terms also sought to use miles for flights and upgrades.

20. *Ginsberg,* 134 S. Ct. at 1433. The invocation of the Department of Transportation was odd in light of Wolen's stress on the fact that the Department of Transportation "lack[s] contract dispute resolution resources." *Wolens,* 513 U.S. at 234.

21. *Ginsberg,*134 S.Ct. at 1432; see also *Wolens,* 513 U.S. at 228–29.

22. *Ginsberg,*134 S.Ct. at 1429–30.

not its form . . . ."[23] The Court unfortunately took no time to consider the different forms and attendant procedures of the production of statutory versus common law and how those differences might bear on the content and function of the law. All of these arguments seem flawed, but, as I will now elaborate, the claims about contracts, good faith, and common law merit a special rebuke from a communicative perspective that values law as a forum of public communication and transmission of public values.

IS THE DUTY OF GOOD FAITH A DISCRETE, STATE-IMPOSED OBLIGATION OR IS IT IMPLICIT IN THE PARTIES' PROMISES?

To begin, the division that the Court drew between the state's imposition of a duty of 'good faith' and the parties' voluntary undertakings is strange.[24] After all, the duty of good faith (and cousin doctrines like

23. *Id.* at 1430.

24. It recalls another strange distinction the Minnesota Supreme Court drew in *Cohen v. Cowles Media Co.*, 457 N.W. 2d 199, 203–205 (1990). That case distinguished between contract claims based on promissory estoppel, which, when involving promises by the press of confidentiality for a source, it represented as raising special state action and First Amendment concerns, as contrasted with those contract claims based on consideration which the Court regarded as private action, whose enforcement thus did not raise First Amendment concerns. On review, the US Supreme Court found that enforcement would not violate the First Amendment and took no strong stand on the distinction between consideration contracts and promissory estoppel. Nonetheless, it affirmed that enforcement of the promise, under a theory of promissory estoppel, would constitute state action and cited without criticism the Minnesota Court's holding that promissory estoppel "created obligations never explicitly assumed by the parties." 501 U.S. 663, 668 (1991). Largely, most common law jurisdictions in the United States now regard these as different voluntary pathways through which contracts are formed—one by *voluntarily* making representations that reasonably invite and elicit reliance and the other by *voluntarily* exchanging consideration. All contractual interpretation and enforcement by courts involve state action, as Justice O'Connor has eloquently noted. See *Wolens*, 513 U.S. at 248–50 (O'Connor, J., dissenting); see also Shelley v. Kraemer, 334 U.S. 1 (1948) (holding that judicial enforcement of a racially discriminatory housing covenant constitutes state action); Morris R. Cohen,

'best efforts') is largely understood as a way to interpret the meaning of those voluntary undertakings. It requires that one interpret the content of the parties' agreements through active engagement with their underlying purpose and not by relying only on a superficial fixation on what is explicitly detailed.[25] The duty of good faith might be considered a kind of secondary duty that flows from the primary commitments—a secondary duty that demands attentiveness to the spirit of the bargain in certain contexts as a way of ensuring that parties honor the agreement and its primary commitments. What those contexts are and whether the parties' identities or mutual standing affects the stringency of the good faith obligation may vary

"The Basis of Contract," *Harvard Law Review* 46, no. 4 (1933): 553–92, at 562 (arguing that judicial enforcement of contracts involves public, not merely private, interests and "puts the machinery of the law in the service of one party against the other"). Courts do not treat estoppel-based claims as quasi-contract or otherwise *distinctively* a product of the state as opposed to those contracts created by the exchange of consideration. See Susan M. Gilles, "Promises Betrayed: Breach of Confidence as a Remedy for Invasions of Privacy," *Buffalo Law Review* 43, no. 1 (1995): 1–84, at 64 ("[T]he decision to enforce a contract is as much a policy decision as is a state court's decision to enforce promissory estoppel . . . ."). For criticism that the Court's citation of "ordinary contract principles" is not accompanied by sufficient grasp of them in the domain of interpretation, see Robert A. Hillman, "The Supreme Court's Application of 'Ordinary Contract Principles' to the Issue of the Duration of Retiree Healthcare Benefits: Perpetuating the Interpretation/Gap-Filling Quagmire," *ABA Journal of Labor & Employment Law* 32 (2017): 299–325 (discussing *M & G Polymers USA v. Tackett*).

25. See, e.g., U.C.C. § 2-313(b); Daniel Markovits, "Good Faith as Contract's Core Value," in Gregory Klass, George Letsas, and Prince Saprai eds., *Philosophical Foundations of Contract Law* (Oxford: Oxford University Press, 2014), 272–94, at 284 (explaining that good faith is not a "separate undertaking" of contracting parties, but rather "recognize[s] the authority of the contract, and hence the authority . . . to insist on performance according to the contract's terms"); Steven J. Burton, "Breach of Contract and the Common Law Duty to Perform in Good Faith," *Harvard Law Review* 94, no. 2 (1980): 369–404, at 371 (noting that the doctrine of good faith is a tool for interpreting contracts). Notably, the duty of good faith only applies after formation of a contract and not to pre-contractual negotiations. See Restatement (Second) of Contracts § 205 cmt. c (Am. Law Inst. 1981) (noting that contractual good faith protections generally do not apply to negotiations preceding contract formation); see also U.C.C. § 1-203 (Am. Law Inst. & Unif. Law Comm'n 2015) (imposing good faith protections in the "performance or enforcement" of contracts).

in different jurisdictions and with respect to different subject matters.[26] Still, whether the duty of good faith is understood to be robust or modest,[27] variant interpretations of the duty converge on this point: to understand the scope of the parties' commitments and whether their actions honor them, one must ascertain the purpose of their transaction and judge whether the parties' own interpretations and actions represent a good faith effort to redeem it.

That is, doctrines like 'good faith' and 'unconscionability' offer interpretive guidance to fill in those gaps arising between an agreement's objective meaning and its explicit terms.[28] The interpolation

26. See Restatement of Contracts (Second) § 205, cmt. a (Am. Law Inst. 1981) (defining good and bad faith by reference to "community standards of decency, fairness or reasonableness"). Compare Fortune v. National Cash Register, 364 N.E. 2d 1251, 1256 (Mass. 1977) (finding a good faith requirement for terminations of at-will employment when commissions are part of compensation) with Hartle v. Packard Electric, 626 So. 2d 106 (Miss. 1993) (holding that at-will employment relationships are not subject to the implied covenant of good faith). See also Dirk Broad Co. v. Oak Ridge FM, 395 S.W.3d 653, 655–66 (Tenn. 2013) (describing jurisdictional variation about whether refusals to permit assignments of a commercial sublease governed by a "silent consent" clause must comply with an implied duty of good faith and adopting the "modern" position that unreasonable refusals violate an implied duty of good faith).

27. Some courts articulate the duty in spare terms, e.g., the duty bars "one party [from] 'unjustifiably hinder[ing]' the other party's performance of the contract." In re Hennepin Cty. 1986 Recycling Bond Litig., 540 N.W.2d 494, 502 (Minn. 1995). Some jurisdictions equate a violation of the duty of good faith with the presence of bad faith. See, e.g., De La Concha of Hartford v. Aetna Life Ins. Co., 849 A.2d 382, 388 (Conn. 2004) (acts constituting breach of implied duty of good faith must have been taken in bad faith where "bad faith" means more than mere negligence but "some interested or sinister motive," a dishonest purpose). Others distinguish between the two, requiring that plaintiffs show only a lack of good faith. See, e.g., *Nickerson, supra* note 15, at 704. See also E. Allan Farnsworth, "Good Faith in Contract Performance," in Jack Beatson and Daniel Friedmann eds., *Good Faith and Fault in Contract Law* (Oxford: Clarendon Press, 1995), 153–71, at 159–69 (describing doctrinal and theoretical disagreements about the meaning and extension of "good faith").

28. Harold Dubroff, "The Implied Covenant of Good Faith in Contract Interpretation and Gap-Filling: Reviling a Revered Relic," *St. John's Law Review* 80, no. 2 (2006): 559–619, at 562. The ambition of interpretative canons may be to do the same for law, with famously mixed opinions about the results. For optimism, see John F. Manning, "Legal Realism & the Canons' Revival," *Green Bag 2d* 5 (2002): 283–95; for pessimism, see Karl N. Llewellyn, "Remarks on the Theory of Appellate Decision and the Rules or Canons of About How Statutes Are to Be Construed," *Vanderbilt Law Review* 3, no. 3 (1950): 395–406.

of the duty of good faith is often necessary to save what was clearly meant to be a contract from what would otherwise fail for want of consideration, given one of these gaps. For, if performance or termination is at one party's unbridled discretion, then she has made no commitment at all, but if it is at that party's discretion *in good faith*—that is, her discretion is constrained—then there can be a commitment and hence, consideration.[29]

Why are there such gaps? Sometimes the absence of prior articulation is the simple product of reasonable efforts at efficiency and economy: we decline to detail every conceivable scenario because their disposition follows from the more general commitments we have made, whether in the contract or through implicit incorporation of the well-established boilerplate of state-supplied default terms. Sometimes we simply fail to anticipate some circumstances, misunderstandings, or disagreements affecting performance. In other cases, we reasonably want to defer premature concretization. Incomplete articulation and specification of terms and the use of open-ended terms like 'reasonable,' 'good faith,' 'fair-dealing,' and 'unconscionable' have the virtue of affording contractors and the law the opportunity to proceed in a principled way while also allowing for more articulate understandings of our commitments to emerge and evolve over time as we observe them in action.[30]

29. See, e.g., Cortale v. Educ. Testing Serv., 674 N.Y.S.2d 753 (N.Y. App. Div. 1998) (given Educational Testing Service's destruction of evidence and internal reviews suggesting bias, a genuine issue of fact remained over whether ETS canceled a score in good faith); *Dalton*, 663 N.E.2d at 293 (finding that ETS's reserved right to cancel any score it found questionable at its own discretion was limited by a duty of good faith to consider any relevant evidence submitted by the test-taker because the contract afforded the test-taker the right to submit that evidence); see also Wood v. Lucy, Lady Duff-Gordon, 222 N.Y. 88, 90–92 (1917) (finding an implied duty of an exclusive agent to make "best efforts" to promote a client's sales).

30. See generally Seana Valentine Shiffrin, "Inducing Moral Deliberation: On the Occasional Virtues of Fog," *Harvard Law Review* 123, no. 5 (2010): 1214–46, at 1222–29 (arguing that legal standards encourage moral deliberation by courts and citizens about the underlying moral purposes of law, deepening the motivational foundations of compliance

Thus, the Court's preoccupation with the fact that Minnesota did not permit parties to contract around the covenant of good faith is peculiar. A failure of good faith is a way a contract may be breached, but derogation of the duty of good faith does not underpin an independent cause of action.[31] The duty of good faith is not a discrete, state-imposed duty, such as a requirement to post a bond or to self-insure in a specified way. Furthermore, many rules of contract are fixed and not up to the parties, including some rules of interpretation, consideration, and damages, but that does not render the contracts made against that backdrop any less voluntary undertakings. The parties still must choose whether to contract in the first place, and (unlike some other mandatory rules) the content of the duty of good faith closely tracks the content of the discretionary aspects of their voluntary undertaking.[32]

with law and promoting an evolving understanding of the law's content). See also Charles Fried, *Contract As Promise* (Cambridge: Harvard University Press, 1981), at 87–88 ("One sometimes cannot know what is specified in the system [of background expectations] until the question arises").

31. This is explicit in the U.C.C.'s comments about good faith. "This section does not support an independent cause of action for failure to perform or enforce in good faith. . . . [T]he doctrine of good faith merely directs a court towards interpreting contracts within the commercial context in which they are created, performed, and enforced, and does not create a separate duty of fairness and reasonableness which can be independently breached." U.C.C. § 1-304 cmt. 1 (Am. Law Inst. & Unif. Law Comm'n 2015). See also Markovits, *supra* note 11, at 276. See also Cramer v. Ins. Exch. Agency, 675 N.E.2d 897, 903 (Ill. 1996) (noting that the "good-faith principle, however, is used only as a construction aid in determining the intent of contracting parties" and does not ground an independent cause of action in tort).

32. See, e.g., Metcalf Constr. Co. v. United States, 742 F.3d 984, 991 (Fed. Cir. 2014). The *Metcalf* court noted that some violations of good faith, like subterfuge, may be identified independent of the specific contractual terms, but "[i]n general, though, 'what that duty entails depends in part on what that contract promises (or disclaims),'" quoting Precision Pine & Timber, Inc. v. United States, 596 F.3d 817, 830 (Fed. Cir. 2010). "[R]epeated formulations . . . capture the duty's focus on 'faithfulness to an agreed common purpose and consistency with the justified expectations of the other party' (Restatement § 205 cmt. a)." *Metcalf Constr. Co. at 991.*

DEREGULATING GOOD FAITH?

Moreover, leaving the market to police bad faith as though that delegation naturally follows from a commitment to price deregulation represents a confusion. Deregulation of 'good faith' is not on all fours with price deregulation. To the contrary, the attraction of setting prices through the free market's operation depends on the background assumption that the state will enforce the contracts the parties arrive at with their agreed-upon prices for services or goods in return. So understood, the Court's decision does not elaborate the deregulation commitment but is in tension with its presuppositions. After all, Ginsberg and Northwest concluded many agreements about flight tickets in a context including the enticement of a frequent flyer program informed by the implicit duty of good faith, but this decision declines to enable their enforcement.

If one sought a 'good faith' analogy to price deregulation, it would not involve the sheer elimination of the common law standard of good faith with nothing but the commentary of market watchdogs to replace it. Price deregulation neither involves the elimination of prices nor judicial indifference to nonpayment of agreed-upon prices. The 'good faith' analogy to price deregulation would involve an instruction to the parties to devise for themselves an agreement about interpretative standards as a prerequisite to contracting (just as an agreement about price is a prerequisite to contracting), coupled with a commitment to enforce that agreement.[33] It is difficult to imagine that the ADA implicitly contains that burdensome instruction. Furthermore, it is unlikely that the putative advantages of price deregulation and price competition

33. It would then be a nice question for many theorists of contract whether interpretation of the parties' interpretative standards would itself require judgments about good faith.

carry over to market-based (or predictably corporate-dictated) systems of legal interpretation, given transaction costs, asymmetries of knowledge and information, and the complexity of law relative to price.[34]

The analogy between deregulating price and deregulating 'good faith' thus cannot survive careful scrutiny. An incomplete grasp of the public commitment to have a contract law fuels that defective analogy. That commitment and its animating purposes may be understood thinly, predominantly as a mechanism to facilitate efficient markets and transactions between strangers or, more robustly, as a way to foster practices of reliance, protect the vulnerable, vindicate solicited expectations, or structure and nurture a culture of trust. However it is understood, though, a coherent public commitment to upholding private commitments requires, first, that *we* uphold those private commitments and, second, that *we* do so according to publicly articulated and fairly administered standards. In other words, treating price and law as interchangeable is a symptom of the Court's implicit denigration of the significance and complexity of law.

Consider more closely the claim that there is no need for the common law regulation of good faith because the free market and Department of Transportation *could* adequately police bad faith.[35] Even assuming the best of the market and the Department of Transportation, the implicit suggestion that the question is just *which agent* will protect frequent flyers assumes that the issue is

34. Parties may usually grasp the significance of prices, at least simply structured ticket prices, whereas legal standards and their significance are harder to grasp quickly, especially by non-experts. Price is also relatively simple to bargain over, while bargaining over the complexities and precision of legal standards carries high transaction costs and is often unavailable where one party insists on standardized agreements. Furthermore, comparison-shopping for standards also carries high transaction costs and may be unavailable where one party obscures its terms or practices.

35. See *Ginsberg*, 134 S. Ct. at 1433.

one of episodes of bad behavior, according to unspecified criteria, rather than the development of standards of interpretation that delineate what counts as compliance and what counts as non-compliance with the parties' voluntarily assumed contractual duties. Contractual provisions do not interpret themselves and do not contain provisions for every circumstance or controversy. If the standards of interpretation are left to the free market, then, as with the side effect of the widespread invocation of arbitration clauses, we exit the realm of law and reenter the Wild West, where the powerful dictate terms and their meanings and abide by them only at their pleasure.

In this case, the Court's elimination of governance by law is no side effect, but is explicit, direct, and intentional. Delegation to the Department of Transportation might seem better, but it is, in fact, a bait and switch. For, here is what the Aviation Consumer Protection division's website reports about frequent flyer programs:

> The Department of Transportation does not have rules applicable to the terms of airline frequent flyer program contracts. These are matters of individual company policy. If you are dissatisfied with the way a program is administered, changes which may take place, or the basic terms of the agreement, you should complain directly to the company. If such informal efforts to resolve the problem are unsuccessful, you may wish to consider legal action through the appropriate civil court.[36]

36. *Frequent Flier Programs,* U.S. Dep't of Transp., https://www.transportation.gov/airconsumer/frequent-flier-programs (last updated January 21, 2015). While the US Department of Transportation (DOT) accepts consumer complaints, its reports themselves concede that the agency does not investigate the complaints' validity. See, e.g., Aviation Consumer Prot. Div., U.S. Dep't of Transp., Air Travel Consumer Report 35 (Nov. 2016), https://www.transportation.gov/sites/dot.gov/files/docs/2016NovemberATCR.pdf ("DOT has not determined the validity of the complaints").

What if the Department of Transportation did more than merely collect complaints and distribute the runaround? What if the Department of Transportation actually read and resolved them—by dismissing the unsupported ones and by issuing favorable rulings, backed by fines or what have you, for the legitimate ones? Even if the consumers' complaints would each, episodically, be satisfactorily addressed, the idea that dispute resolution is the principal function of law overlooks the importance of the public articulation of legal standards—in this case, the standard of good faith that common law jurisprudence provides.[37] The *Ginsberg* decision, through preemption, deprives the appropriate civil court of the relevant legal resources to apply. As a consequence, there are no applicable legal standards, whether for the frustrated party or for an airline eager to comply with the law.[38] My point is not to insist that we must, finally, tackle frequent flyer reform or to drive home that the Court offered flyers a false panacea. The details illustrate a more theoretical point about the value of law. It is hard to explain why we bother to have a social institution of contract—a public commitment to commemorate, facilitate, and honor private commitments—but we then fail to see our public commitment through.

37. Cf. Alexander M. Bickel and Harry H. Wellington, "Legislative Purpose and the Judicial Process: The Lincoln Mills Case," *Harvard Law Review* 71, no. 1 (1957): 1–39, at 5 (complaining that a brief per curiam opinion that stated the holding but no reasons to support it "does not make law in the sense which the term 'law' must have in a democratic society").

38. As the overturned appellate court predicted, "if common law contract claims were preempted by the ADA, a plaintiff literally would have no recourse because state courts would have no jurisdiction to adjudicate the claim, and the DOT would have no ability to do so. Effectively, the airlines would be immunized from suit—a result that Congress never intended." Ginsberg v. Nw., Inc., 695 F.3d 873, 879 (9th Cir. 2012), *rev'd*, 134 S. Ct. 1422 (2014).

ARE STATUTORY LAW AND COMMON LAW INTERCHANGEABLE?

Treating price and law as analogous is only one disturbing aspect of *Ginsberg*. So is the Court's abrupt dismissal of the suggestion that preemption of a state statute and preemption of a common law claim may raise distinctive issues. In its reading of the ADA's language that preempted state "law[s], regulation[s] or other provision[s] having the force and effect of law related to a price, route, or service of an air carrier"[39] to encompass general principles of state common law, what the Court said was not exactly wrong: both statutes and common law have the status of law; both *could*, depending on content and effect, conflict with the ADA's deregulatory aim.[40] These observations, however, are unsatisfying when offered as a complete justification for equating statutory law and common law in this context and thereby eliminating the application of common law in this domain. After all, the abstract possibility that the application of some common law rules *could* frustrate a statutory purpose does not show that purpose is frustrated in the specific case. A requirement that a program be administered in good faith does not amount to a regime of price controls. The Court's larger, simplistic reasoning was that if there is state action with the force of law around which the parties cannot contract, then the state has imposed a legal duty. Hence its only (easy) question was whether common law has the force of law. As I have already suggested, this is unconvincing because the duty in question is embedded within a complex, voluntary undertaking peppered with elected terms.

By analyzing only their impact in the instant case (would both statutory law and common law exert legal force?), the Court's

39. 49 U.S.C. § 41713(b)(1).
40. See *Ginsberg* at 1429–30.

result-oriented, reductionist approach to whether common law and statutory law differ for preemption purposes neglects some of the special strengths of common law as a form of collective moral articulation.[41] First, the process of generating common law has some distinctive democratic virtues. Although any piece of common law jurisprudence is generated by a single judge or a handful of judges at most, through explicit reasoning, practices of precedent, and taking notice of other jurisdictional approaches, common law judges are in conversation with litigants, amici, and other judges over the generations and throughout the states. The issues themselves arise from the grassroots, in a way, as problems occur. Any party who may allege a prima facie cause of action may present arguments, have them heard, and elicit a reasoned response. This process contrasts favorably in many respects with the current state of legislative access which is highly and disproportionately responsive to organized lobbying and donors. Even in its more ideal forms, given the cumbersomeness of legislating, legislative responsiveness is slower to come by and predictably more keyed to larger problems and the needs of large (or highly organized) groups. Thereby, the common law process embodies a judicial manifestation of the equal importance of each citizen, a process less sensitive to affiliation and social power than many manifestations of the legislative process.[42]

41. Indeed, I am tempted by an argument that either the *Ginsberg* decision is difficult to square with *Erie v. Tompkins* or, worse, it generates something approximating a lawless zone. If contracts are inherently incomplete, then their meanings will necessary demand interpretation (a traditionally common law endeavor) and that interpretation will rely on rules of interpretation (whose articulation is also, traditionally, a common law endeavor). If federal law preempts the state law rules of interpretation but does not offer an explicit standard of interpretation in its place, then what takes the place of the state law of interpretation? The general federal common law of contract interpretation, which *Erie* did away with? See also *infra* note 44.

42. Cf. Robert C. Hughes, "Responsive Government and Duties of Conscience," *Jurisprudence* 5 (2014): 244–64, at 261 (making the related point that litigation permits access to democratic deliberation to minority groups who may lack the political power to garner legislative attention).

Second, the scope of the common law is broader and often more trans-substantive than statutory law: common law jurisprudence articulates law as cases present themselves. Its mission is not confined to the agenda articulated, however broadly construed, by statutory text. For some problems, such evolution may reflect a more considered and measured expression of our joint moral commitments than is contained within pieces of legislation that attempt to anticipate and resolve all issues at once. Thus, some statutes may be more effective when they emerge downstream from the development of common law so they can benefit from the uncovering of the issues and legal developments first forged in common law.

The common law's power to evolve, responsively, traces in part to a common law notion that a legal commitment's full scope may be difficult to articulate completely in any one explicit effort. (So, too, it is a truism that no contract is or could be complete, which is to say that no contract could, explicitly, provide for all possible contingencies of interpretation and performance.[43] This is one reason why the doctrine of good faith and companion interpretative doctrines are necessary for a coherent and complete contract law.) For related reasons, whereas statutes tackle specific issues (airline safety and deregulation, fair housing, food quality) and often generate norms associated with those issues and the specific statutory approach dedicated to them, the common law ranges across issues and deploys the same concepts trans-substantively, facilitating the development of a topic-independent understanding of such concepts, as with the standard of good faith and a methodology of interpretation guided by

43. Indeed, the Restatement is explicit about this feature of "good faith," explaining that "[a] complete catalogue of types of bad faith is impossible." RESTATEMENT (SECOND) OF CONTRACTS § 205 cmt. d (AM. LAW INST. 1981); see also Roger J. Traynor, "No Magic Words Could Do It Justice," *California Law Review* 49, no. 4 (1961): 615–30 (arguing that fear of judge-made law, resulting in excessive deference to the legislature and to precedent, hinders the law from evolving to respond to changing circumstances and data).

the directive of good faith, forged as different cases arise, understood in terms of its underlying moral principle, and not reduced to a discrete list of actions. Because common law reasoning places greater pressure on courts to think comprehensively about how a concept's interpretation will fit into the legal system as a whole, there is some structural pressure for common law reasoning to generate greater trans-substantive unity than the more focused agenda enacted by statutes.

Third, because they are not bound as tightly by a statutory text and the limits associated with its administering agency, common law courts may enjoy greater versatility to articulate law that responds to the entirety of the circumstances presented. This versatility is particularly well suited for the sort of "clean-up" duty that doctrines like "good faith" can perform where a problem arises in the interstices of what drafters anticipate and specify.

Thus, while both common and statutory law have the force of law, common law jurisprudence serves a distinctive function in giving principled voice to a local, emergent understanding of our mutual moral relations, one that underpins the governing culture and expectations citizens form about each other. In this example, the doctrine of good faith plays an important role in publicizing and enforcing expectations about the significance of making a binding agreement. Through interpretation of the duty of good faith, courts contribute to the development of a public articulation of how to assess the spirit of a bargain and what it means to respect it in one's reasons when exercising discretion. How good faith is enforced and interpreted—whether the parties can expect that their agreements will be interpreted to have robust meaning or whether they should regard themselves more warily as at extended arms-length—in turn has an influence on the scope of trust that it is safe for a contractual party to invest in her partner; the narrower that scope, the more anxious parties may be to attempt to devise explicit constraints to insert into their agreements.

Indirectly and directly, the legal doctrine contributes to the nature of the local social-moral culture.

Given the trans-substantive, unifying function of many common law doctrines like this one, a piecemeal preemption practice that carves out distinctive rules concerning, say, unconscionability or good faith for particular industries leaves a hole in the moral fabric woven by the state common law. This, in turn, interferes with the cultivation of a general moral culture in which even non-specialists may develop the social-moral intuitions to navigate through it and rely on it.[44] That problem is compounded in the instant case where there are no rules that replace the state common law, but instead just a void. Even were the free market and the Department of Transportation to handle some specific cases of bad faith well, their disposition would not be public and deliberate. They would not generate a public record, give reasons for decisions, or generate precedent. When preemption goes beyond the piecemeal, those holes may further fray the local legal mechanisms that build a purposive and distinctive legal culture that makes law morally comprehensible and responsive.

Taken together, the distinctive features of common law adjudication do not establish its general superiority. The different attributes of common law and statutory law complement each other well. Instead, these factors offer reasons to value that complementarity, to resist any easy equation of the preemption of common law and the preemption of state statutes, and, more generally, to pay greater heed to whether preemption might displace, disrupt, or render discontinuous the special contribution common law makes to generating a continuous,

44. The interest in cultivating a general, trans-substantive moral-legal culture gives reason to worry that further development and application of federal common law to those piecemeal cases where federal preemption applies would not constitute a fully adequate solution.

morally articulate body of law and to establishing a baseline moral culture and identity.

CONCLUSION

I have used the seemingly minor case of *Northwest v. Ginsberg* to illustrate a number of themes about the significance of law from a democratic perspective and about its form. First, it is a mistake to locate dispute avoidance and dispute resolution, divorced from a conception of how they are achieved, as the sole or central significant purposes of the generation and application of law. In ways both small and large, that undervaluation of law facilitates arbitrary domination by more powerful actors. It also ignores the intrinsic importance of articulating mutual moral understandings and generating transparent, public, mutual expectations. Dispute avoidance and resolution figure among the salutary consequences and benefits of such articulation but they are not its single driving point.

Second, the democratic importance of generating and articulating law should not be mistakenly translated into a preference for statutory law in particular. What form law should take and how it should be generated depends a great deal on its specific purposes, including, always, its communicative aims and how they are best achieved in the relevant context. The need for common law roughly parallels the need for good faith (and a doctrine of good faith) in contractual relations. Morally healthy and successful contractual relations are well served by expecting parties to act in good faith in light of the significant aspects of their agreement, rather than placing an onus on parties either to plan for every contingency, explicitly and in advance, or take their chances. Such planning attempts are not only a costly exercise in futility, they encourage a counterproductive form of rigidity that deprives the relationship of the flexibility to serve as a locale for the development and redemption of trust and to evolve as circumstances change and as awareness of the values served by the agreement deepens. By contrast, mutual expectations of good faith can complement explicit understandings to preserve such opportunities, thereby advancing the purpose of the parties' specific understandings but also realizing the highest aims of a legal culture of contract—to facilitate and protect deliberate relations of trust.

In a similar vein, it may be both futile and counterproductive to attempt a complete and final articulate understanding of our joint moral commitments in one fell statutory swoop. As with other occasions for moral understanding, our apprehension may need time to evolve and crystallize through ongoing conversation. With respect to some questions, such evolution may be more deliberate if it is gradual and formulated in response to issues as they arise and not only as they may be predicted to arise. The quality and depth of our apprehension may improve as we hear from a variety of those most affected by the issues and as we responsively refine our preliminary articulated understandings of our commitments through reasoned reactions to their arguments. Finally, for some values, they may be better served through a trans-substantive approach, especially an approach that contributes to the fostering of a distinctive local culture. If, as the democratic approach alleges, a driving purpose of law is to give voice to mutual moral commitments we must make to one another, the common law's distinctive strengths in these very regards should be celebrated and not eclipsed.

Chapter 3

Constitutional Balancing and State Interests

SEANA VALENTINE SHIFFRIN

INTRODUCTION

In Chapter 2, I articulated a democratic case for celebrating the common law and preserving greater room for its development given the common law's role in articulating and concretizing a coherent web of collective moral norms. Given *Erie v. Tompkins,* that case is closely connected to the ability of states to exercise autonomy and develop distinctive forms of moral culture. I am not, however, delivering a states' rights manifesto. There are well-known hazards to overinvesting confidence in local authority, including that local authorities may be prone to encroach on foundational constitutional values, ones that underwrite our national identity and represent our fundamental commitments. In this chapter, I want to pursue an underdiscussed issue about constitutional balancing and state interests that is pertinent to the aim of striking an appropriate balance between local authority and constitutional values. The issue concerns when a state actor *has* a qualifying state interest that may be "balanced" against

Seana Valentine Shiffrin, *Constitutional Balancing and State Interests* In: *Democratic Law.*
Edited by: Hannah Ginsborg, Oxford University Press.
DOI: 10.1093/oso/9780190084486.003.0004

constitutional interests, such as liberty interests, in the process of determining whether state action threatens a constitutional right.

This issue becomes more apparent when one adopts a communicative conception of democratic law of the sort described in Chapter 1, a conception that emphasizes that certain normative stances may require commitment and other behaviors alongside articulate understanding to be appropriately and sincerely communicated and, in turn, to be worthy of reciprocal respect. On the one hand, as just discussed in Chapter 2, our jurisprudence sometimes neglects the values of a more unified, local collective moral culture, one that is typically nurtured at the state level. In other respects, in the way we currently identify what interests a state actor has, our constitutional jurisprudence seems overly deferential to the mere appearance and assertion of a local moral culture but insufficiently demanding of its actual development.

The predominant method of resolving constitutional challenges putatively "balances" constitutional interests against asserted "state interests." When a court hears a challenge to a law or regulation, one that alleges that a law (or other form of state action) violates a constitutional right, that challenge typically triggers the application of a test that putatively balances the constitutional interests at stake against the "state" interests on the other side and indicates what level of strength is required for the state interest to tip the balance. Roughly speaking, the product of this balance produces the content and limitations of the right.

The sort of balancing used depends on which constitutional interests may be threatened or affected by the state action. For instance, alleged impingements on the freedom to speak one's mind about politics invoke strict scrutiny, for which we ask whether the law actually restricts the freedom to speak and, if so, whether the restriction uses the least restrictive means to serve a compelling state interest.[1]

1. Kathleen Sullivan, however, reserves the label 'balancing' for cases subject to intermediate scrutiny because it is only in those cases that the outcome is not a fait accompli, already

Alleged gender discrimination attracts lesser, "intermediate" scrutiny. To determine if the guarantee of equal protection is violated, we ask whether there is discrimination by the state and, if so, whether it substantially serves an important state interest.[2] Implicit in these tests is the idea that the content of an enforceable constitutional right involves a balance between constitutional interests and state interests.[3]

An extraordinary amount has been written about constitutional balancing, including what tests are appropriate, what evidence is required to show the state action actually promotes relevant state interest, and whether courts actually apply these tests in a meaningful way. Of course, some have challenged whether constitutional interests may appropriately be *balanced* at all against state interests, whether on a specific occasion of enforceability or at the more general level of determining the content of the right. I do not aim to settle that challenge but instead to offer a charitable reading of what the model of balancing would require if taken seriously and to identify an important respect in which adhering to the model would be more demanding than is often recognized.

determined by the determination of the appropriate level of scrutiny. See Kathleen M. Sullivan, "Governmental Interests and Unconstitutional Conditions Law: A Case Study in Categorization and Balancing," *Albany Law Review* 55, no. 3 (1992): 605–18, at 606–608, 610, and 617. Because I am less focused on which cases remain open questions at litigation and more on how we conceptualize the architecture underlying our articulation of a right, I use the common, broader use of 'balancing.'

2. See, e.g., Craig v. Boren, 429 U.S. 190, 198 (1976) (applying intermediate scrutiny to gender-based age classifications for beer sales); Reed v. Reed 404 U.S. 71, 75 (1971) (applying intermediate scrutiny to gender-based executor scheme in probate).
3. Others use different language to describe the same process. For instance, Richard Fallon uses 'triggering right' to refer to the constitutional interest against which the state interest is balanced and 'ultimate right' to refer to the product of that balance. See Richard H. Fallon, Jr., "Strict Judicial Scrutiny," *UCLA Law Review* 54, no. 5 (2007): 1267–1337, at 1316–18. I use 'constitutional interest' rather than 'triggering right,' both to avoid semantically induced concerns about balancing incommensurables and to use more ecumenical language with respect to the debate about whether rights are absolute or near-absolute trumps or whether they are strong barriers to action that may nevertheless be overcome.

Hence, in what follows, I will not address the important debates just mentioned but instead seek to introduce a distinct issue about what should qualify as a state interest for purposes of constitutional balancing. Despite the ubiquitous invocation of state interests in constitutional law, we have dedicated insufficient attention to what it means to say, in a constitutional controversy, that a state (actor) *has* an interest, whether compelling, substantial, or legitimate, to be weighed against the constitutional interests at stake. Therefore, at a theoretical level, we still have not fully confronted what balancing normatively requires. It often seems implicitly assumed that the question of what interests a state has may be resolved entirely through armchair, a priori reasoning. But a priori reasoning could not settle which assertions of state interests should be taken as actual and sincere as opposed to hypothetical, aspirational, fledgling, or ambivalent.[4]

The academic literature and the courts have extensively considered what aims might be *disqualified* from serving as a legitimate state interest, emphasizing that the state cannot designate as an interest the frustration of citizens' rights, the diminution of the status of equal citizens, or those interests that essentially are cover for state (or private) motives of animus and exclusion.[5] A state actor cannot

4. Although in the preemption domain, the term 'state' refers to one of the fifty political units in our union, they are not the exclusive referents of the term 'state' when discussing the 'state' interest in constitutional balancing; rather, the term 'state interests' refers more broadly to the interests of any sort of governmental actor. Nevertheless, many of the examples of interest to me also concern state governments. They will be my primary focus in what follows, although much of what I contend should also apply to other state actors as well.

5. See, e.g., Romer v. Evans, 517 U.S. 620, 632–35 (1996) (overturning Colorado's Amendment 2, which prohibited any government entity in the state from protecting lesbian, gay, or bisexual [LGB] people because the law singled out LGB people from "the right to seek specific protection from the law" and appeared to be animus-based); City of Cleburne v. Cleburne Living Ctr., 473 U.S. 432, 448, 450 (1985) (striking down a law requiring a special permit for the operation of a group home for the mentally disabled because the law seemed to enact private citizens' negative attitudes and irrational prejudices toward the mentally disabled);

assert a legitimate interest in the violation of a constitutional right, conceived of as an end in itself.[6] Furthermore, a state cannot assert an interest in a matter outside its jurisdiction, such as to discharge an exclusively federal mandate.[7] That a priori part yields a tolerably good understanding of what a legitimate state interest could not be but little positive understanding of what it could be and whether a state possesses it.[8] Apart from a small handful of religious freedom cases,

Palmore v. Sidoti, 466 U.S. 429, 433 (1984) ("Private biases may be outside the reach of the law, but the law cannot directly or indirectly, give them effect"); Miss. Univ. for Women v. Hogan, 458 U.S. 718, 729 (1982) (finding the declared state interest in a same-sex nursing school to remediate past discrimination against women a pretext for stereotype-based discrimination against men). See also Justice O'Connor's quick dismissal of the proposal that Mississippi University for Women's interest in maintaining a same-sex college was to "provide opportunities for women which were not available to men." *Hogan*, 458 U.S. at 727 n. 13.

6. See, e.g., *Cleburne*, 437 U.S. at 448 ("It is plain that the electorate as a whole, whether by referendum or otherwise, could not order city action violative of the Equal Protection Clause" [citing Lucas v. Forty-Fourth Gen. Assemb. of Colo., 377 U.S. 713, 736–37]). Furthermore, at least federal interests (even asserted "compelling interests") must be formulated in ways consistent with other federal statutory commitments. See also Gonzales v. O Centro Esp. Beneficente União do Vegetal, 546 U.S. 418, 436 (2006) (rejecting federal government's asserted and generally framed interests in uniform compliance with narcotics laws given the regime of exceptions contemplated in the Religious Freedom Restoration Act).
7. See, e.g., Arizona v. United States, 567 U.S. 387, 399 (2012) ("States are precluded from regulating conduct in a field that Congress, acting within its proper authority, has determined must be regulated by its exclusive governance").
8. Some related concerns surface when the Court discusses under-inclusivity. Usually, however, that complaint cashes out as a concern that the legislation would be ineffective at achieving its putatively justifying purpose, that the under-inclusivity of the legislation suggests a pretextual motive or constitutes an impermissible pattern of regulation, or both. See, e.g., Whole Woman's Health v. Hellerstedt, 136 S. Ct. 2292, 2320–21 (2016) (Ginsburg, J., concurring) (arguing that the under-inclusivity of surgical center requirements revealed purpose of regulations was to obstruct access to abortion); Republican Party of Minnesota v. White, 536 U.S. 765, 780 (2002) (under-inclusivity of restrictions on judicial speech challenge the credibility of the state's cited purpose for speech restrictions on judicial candidates); City of Ladue v. Gilleo, 512 U.S. 43, 52 (1994) (noting that under-inclusiveness "diminish[es] the credibility of the government's rationale"); Church of the Lukumi Babalu Aye, Inc. v. City of Hialeah, 508 U.S. 520, 536–38, 544–46 (1993) (using examples of under-inclusivity to demonstrate legislation embodied a form of discriminatory treatment of religious practice); Florida Star v. B.J.F., 491 U.S. 524, 541–42 (1989) (Scalia, J., concurring) (decrying the ineffectiveness and therefore the unjustifiability of an under-inclusive speech regulation).

investigations into pretextual rationalizations to disguise illegitimate motives,[9] and some of Justice Brennan's opinions,[10] our jurisprudence does not typically dwell on whether the particular state agent is truly committed to an asserted interest in a way that would justify that interest's exerting weight in a balancing test.[11] This nonchalance

9. See, e.g., *Church of the Lukumi Babalu Aye*, 508 U.S. at 534–43 (1993) (finding that a facially neutral ordinance regulating animal sacrifice was improperly motivated by a desire to suppress Santeria worship despite the state's asserted interests in the maintenance of public health); Wisconsin v. Yoder, 406 U.S. 205 (1972).

10. Justice Brennan's opinions showed sensitivity to the issues I explore here, although he was often in the minority; my argument may be understood as offering a philosophical argument for the more regular application of his approach. A few examples: in *Michael H.*, Justice Brennan criticizes the majority for an approach that does not consider whether the asserted state interest in presumptive determinations of paternity bolstering the state's paternity rule "has changed too often or too recently to call the rule embodying that rationale a 'tradition.'" Michael H. v. Gerald D., 491 U.S. 110, 140 (1989) (Brennan, J., dissenting). His dissent in Cruzan also noted that Missouri's own enactments did not support the conclusion that Missouri had an unqualified interest in life given its absence of a health insurance scheme and its legislative support for living wills. Cruzan v. Dir., Missouri Dep't of Health, 497 U.S. 261, 314 n. 15 (1990) (Brennan, J. dissenting). In Capital Cities Cable, Inc. v. Crisp, 467 U.S. 691, 715 (1984), Justice Brennan's majority opinion cited the "the selective approach Oklahoma has taken toward liquor advertising" as a reason to assess its state interest in regulating alcohol consumption as "modest." See also Katzenbach v. Morgan, 384 U.S. 641, 654 (1966) (Brennan, J.) (expressing doubt that New York's English literacy requirement for voting served the interest in incentivizing English literacy and informed voting given the exceptions to the requirement and the evidence of prejudiced motives). I do not, however, mean to defend his insistence on *actual* legislative purpose, which I regard as a distinct issue. See United States Retirement Bd. v. Fritz, 449 U.S. 166, 188 (1980) (Brennan, J., dissenting) and discussion *infra* in note 52.

11. How the state interest should be framed and at what level of generality are also strangely neglected questions. See Fallon, *supra* note 3, at 1271, 1324–25 (observing that the Court has not addressed the level of generality at which a government interest should be framed); see also Dov Fox, "Interest Creep," *George Washington Law Review* 82, no. 2 (2014): 273–357, at 275–78 (analyzing "interest creep," a phenomenon in which courts justify uncontroversial government actions by referencing a broad state interest and subsequently justify more controversial government acts with reference to the same broad interest). Its neglect is particularly odd given the demands that the constitutional interest must be stated with particularity and supported with a historical pedigree. See, e.g., Washington v. Glucksberg, 521 U.S. 702, 720–21, 723 (1997) (noting that a constitutional right must be narrowly framed and historically defensible, and articulating the constitutional right at issue as a "right to commit suicide which itself includes a right to assistance in doing so"); Reno v. Flores, 507 U.S. 292, 302–03 (1993) (providing that an asserted right must have a "careful description" and be "so rooted in the traditions and conscience of our people as

is difficult to understand, particularly given all the careful attention paid to whether plaintiffs have standing as well as whether a real constitutional interest is under threat and how to frame it. The way our constitutional tests are structured suggests that, in characterizing the scope or extension of a constitutional right, we are balancing individual constitutional interests against state interests. If we are truly balancing, then a compromise of sorts is being brokered. But compromises carry legitimacy only when real—as opposed to hypothetical, potential, or aspirational—interests are at stake between the opposing positions.[12] So why don't we regularly investigate whether the state has real interests that merit compromise?

The issue of whether the state has a substantial investment meriting compromise arises most pointedly with what I will call 'discretionary interests,' as opposed to 'mandatory interests.' Mandatory

to be ranked as fundamental"(quoting United States v. Salerno, 481 U.S. 739, 751 (1987); Snyder v. Massachusetts, 291 U.S. 97, 105 (1934)); *Michael H.*, 491 U.S. at 122–23, 127 n. 6 (emphasizing the importance of history and tradition in asserting a constitutional right and providing that the relevant tradition should be framed at "the most specific level at which a relevant tradition protecting, or denying protection to, the asserted right can be identified"). Yet no such efforts are made with identifying the relevant state interest. Historical tests are not applied to identify whether an interest is constitutionally protected. Furthermore, the Court has recently declared that historical precedent limits membership into the category of unprotected speech that falls *outside* the scope of First Amendment protection. See United States v. Stevens, 559 U.S. 460, 468–72 (2010) (striking down a law banning depictions of animal cruelty based in part on a finding that such depictions do not fit into any historically defined categorical exception to the First Amendment and declining to adopt a balancing test to create new exceptions based on a general presumption in favor of speech protection). Only four justices, however, endorsed this approach in United States v. Alvarez, 567 U.S. 709 (2012); five justices adopted a different methodological approach to assessing whether a federal law prohibiting lies concerning one's military honors violated the First Amendment. See the discussion in Steven H. Shiffrin, *What's Wrong with the First Amendment?* (New York: Cambridge University Press, 2016) at 74–76.

12. Some attention is paid to whether there is credible evidence that a state interest would actually be under threat absent the state action under challenge. These are factual questions, often connected to normative issues about who should decide them and whether the court should adopt a posture of deference. Similarly, demands that the law be well-tailored to fit the state interest will provoke some questions about legal design and whether the state action is a well-crafted means to the state end.

interests may be defined more or less broadly and in ways more or less associated with textual commitments. A narrow textual approach would identify mandatory interests as those interests the Constitution, through its explicit language, requires state actors to have, such as an interest in equally protecting the rights of its citizens, protecting the free exercise of religion, and providing for the common defense. A wider textual approach might locate mandatory interests in implicit, as well as explicit, textual commitments elaborated in the Constitution, drawing on the justifications, purposes, and preconditions of textual commitments in order to flesh out a full specification of the relevant interests. Less textually centered approaches might ask what interests a state must have to fulfill its functions as a state full stop; what interests a particular state must have in light of its history, traditions, and culturally understood commitments; or, alternatively, what interests a state must have when it is conceived of as a political entity dedicated to establishing and maintaining justice.[13] This last framework might categorize foreign humanitarian aims as mandatory, while the other approaches would cast them as discretionary.

Discretionary interests are those that would be permissible for a state actor to entertain or promote, but are not required; that is, they are permissible interests that are not mandatory interests.

13. One might object that cases like *DeShaney* belie the claim that there are any recognized mandatory interests within our constitutional framework because the decision of when, how, whether, and how vigorously to pursue what I call mandatory interests is left entirely to the discretion of the state, and, further, the state is not judicially accountable to its citizens for its failures to pursue them. DeShaney v. Winnebago Cty. Dep't of Soc. Servs., 489 U.S. 189, 202–03 (1989) (holding that the Due Process Clause of the Fourteenth Amendment did not impose an affirmative, judicially enforceable right on the state to protect a child against abuse). I join those who regard *DeShaney* as a monstrously bad decision. I would endorse a more robust theory of mandatory interests that articulated a more reasonable delineation of the state's discretion in implementation. Still, despite the shortcomings of *DeShaney* and its progeny, the inability of the state to contradict or explicitly to deny a mandatory interest serves to underwrite a distinction between mandatory and discretionary interests. See *supra* note 5.

Discretionary interests may be disavowed. Examples include interests in protecting fetal life, in protecting life irrespective of its quality, or in maintaining the integrity of the legal profession. The range of potential discretionary interests may not be capable of being jointly affirmed by one state at once. Washington State's assertion, at one time, of an "unqualified" interest in preserving life, even against a patient's will, is incompatible with Oregon's interest in facilitating patients' choices regarding the timing of their deaths, betraying a more qualified interest in preserving life when disvalued by its bearer.[14] Given their elective quality, the question arises whether the mere articulation and in-principle defense of a discretionary interest could establish that a state *has* that interest for constitutional balancing purposes.

As I argued in Chapter 1, certain commitments and attitudes, such as respect or gratitude, may require certain forms of explicit action as a condition of their sincere, apt conveyance. If it were only a matter of dispelling communicative ambiguity, inventing more finely calibrated conventions of communication to convey our attitudes with greater precision could serve as a solution. That sort of ambiguity is not the only driver behind the requirements of action. Rather, to have the relevant commitment or attitude in full, one that is worthy of the sort of moral response it appropriately invokes, involves perceiving what actions are to be done to respond to the judgments

14. It need not be that, for any discretionary interest, its contrary could be affirmed by another state. For example, a state could adopt an interest in protecting its citizens from private censorship (and might pursue that interest through laws preventing retaliatory discharge in employment based on employee speech). The adoption and pursuit of that interest are not required by the First Amendment, yet a state could not affirmatively adopt an interest in promoting private censorship without raising First Amendment concerns. Cf. Reitman v. Mulkey, 387 U.S. 369, 376–77, 380–81 (1967) (establishing that the state could adopt measures to prohibit private discrimination and that it could repeal those measures, but that it could not adopt measures explicitly authorizing or encouraging private discriminatory activity).

underlying the commitment or attitude and also involves their pursuit, should the opportunity arise.

Similar claims may be made about *having* the sort of interest that exerts moral force, for both individuals and the state. In the individual case, whether one has made and honored a commitment or formed and pursued an interest does not depend (only) on her subjective mental states, but also on whether her objective representations and behavior underwrite sufficient objective indices of sincerity. We may say the same about the state. Hence, countering calls for sincerity with a rehearsal of the challenges of assessing legislative motive given the panoply of diverse legislative actors and their multiplicity of individual motives seems beside the point. The alleged futility of reliably discerning legislative motive should not preclude inquiries into whether a state actor, even a collective state actor, has evinced objective patterns of commitment to an interest. The coherence of balancing depends on there being such objective indices of investment in an interest in addition to recitals of that interest and demonstrations of its a priori acceptability.

INDIVIDUAL INTERESTS

I will illustrate the importance of actual investment by starting with individual, discretionary interests. By 'interest,' I mean something more than desire or preference; rather, something whose pursuit or success significantly contributes to the objective well-being of the agent who has it. A 'discretionary' interest is one that the agent chooses to develop, where neither prudence nor morality dictate that choice. For instance, an individual may reasonably and morally take an interest in musical theater, dance, community beautification, tutoring students in need, or learning a foreign language. Some such projects are predominantly self-regarding, while others have wider moral value. Should she dedicate substantial time and energy to it, the success of her endeavor or at least her access to participation would come, over time, to constitute an interest *of hers* in a robust sense, perhaps looming large enough to play a role in her characterological identity.[15] Her freedom, welfare, and even her life's meaning may suffer should her success or access be thwarted—especially if by sources outside herself.

As fellow community members, we would have moral reasons to adjust our plans to avoid thwarting her interests, where possible. If the most convenient time for a weekly neighborhood watch meeting conflicted with her regular dance class and if the other times, while less convenient or even costly, did not thwart any of our *interests* in this particular sense, we should adjust our meeting time to accommodate her interest. If adjusting the time affects others' interests, we would have reason to ask how great the imposition was on others, whether that imposition could be mitigated, and to search for some fair way to distribute the burden. Whichever form of accommodation is apt, the justification for our absorption of some costs on her behalf depends on her actually *having* that interest. That possession depends on a certain level of dedication and involvement. If she were merely considering or had only just begun attending class, the opportunity to continue would matter but would not be of a different caliber than the reasons why the time is more convenient for us; same if she is an occasional drop-in but often foregoes the class for dinner with friends, a good book, or to save money. Her assertion of her "interest" in attending despite her only episodic participation might be sincere in the sense that she subjectively wants to dance more and dancing figures among the activities that matter to her. Such assertions matter and may represent an aspiration to make dancing her

15. This concept differs from the philosophical notion of personal identity that tracks persistence over time as the same person.

interest. Still, the moral significance of such aspirational, fledgling, or ambivalent discretionary interests differs from the case where she actually has substantially incorporated a commitment to dance into her life. The sincerity of the occasional dancer's assertion that dancing is an important interest of hers is partially compromised not by subjective ambivalence but by her failure to act consistently to realize these intentions in a morally significant way.

We may take a different view about mandatory interests. If the contested time is the only time our neighbor could go to needed physical therapy or to help her child with his homework, we may be obliged to ensure that that time is free—even if our neighbor has neglected her health in the past or failed to make homework a priority and, even if at present our neighbor shows an inconsistent pattern of concern for her recovery or her child's academic success. We should not preclude the possibility of her fulfilling her duties to self or others although we might reasonably ask for evidence of a feasible plan to pursue the mandatory interest and eliminate impediments to its achievement. Still, in many cases at least, we should be willing to compromise with respect to our desires and discretionary interests to preserve the possibility of the fulfillment of her duty. With discretionary interests, however, our obligations to attempt to accommodate them depend on a person's actual, demonstrable, and developed investments in them.

The sustained pursuit involved in the substantial incorporation of a discretionary interest into a life demonstrates that the interest is actual as opposed to aspirational, that it has duration as opposed to its being impulsive or impetuous, and that the agent has considered what its execution involves in terms of appropriate means and opportunity costs. Substantial incorporation not only speaks to a tight connection to her characterological identity and her life's meaning, but it also provides stronger deliberative credentials about the worthiness of the choice in light of its actual and not merely its imagined features and costs. These credentials matter morally. Partly, this is for reasons of reciprocity. Other things equal, it may be appropriate to ask others to bear costs on one's behalf only for those things one is willing to bear costs for oneself. Partly, these credentials matter morally because shouldering those costs and forsaking other possibilities lends deliberative credibility to one's assertion of the interest's worthiness. Tellingly, shouldering them often heralds revisions in the articulation of one's exact interest.

STATE INTERESTS

When an individual asserts theoretically legitimate discretionary interests that are predominantly only aspirational, fledgling, or ambivalent, their precarious status may diminish their moral force. Shouldn't these same considerations hold true when the state cites a discretionary interest as a reason for citizens to be afforded a narrower range of opportunities to pursue their constitutional interests? States also may assert legitimate interests that are only discretionary and that, for those actors, are predominantly aspirational, fledgling, or ambivalent.

Consider the state interest asserted in the right-to-die litigation in *Washington v. Glucksberg*,[16] a 1997 Supreme Court case that dismissed a constitutional claim mounted by suffering, terminally ill patients who alleged that a fundamental right to die invalidated Washington State's prohibition, as applied, on suicide and its assistance.[17] Chief Justice Rehnquist's majority opinion emphasized that "Washington has an '*unqualified* interest in the preservation of human life.'"[18]

16. 521 U.S. 702 (1997).
17. *Id.* at 708.
18. 521 U.S. 702 (1997), at 728 (emphasis added) (quoting Cruzan *ex rel.* Cruzan v. Dir., Mo. Dep't of Health, 497 U.S. 261, 282 (1990)).

Even assuming the theoretical legitimacy of such an interest,[19] its assertion by Washington might startle those familiar with the death-penalty map. Washington was not then and is not now an abolitionist state. Its penalty sentencing practice suggests, to the contrary, that Washington's interest in preserving life was entirely qualified and fledgling at best. Strangely, no effort was made to reconcile its asserted "unqualified" interest in life with its willingness to declare some lives ineligible for preservation. Indeed, no evidence whatsoever was assembled showing that *Washington* embraced this unqualified interest. There was no survey of Washington's historical efforts in workplace and traffic safety, no descriptions of unstinting support for medical funding of the severely disabled and the elderly, and no description of a state educational curriculum dedicated to instilling equal respect for the lives of all of its citizens. The Court did not explicitly glean a commitment, beyond the assertions in briefs, from the preambulatory language of the statute, commitments voiced in prior cases, or the amicus practice of the state of Washington in other cases involving end-of-life issues, expressions that might have supported a distinction, however specious, between "innocent" lives and the lives of criminals.

Bizarrely, to support the assertion of Washington's alleged interest, Justice Rehnquist instead cited his own prior opinion in *Cruzan*, a case affirming that *Missouri* could require "clear and convincing evidence" that a patient in a permanent vegetative state had wished to refuse treatment.[20] Right topic, wrong

19. I will assume for the purposes of this paper that the asserted interests I discuss are permissible ones for a state to assert. Objections may be raised to them, however. See, e.g., Ronald Dworkin, *Life's Dominion: An Argument About Abortion, Euthanasia, and Individual Freedom* (New York: Knopf, 1993) at 160–66 (exploring whether some articulations of the state interest in the preservation of human life may be inconsistent with First Amendment values).

20. 497 U.S. 261 (1990).

state.[21] The *Cruzan* opinion had a similar *ipse dixit* quality, making assertions about Missouri without reference to its history, policies, or prior cases apart from the instant case, gliding from the claim that Missouri was *permitted* to *assert* an unqualified interest in life to concluding Missouri *had* that interest.[22] To be fair, in *Glucksberg*, there were citations to the very law at issue and to the defeat of a referendum that would have allowed physician-assisted suicide.[23] Those citations only seem to prove, however, that Washington had the very law under challenge, not that that law was justified by a general pattern and commitment by Washington State to protecting lives, no matter what their quality.[24]

We should be puzzled by a constitutional approach that affords much weight to Washington's asserted interest given its exhibited ambivalence about the unqualified value of life, troubled by the Court's failure to demand substantiating evidence of its commitment, and perplexed by its substitution of one state's purported commitment to testify to the commitment of another's. It is not as though the states are univocal on this matter. Not long before *Glucksberg* upheld the constitutionality of Washington's prohibition on assisted suicide, its neighbor, Oregon, passed a law acknowledging a right to

21. At least, you might think, the Court's peculiar understanding of "unqualified" was consistent across cases. Missouri also has (and had) the death penalty. See, e.g., Mo. Rev. Stat. § 546.720 (1990) (describing procedures for administering death penalty); *id.* (2016); Mo. Rev. Stat. § 565.020 (1990) (imposing death or life without parole for conviction of first-degree murder); *id.* (2016).

22. *Cruzan*, 497 U.S. at 281.

23. *Glucksberg*, 521 U.S. at 716–17.

24. *Glucksberg* did contain a more extensive history of New York State's record of deliberating about issues concerning the end of life, as well as California's. The relevance of California's position to the case escapes me, but at least it was appropriate to discuss New York, given the companion case, *Vacco v. Quill*, which dismissed an equal protection challenge to New York's ban on assisted suicide. 521 U.S. 793, 797 (1997). California, like Washington, has since altered its position and permits assisted suicide for competent, terminally ill California residents. See End of Life Option Act, Cal. Health & Safety Code § 443 (2016).

die and creating an administrative system for regulating assisted suicide.[25] In the light of these competing discretionary interests, why was Missouri's interest taken as dispositive evidence of the seriousness of Washington's interest? If we are looking to the opinion of other states, why wasn't Oregon's rejection of an unqualified interest grappled with as a counterweight to Missouri's interest? Oregon's divergent path reveals a defect in *Gluckberg*'s methodology; citing one state's interest as evidence of another's seemed a rather thin veneer for assuming that there was only one acceptable commitment a state could have. When there is an actual diversity of possible interests, establishing one particular state's interest requires more than a priori reasoning; it demands a more searching inquiry into the depth and breadth of the state's commitment.

Variation in the content and level of commitment to discretionary interests is not restricted to the right to die and the divergent interests putatively embraced by Washington and Oregon in the late 1990s. There are other cases in which a state has asserted a non-pretextual,[26]

25. Oregon Death with Dignity Act, Or. Rev. Stat. § 127.800 (2015). It was enacted by ballot measure in November 1994 and went into effect that December. When Oregon's law was constitutionally challenged because plaintiffs alleged that the law had inadequate safeguards to protect the incompetent from involuntarily choosing suicide, Oregon's interests were specified as "(1) avoiding unnecessary pain and suffering; (2) preserving and enhancing the right of competent adults to make their own critical health care decisions; (3) avoiding tragic cases of attempted or successful suicides in a less humane and dignified manner; (4) protecting the terminally ill and their loved ones from financial hardships they wish to avoid; and (5) protecting the terminally ill and their loved ones from unwanted intrusions into their personal affairs by law enforcement officers and others." Lee v. Oregon, 891 F. Supp. 1429, 1434 (D. Or. 1995) (invalidating the law on equal protection grounds), *vacated*, 107 F.3d 1382 (9th Cir. 1997) (citing lack of standing), *cert. denied*, 522 U.S. 927 (1997).

26. Facts that raise concerns about the level of commitment may also raise independent, more foundational concerns about pretextuality, whether with respect to the interest asserted or with respect to the means that the state asserts are necessary. For instance, in a recent abortion case, the Court noted that Texas did not evince the same level of concern for health and safety for procedures such as colonoscopies and home births as it did for abortion. See *Whole Woman's Health*, 136 S. Ct. at 2315. That inconsistency could be interpreted in at least two ways. First, coupled with other evidence that Texas' regulations were

legitimate, but not obligatory interest, but, nonetheless, the state's level of commitment to that interest is questionable—either predominantly aspirational (apart from the state action in question), fledgling, or ambivalent. For example, since *Roe,* the Court has taken the stance that the state may take an interest in the health of the embryo or fetus, but there is no suggestion that it must.[27] Importantly, no one other than the state has standing to assert the fetus' interest, and the fetus has no standing to object should the state decline to regulate to protect the life or health of the fetus as such.[28] When a state asserts a discretionary interest in fetal life *as a reason* to restrict the scope of exercise of women's right to abort, it seems fair to ask whether the state's assertion goes beyond the aspirational, the ambivalent, or the fledgling.[29]

unnecessary or counterproductive means of serving women's health, Texas' cited interest in women's health might be taken as pretextual, as a cloaked effort to obstruct access to abortion, as a rationally defective means of protection, or both. Or, second, Texas had yet to form a thorough, committed interest in health or a consistent method of its pursuit, although such an interest would of course be appropriate. See also City of Cleburne v. Cleburne Living Center, 473 U.S. 432, 449–50 (1985) (noting inconsistencies in policy with respect to asserted interests in safety and liability and concluding these were pretextual assertions to mask illegitimate prejudice against the disabled).

27. I take those regulations justified by appeals to women's health as appeals to a mandatory interest. Despite all these areas of deference to the state's judgment about how and to what degree to pursue an interest in women's health (or children's protection) is discretionary, the interest itself is not. Were the state to declare that it did not care about protecting the health of women, or children, or all of its residents, I take it that there would be an equal protection violation in the former case and a due process violation in the latter. Although the interest is mandatory, its citation is often pretextual and the regulations unnecessary or deleterious to women's safety. See, e.g., *Whole Woman's Health,* 136 S.Ct. at 2315–16 (2016) (discussing the lack of reasonable relationship between requirements for surgical centers for early-term abortions and the interest in ensuring safe procedures); see also *id.* at 2320-21 (Ginsburg, J., concurring) (arguing that surgical center requirements for abortion endanger women's safety).

28. See Diamond v. Charles, 476 U.S. 54, 67 (1986) (holding that a pediatrician lacked standing to assert an unborn fetus' constitutional interests because only the state may assert such an interest). Failures to take measures to ensure the health of any future child may be a different matter.

29. It seems particularly reasonable since the standing doctrine generally requires that the plaintiff's interests be actual and not hypothetical. See Lujan v. Defs. of Wildlife, 504

There are often reasons to doubt the robustness of the state's asserted interests in fetal life. Take, for example, the regulations considered in *Planned Parenthood v. Casey*.[30] Pennsylvania compelled women to attend an education session followed by a 24-hour waiting period before they could abort, justifying these restrictions by appeal to the state's interest in the life and health of the embryo or fetus. Yet, for embryos fabricated through in vitro fertilization (IVF) procedures, Pennsylvania required only reporting on the preservation, protection, and disposal of embryos.[31] It permitted their destruction at the election of either genetic parent without any waiting period or compulsory education.[32] The failure consistently to pursue measures reflecting an interest in the embryo may well substantiate charges that the cited interest is pretextual, meant to disguise the intent to bully or otherwise to impose an undue burden on women.[33]

U.S. 555, 560 (1992) (requiring plaintiffs to demonstrate that they suffered "injury in fact" for standing).

30. Planned Parenthood of S. Pa. v. Casey, 505 U.S. 833 (1992).

31. Pennsylvania's regulations governing the destruction of embryos created through IVF at present and at the time of the passage of the mandatory education for abortion statute only require quarterly reports from staff who perform IVFs of the number of fertilized eggs created, the number destroyed, and the number of implantations. 18 PA. CONST. STAT. 3213 §(e) (adopted 1988).

32. In Reber v. Reiss, however, a Pennsylvania Superior Court held that in a divorce dispute over embryos in which one partner wanted to implant and the other wished to avoid further procreation, the wife could gain full custody over them with the purposes of implantation because they represented her best chance at biological parenthood. Notably, the interests in fetal health and life were not raised. Reber v. Reiss, 42 A.3d 1131 (Pa. Super. Ct. 2012).

33. My concern is related to, but distinct from, the concerns that drive many charges of hypocrisy. Charges of hypocrisy often focus more on an agent's pursuit of contrary aims. Conflicting pursuits may sometimes represent evidence of insincerity or pretextualism. Charges of hypocrisy may also reflect an inchoate sense that the state's ambivalence is a sign of an incomplete or partial commitment. That is my focus, but my concern may arise even where an agent does not pursue contrary aims. Unlike charges of hypocrisy, the concern about incomplete commitment need not be accompanied by connotations of venality or bad faith.

Alternatively, it may simply show that the state's commitment to the interest was not well-considered and fully fledged, thereby depriving the state of the normative standing to burden the exercise of a recognized constitutional interest. Skepticism about the depth of the state's commitment and of its deliberation should not seem out of place here; after all, these regulations are predicated on skepticism that women seeking abortion have adequately deliberated, thus forcing deliberative measures on women to ensure the depth of their commitment to the procedure. It seems only fitting to make an analogous demand of the state. If it requires such indignities of women as a condition of their pursuing a constitutional interest, then it should offer a reciprocal showing of its commitment to the asserted state interest as a sign of its deliberative credentials.

Life-and-death issues challenge some people's confidence in their judgments, so consider a less taxing but hypothetical example concerning lawyer licensing. In 1978, when upholding restrictions on lawyer solicitation, the Supreme Court in *Ohralik* cited Ohio's special interest in maintaining standards among members of the licensed professions.[34] Suppose that, thereafter, Ohio were persuaded by market or free speech libertarians that the state has no business restricting the practice of law. It will no longer license lawyers or require licensing but will leave it to private accreditation associations to offer certifications and will leave it to the public to choose whether to

34. Ohralik v. Ohio State Bar Ass'n, 436 U.S. 447, 460 (1978). Perhaps the state has a mandatory interest in maintaining the quality of attorneys given the role attorneys play in the articulation of law, the state's primary mode of expression, and its fair administration. With respect to other licensed professions, though, that argument may be harder to make. Take the state's professed interest in maintaining high professional standards in the medical field and preserving the public's confidence in doctors. See, e.g., Gonzales v. Carhart, 550 U.S. 124, 157 (2007) (offering this interest as one reason to prohibit intact dilation and extraction procedures). If the state deregulated medical licensing but cited this interest to justify restrictions on abortion, it seems reasonable to question whether the state's dedication to this interest is serious enough to justify burdening women's constitutional interest in access to abortion.

hire accredited lawyers or not. Suppose further that Ohio does not repeal its solicitation restrictions. Now suppose that the solicitation restrictions are challenged anew. Would it be credible against a First Amendment challenge to rehearse the same arguments about Ohio's (or California's) special interest in maintaining the integrity of the legal profession? Although this is a credible state interest, shouldn't it matter that Ohio has abandoned a special commitment to this value?

Although this last example is hypothetical, in the coming years, litigation about issues involving discretionary interests and their relationship to constitutional interests will likely continue.[35] We may also see states pursue divergent stances on other issues such as privacy, narcotics use, and state cooperation with immigration control measures, where some states abandon their traditional commitments for stances that are more experimental, some at odds with federal policy and some in tension with acknowledged constitutional interests.

I have been arguing for two principles that should inform our approach to these constitutional balancing questions:

A. Mere assertion of a legitimate state interest should not always suffice to establish that a state [actor] *has* that interest in the sense that should be relevant to constitutional balancing.
B. At least for discretionary interests, a demonstrable commitment (that shows more investment than the assertion of a mainly aspirational, fledgling, or ambivalent interest) is necessary to establish that the state *has* that interest.[36]

35. See, e.g., People ex rel. Becerra v. Sup. Ct., 29 Cal. App. 5th 486, 505 (2018) (litigation over the constitutionality of California's right-to-die statute); North Carolina St. Bd. of Dental Examiners v. F.T.C., 135 S.Ct. 1101 (2015) (identifying limits to licensing boards' immunity from antitrust regulations that may inaugurate fresh scrutiny over exclusionary practices of licensing boards).

36. I bracket the question whether the degree of commitment might permissibly vary depending on the level of scrutiny appropriate to the constitutional interest at stake, whether rational basis, intermediate scrutiny, or strict scrutiny.

My argument has been that to make normative sense of the balancing tests that dominate our constitutional jurisprudence, we must inquire about the strength of a state's commitment to a discretionary interest just as we undertake a similar inquiry in the interpersonal case. If a major function of democratic law is to express our joint moral commitments, our constitutional jurisprudence should do more to unearth what actual, rather than hypothetical or aspirational, commitments our laws express and should demand that a sufficiently developed and sincere expression of those interests be identified before acknowledging a permissible limitation on the scope of constitutional interests.

THE RELEVANCE OF DEMOCRATIC EXPRESSION: MANDATORY INTERESTS

In what follows, I elaborate on my claim that contemporary democratic activity should influence our understanding of constitutional rights. My focus will soon return to the democratic treatment of discretionary state interests. I will begin, however, with some preliminary remarks about the democratic component of mandatory state interests. Mandatory ends will form the basis of many state interests whose pursuit may constrain the available range of opportunities to express and pursue individual constitutional interests. National security may come to mind. If we constitute a state to achieve mandatory moral purposes, our ability to maintain and continue this collective project against actual threats to its existence seems like an essential, even compelling, state interest. Because that interest is not discretionary, asking for evidence of the state's prior demonstrable commitment to it may seem overly demanding. For if the state has not been committed, it should have been, and we should extend the necessary deference to it to enable its pursuit once the state has so embarked.

That idea seems straightforward. Its obviousness may explain why we might readily concede that national security is a compelling state interest. In turn, then, our closer attention would naturally concentrate on subsidiary empirical questions, such as whether specific allegations that the exercise of a constitutional interest would threaten it represent careful assessments or panic-fueled exaggerations; whether the state action in question will actually further that interest; and the social engineering question of whether it is possible to accommodate both—that is, to provide room for the constitutional interest so that it does not threaten the state interest. Similar points may be made about individual security, public order, and the state interest in securing equality.

There is no gainsaying that these empirical questions are crucial ones, but they should not eclipse lingering normative questions. Once we have a clear, compelling, mandatory interest in hand, further normative questions implicating the democratic process remain about whether the interest appropriately triggers the balancing test. Constitutional balancing is no simple balancing act, to be sure. Take a putative mandatory interest like (territorial) national security.[37] If empirically demonstrable, a threat to it might (as the balancing test would have it) justify some suppression of speech, a well-recognized constitutional interest, if that suppression would defuse the threat.[38] The boundary of the speech right ends where national security is threatened not because there is no free speech interest there but because of the compelling nature of national security "outweighs" it. Even on this model, we still must ask *which* threats to national security

37. See Fox, *supra* note 11, at 275–76, for a short discussion of the frequent elision in invocations of "national security" from notions of territorial security to vague conceptions of national interest.

38. See Brandenburg v. Ohio, 395 U.S. 444, 447 (1969) (forbidding restraints on incendiary political speech except where "such advocacy is directive to inciting or producing imminent lawless action and is likely to incite or produce such action").

count as relevant threats? Private speech that supplied security codes to enemies at war counts, but surely private speech that convinced the public to vote for open-source laws or that convinced the public to dismantle the military would not.[39] What counts as a threat cannot be assessed merely by considering the brute consequences of the speech; we must consider *how* the speech would bring about that outcome and whether that pathway is normatively significant.

Even if we embrace the basic idea behind the balancing framework, which pathways constitute threats to appropriately weighty state interests and which constitute protected, even if costly, mechanisms of individual and collective freedom are independent normative questions. What counts as a breach of national security will depend on what values and commitments are essential to us.[40] To get to the point where we might balance constitutional interests against state interests, we must show that the conflict is the relevant kind. Not all conflicts between their realization should trigger balancing but only those conflicts that, to lack a better term, do not represent the point of the constitutional interest and its core, proper exercise.[41] Our conceptions of what constitutes a threat and what constitutes a

39. To take another example, whether speech causes a *regulable* threat to individual safety may depend on whether a private person takes it upon herself through her private speech to threaten or incite violence against another (regulable) or whether speech persuades the polity to divert funds to invest more in park maintenance than in police patrols (non-regulable). The effects may be the same but the way the speech brings about the outcome is normatively significant and independently makes a difference to its regulability.

40. Some state interests (such as the fundamental commitment to equality and to roughly democratic means of governance) may be (implicitly and justifiably) entrenched and impervious to significant democratic alteration.

41. This implicit limitation on what conflicts "reach" the balancing test reflects a respect in which the balancing regime incorporates the notion that rights are trumps. Some core exercises of constitutional interests seem protected despite their consequences when those same consequences, if arrived at through less direct pursuits of the interest, might be reasons to curtail such expressions of the interest. I discuss the relation of this idea to the secondary effects doctrine in "Speech, Death, and Double Effect," *New York University Law Review* 78, no. 3 (2003): 1135–85.

state interest cannot be so capacious as to eclipse a generous sphere of operation for constitutional interests. Calmly and rationally persuading the polity to cede land to another power cannot count as an actionable threat to national security. An autonomous, competent decision to refuse medical care cannot count as an actionable threat to a citizen's personal security.[42]

Thus, democratic actions such as persuading and being persuaded may have an influence on what counts as a state interest or as a threat to a state interest. The protection of national security may be a mandatory end of a compelling nature, but at least some aspects of what constitutes the essential part of the nation (and hence what sort of attack to it would threaten national security) may be subject to democratic adjustments. What counts as a threat to a state interest, even to a mandatory state end, may change, not just as empirical facts shift, but normatively, as the democratic community changes its mind about what matters. Even the scope of our realization of mandatory ends will have some give as they are applied and related to other collective ends.

42. See *Cruzan*, 497 U.S. at 269, 278–79; *Glucksberg*, 521 U.S. at 720. The parallel position should have been arrived at in *Gonzales v. Carhart*, 550 U.S. 124, 159 (2007) about whether consensual abortion constituted an actionable threat to the mandatory interest in women's health or to the more discretionary interest of preventing women from experiencing regret. These are all cases in which to protect a constitutional value, its operation cannot be deemed an actionable threat to another constitutional interest even if its exercise affects the achievement of the latter. One could also see them as cases in which, although the interest may be adversely affected, to recognize some activity as a threat to a state interest would threaten a constitutional value. That latter frame may encompass *Palmore v. Sidoti*, 466 U.S. 429, 434 (1984), which refused to recognize involuntary exposure to others' private racial discrimination as a legitimate rationale for depriving a parent of child custody to further the mandatory interest of a child's best interests (the refusal to permit others' bigotry to serve as a rationale for altering custody protecting both the constitutional interest associated with parenting but also that of equal protection by defusing bigotry of some of its effective force). See also *Cleburne*, 473 U.S. 432, 448 (1985) (disallowing the "mere negative attitudes, or fear, unsubstantiated" of neighbors to mentally disabled people to ground asserted state interest in assuaging neighbors' fears).

An example of this "give" is often implicit in how courts apply these tests. For the balancing idea to be plausible, it surely cannot be enough to warrant a constitutional interest's restriction that its exercise poses a relevant threat to an eligible state interest of sufficient importance. After all, the provision and protection of a wide sphere of exercise of constitutional freedoms is also a mandatory state end. We should ask not only how significant (and irreversible) is the incursion by the exercise of the constitutional interest into the hefty state interest but also how significant (and irreversible) restrictions on the constitutional freedom would have to be to restrict that incursion. In some cases, for example, speech might verily pose a threat to national security, but the restriction necessary to avert that threat might be too sweeping or invasive to merit its restriction. That is one way to put some of the opposition to the National Security Agency (NSA)'s vast spying enterprise. Our articulation of the relevant constitutional test should have a more obvious way to register the structure of this opposition.

These remarks about the relation between constitutional interests and mandatory state ends aim to highlight the often-submerged dependence of some features of the constitutional balancing model on ongoing democratic activity. These points may be underappreciated or underemphasized in our constitutional discourse, but they are fairly straightforward and could be easily incorporated into the routine of applying constitutional balancing tests.

With respect to discretionary state ends, however, a coherent balancing model must involve a further form of attention to democratic activity, to what are our actual commitments. Indirectly, we sometimes pay attention to our actual commitments when we try to smoke out pretextual justifications for illicit motives. But, partly because we have conflated issues about actual interests with the issues about the discernibility of subjective legislative motive, we have neglected to give the matter of discretionary interests the attention that it deserves.

STATE INTERESTS AND THE BALANCING MODEL

One may object that the inattention to the state's investment in a discretionary interest is neither surprising nor objectionable. When we entertain a constitutional challenge to a law or other form of state action, we begin with the direct or indirect product of a democratic process. It is natural to infer that a statute represents a state interest substantial enough to warrant passage; asking for a historical pedigree of commitment would belie the dynamic nature of democracy. The only interesting issue, one might then think, is whether the pursuit and expression of that interest infringes a constitutional right inadequately represented in the instant democratic process. Hence, the jurisprudence centrally focuses on whether the relevant state action unjustifiably infringes on a sufficiently important constitutional interest, taking for granted the bona fide possession of the state interest.[43]

If you took a positive political scientist along for an excursion, the two of you might have a field day questioning the idea that a law's passage supports an inference that a sufficient number of legislators judged that the state had an interest in its methods or its effects rather than that its passage apparently fulfilled the personal ambitions of a majority of legislators. The less cynical might simply observe that because a range of interests might justify a law, its passage serves as poor evidence of adherence to any particular cited interest. It might also be replied that constitutional review does not merely consider the unexamined point of view; a constitutional challenge does not

43. Note, though, that this explanation still leaves mysterious why the constitutional interest, but not the state interest, must be framed at a low level of abstraction.

wither just because the legislature considered the constitutional interests that might be affected by the law's passage.[44]

Furthermore, the structure of the relevant tests belies the notion that constitutional review seeks to ensure that constitutional interests were considered. If our position was that an enacted law, a vetted regulation, or a police officer's activity deserved deference by virtue of being the product of a democratic process and that our only question was whether it misstepped onto the protected territory of individual rights, then we would inquire into what the alleged constitutional interest was only to see whether it was threatened and whether it is in fact a right. Sometimes, that seems to be the procedure—think of Justice Kennedy's opinion in *Obergefell*[45] in which he devoted his complete attention to adumbrating the constitutional interest and its importance without any overt glance at any putative state interest. I attribute this to the fact that the right at stake was a core expression of the relevant constitutional interest. There was no call to balance because we were not settling a question of the boundaries of the right beyond its core expression. More often, the relevant constitutional test and asserted state interest are recited. Inquiries then proceed about the weightiness of the adverse state interest and whether the state action bears a sufficiently tight connection to its promotion. What is missing, to my perplexion, is an inquiry into whether the asserted state interest is actual or aspirational.

Of course, some think that the constitutional interest of the individual should always render the state interest irrelevant. Every case should read like *Obergefell*.[46] It does not matter what the state's

44. See, e.g., City of Boerne v. Flores, 521 U.S. 507, 535–36 (1997) (noting that, although it is incumbent that Congress consider the constitutionality of legislation, the Court is authoritative in constitutional interpretation).

45. Obergefell v. Hodges, 135 S. Ct. 2584 (2015).

46. Others, including many First Amendment cases, do. See, e.g., Snyder v. Phelps, 562 U.S. 443 (2011) (after finding that protestors' speech concerned public issues voiced in a public forum, offering no inquiry into the state interests driving the state's tort actions

interest is—either the decisions are the individual's to make or they are not; if the former, then either the state interest is irrelevant or it could never be weighty enough to surmount it.[47] I sympathize, at least with respect to the core cases representing individual constitutional interests that definitively fall into the scope of the right. But part of the challenge of constitutional jurisprudence is that we do not fully understand ex ante and a priori what falls into the larger scope or extension of a right. Different political configurations might each represent if not equally good, then at least equally good faith efforts to respect universal constitutional values. To take one example, Europe arguably realizes a free speech regime, even as many of its member states place greater weight on privacy interests over freedom of speech interests when the two conflict than we do.[48] Perhaps Europe gets it wrong or perhaps we get it wrong; it seems more likely that we have similar core commitments but that, at the margins, our expressions of those commitments differ in part because of our various discretionary interests. Our own commitment to federalism may encapsulate an idea somewhere in this arena. (Indeed, I believe that it has to if we think that the state interests that can be asserted in constitutional

for defamation, "publicity given to private life, or the intentional infliction of emotional distress").

47. This is one version of the "rights as trumps" position, but, despite its familiarity, I regard it as one of its more controversial articulations. Other versions are compatible with balancing by granting a limited role to balancing for cases at the (metaphysical or epistemological) margins of the right, by using balancing to determine the extension and boundaries of the right that, post-determination, then serves as trump.

48. See, e.g., PJS v. News Group Newspapers Ltd [2016] UKSC 26, [2016] 1 AC 1081 (appeal taken from Eng.) (upholding an injunction against press disclosures of the names and details of a celebrity's sexual affairs); Campbell v. MGN Limited [2004] UKHL 22, [2004] 2 AC 457 (appeal taken from Eng.) (finding liability for wrongful disclosure of private information when a newspaper published photographs and a truthful report about a famous model based on observation). See generally Steven Shiffrin, *What's Wrong with the First Amendment?*, *supra* note 11 (comparing the American, European, and Canadian approaches to freedom of speech across a number of domains including privacy, hate speech, and campaign finance).

litigation are the interests of states as opposed to only those of the federal government.) Either way, we might be understood as settling the boundaries of the extension of a right by considering what state interests might be affected by a more or less generous conception of that right.

To elaborate with respect to individual rights: interests of constitutional import represent an essential arena of human activity that each individual must be guaranteed a right to exercise. Some activities, such as declaring disagreement with the powerful, fall clearly in the center of this arena. Other activities are, arguably, on the periphery. They may further the relevant interest of the individual but that interest might also be sufficiently satisfied elsewhere were this activity made unavailable; its unavailability would be a cost or a sacrifice to the individual but would not deny her basic freedom or dignity. In attempting to fix the boundaries of the right at the periphery,[49] we may reasonably ask what other interests are at stake in one boundary determination versus another. Where substantial community interests are compromised by the extension of the boundary in one direction versus another, it may be reasonable to expect citizens to exercise their constitutional interests within a boundary that is compatible with the pursuit of substantial community interests. But the reasonability of expecting citizens to compromise a fuller realization of their constitutional interests on the grounds that substantial community interests weigh in the counterbalance should turn, at least for discretionary interests, on the actuality of the state's commitment to those community interests. I have been arguing that commitment should be demonstrated through a coherent pattern of state action, one that bears out that the asserted interest is more than fledgling or aspirational and that the state's stance is not ambivalent but consistent. To

49. Different models of rights may regard this determination as metaphysical or epistemic; I will stay neutral on that question here.

"ask" citizens to compromise constitutional interests for state interests seems reasonable only where the state actor has itself invested in those interests, thereby absorbing and reflecting the deliberative lessons such investments provoke.

The concept of a discretionary state interest, I admit, is not commonplace in constitutional jurisprudence. In part, this may be because attempts to force the state to pursue and fund mandatory interests have largely been stymied, resulting in a jurisprudence that gives a wide berth to state actors to exercise judgment about the appropriate degree of state investment, the places of emphasis, the best methods of pursuing mandatory interests, and how to weigh various state priorities against each other.[50] Accountability measures for mandatory interests are largely subject to good will, the free press, and the electorate. The discretion associated with how to pursue mandatory interests may have been unthinkingly extended to the *assertion* of discretionary interests.

Theoretically, inattention to discretionary interests may also derive, in part, from the claim advanced by some influential liberals that the state's interests must be limited to those required by justice; to pursue discretionary ends would be infringe on citizens' liberty to devise their own ends. Liberals with such convictions may not attend to the details of applying balancing tests with integrity since they are apt to find balancing tests entirely out of place where discretionary interests are concerned.

I reject such interpretations of liberalism. In brief, there may not always be singular paths to prosecute justice. Rather, in many cases, divergent paths involving distinctive ends along the way may

50. See, e.g., DeShaney v. Winnebago Cty. Dep't of Soc. Servs., 489 U.S. 189, 202–03 (1989) (holding that the Due Process Clause of the Fourteenth Amendment did not impose an affirmative, judicially enforceable right on the state to protect a child against abuse).

be pursued to give people their due within a flourishing polity. Furthermore, the position that discretionary collective moral ends may not be pursued because their pursuit intrinsically infringes on citizens' liberty depends on a highly individualist, crypto-libertarian, and ultimately implausible conception of the state and of property. Although it is a contested matter, some theorists believe that concern for the environment, in itself, or for animals, in themselves, is not a matter of justice, which concerns fair relations between people; for those who think justice is a matter of relations between citizens, concern for the welfare of foreign denizens might be considered discretionary. Even if environmental preservation or foreign welfare were discretionary ends, their pursuit would not intrinsically infringe on citizens' autonomy rights unless we presuppose an implausible maximalist theory of individual property giving each citizen a proportionate right to all the collective property not required to implement justice.[51] Whatever the source of the neglect of discretionary interests, the conditions for their sincere assertion on behalf of a democratic polity merit further attention.

IMPLICATIONS

My contention has been that aspirational, fledgling, or ambivalent interests should not influence the outcome of constitutional balancing in the same way that consistent, realized, and entrenched

51. See, e.g., Jonathan Quong, *Liberalism Without Perfection* (New York: Oxford University Press, 2011), at 106–107. I see no reason to take this view, rather than the position that first, individuals' liberty rights may be defined substantively in terms of what opportunities are available to them and what state motives are antithetical to them, and, second, their individual property entitlements may be determined by virtue of what is required to ensure that they receive the rights and opportunities afforded by principles of justice.

interests should. Balancing discretionary interests against recognized constitutional interests is normatively plausible only where the state demonstrates an actual commitment to that interest beyond its mere articulation. I am not arguing here for any specific test or inquiry to gauge whether a state has the relevant interest. My agenda is more philosophical than pragmatic, so my contention is abstract: greater sensitivity to the question of whether a state actor *has* the interest it asserts should be shown by both judges and nonjudicial state actors as part of the process for constitutional balancing to make sense, at least considering discretionary interests.

With that caveat in mind, the abstract lesson points in some concrete directions and not in others. Despite some protestations to the contrary,[52] in litigation, that demonstration must involve more than the assertion of the interest in briefs. I doubt that we should presume that attorneys charged with defending the state engage in thoroughly principled decisions about what interests to assert, rather than throwing the pasta at the wall to see if it sticks. Why would a state's assertion of an interest in a brief be more telling than its enacted policies? To be sure, my objection is not to the concept of a belated explicit realization of an abiding, but perhaps inchoate, interest immanent in

52. To be sure, proof of actual legislative motive (or, to be precise, a legislative identification of a state interest as a justification) is not a necessary condition of constitutionality. United States Railroad Retirement Board v. Fritz, 449 U.S. 166 (1980); neither, in many circumstances, is a poor legislative motive sufficient to doom an argument that a statute is constitutional. United States v. O'Brien, 391 U.S. 367, 383–86 (1968). The issue about actual legislative motive is related to but distinct from the one that concerns me. The issue about motive concerns whether we can discover and say illuminating things about the motive of a legislature composed of dozens or hundreds of distinct people with differing agendas and often opaque minds. Skepticism about that endeavor drives the idea that we should adopt an objective point of view, where that is understood as assessing the arguments offered to defend the statute without digging deeper to see whether those arguments motivated a sufficient number of legislators. I am not disputing the move to the objective point of view. Still, taking the objective perspective does not entail that what interest a state actor has should be determined by that actor's assertion alone rather than by a more comprehensive combination of that actor's behaviors, assertions, and other commitments.

the social culture and its practices. My objection, instead, is to the idea that its assertion, on its own, is sufficient evidence of its possession. So what would suffice? Preambulatory language may be *some* evidence, but it isn't much and only partly for the reasons cynical political scientists crow about. Putting aside the possibility of loner grandstanding, the assertion in question requires more than episodic attestation.

Requiring evidence of the strength and sincerity of the state's commitment to an interest need not call for the sorts of divinations of legislative purpose that some commentators find problematic.[53] Rather, the requisite inquiry would assess the strength of the state's commitment by reference to whether its actions and prior stances signified a strong commitment to the interest its representatives articulate. A pro tanto case that a state possesses an interest might involve a showing that it has adopted a moderately comprehensive and serious approach to tackling the interest, whether within the legislation or state action at issue or through the combined effect of extant legislation and regulations.[54] An all-things-considered conclusion that it has the interest would have to answer any serious charges that the state simultaneously neglects important measures necessary

53. Mark Greenberg, "Legislation as Communication? Legal Interpretation and the Study of Linguistic Communication," in Andrei Marmor and Scott Soames eds., *Philosophical Foundations of Language in the Law* (New York: Oxford University Press, 2011), 217–56; Todd Rakoff, "*Washington v. Davis* and the Objective Theory of Contracts," *Harvard Civil Rights-Civil Liberties Law Review* 29, no. 1 (1994): 63–99, at 71–74.

54. An approach of this kind may be compatible with the explicit assertion of that interest occurring for the first time post hoc in response to litigation. What interest we have been pursuing all along may be only evident upon the pressure exerted by litigation. I suggest that our approach to discerning the genuineness of the state's interest should not turn on the *timing* of the interest's assertion but on whether the state's actions and commitments support that assertion, whenever it is made. That said, when the initial assertion appears only in response to litigation, that timing may legitimately highlight the need for deeper demonstrations of genuineness. See United States v. Virginia, 518 U.S. 515, 533 (1996) ("the [state] justification [for a gender discriminatory policy] must be genuine, not hypothesized or invented post hoc in response to litigation").

for undertaking and expressing those interests (e.g., the IVF example) or that the state pursues measures contrary to the asserted interest (e.g., the death penalty).

Such sensitivity could conceivably take different forms. Further specification would require confronting a number of issues beyond the scope of this project, including whether different constitutional interests should trigger different standards of adequate possession, just as different constitutional interests trigger different standards with respect to the requisite tailoring and weight of the interest. Although I will not attempt further specification, I will make a few remarks to dispel objections that this sort of sensitivity is infeasible or in tension with long-standing commitments of another sort.

It may be objected that a test demanding particularized evidence of commitment would render it difficult for states to experiment and take initiatives that might have constitutional implications. To launch such an initiative, they would have to enact comprehensive legislation rather than testing the waters and taking a first step. Particularly with respect to the adoption of controversial interests (here I have in mind the Oregon legislation and the commitment to patient autonomy), the wise course may be a gradualist course.[55]

Furthermore, this approach would make it difficult for a state to "change its mind," so to speak. For instance, in 2008, Washington State reversed its position and passed a right-to-die law that seemed to indicate that its priorities now matched its neighbor to the south.[56] Should that law be challenged, perhaps by a patient in a state hospital who wished to live, even with medical conditions compromising her

55. See also Katzenbach v. Morgan, 384 U.S. 641, 658 (1966) (underscoring that the legislature may have good reason to tackle one aspect of a larger problem); Williamson v. Lee Optical Co. 348 U.S. 483, 489 (1955) ("reform may take one step at a time, addressing itself to the phase of the problem which seems most acute to the legislative mind").

56. Washington Death with Dignity Act, WASH. REV. CODE § 70.245.010 (2015). The Act was passed by ballot initiative in 2008 and largely went into effect in 2009.

life quality, contending that the assisted suicide system violated her right to substantive due process by creating the potential for coercion, would Washington State's claim that its law served its substantial interest in facilitating patient control over the means and timing of death be refuted by reference to its prior attestations of a substantial and unqualified interest in the value of life?

The Washington reversal highlights a third objection about variability, whether jurisdictional or temporal. On the approach I am defending, it would seem that the same legal regulations might be constitutional in Oregon while failing to pass constitutional muster in Washington given its more conflicted history. The problem of constitutional variability would not arise only in cases of state reversal of course, but more generally, as states might pass virtually the same legislation but within contexts that manifested quite different levels of historical commitment and other forms of demonstrated devotion to an interest. Temporal variability is also conceivable, especially should the constitutional inquiry not be fixed exclusively on investigations of the state practice and commitment at the time of passage, but also (or instead) take into account the state's ongoing record of commitment to the interest.[57]

57. For instance, a state's invocation of its interest in the "sanctity of life" to defend a twentieth-century abortion statute or statute banning assisted suicide might be called into question should it have failed to adopt a "sanctity of life" approach to policing or to encourage its municipalities to do so after recommendations adopting this approach were first suggested by the Department of Justice in 1999 and further developed and publicized in 2016 by Police Executive Research Forum (PERF), a non-profit organization that develops model practices for police departments and advises many departments. This approach aims to reduce excessive force in policing by stressing the sanctity of life in police mission statements, training manuals, de-escalation training, and other efforts to minimize the use of lethal force. See Community Relations Service, U.S. Department of Justice, "Police Use of Excessive Force: A Conciliation Handbook for the Police and the Community" (1999); Police Executive Research Forum, "Guiding Principles On Use of Force (2016), http://www.policeforum.org/assets/guidingprinciples1.pdf. Many municipalities adopted this approach, including Sacramento, Baltimore, Chicago, Minneapolis, and San Francisco. See Sacramento Police Department, "Use of Force" (2017), https://www.cityofsacramento.org/-/media/Corporate/Files/Police/Transparency/GO-58002--Use-of-Force.

Much of the force of these objections relies on imagining a particularly stark doomsday remedy to finding that an asserted state interest is more aspirational than actual; namely, invalidation of the state action. There are other approaches. We need not assume a harsh, non-dynamic model of constitutional scrutiny, one in which the only remedy is permanent invalidation. One might think by analogy to facial and as-applied challenges, a locale where we are familiar with the idea that the same statutory text may be constitutional in one jurisdiction but unconstitutional in another, but with a twist. When a state actor defends against a constitutional challenge by citing a "hypothetical" interest that, if realized, would suffice to tip the balance in its favor, a judicial judgment to that effect might be thought to show that the statute was valid on its face, *in the sense that there is nothing wrong with it intrinsically*. My point, nonetheless, is that we should demand some evidence *as applied* that the state's level of commitment to a discretionary interest demonstrably ranges beyond the hypothetical. While we normally think that a statute that survives a facial challenge is enforceable until it is shown, as applied, to generate constitutional harm, in this case, surviving a facial challenge on the basis of a merely hypothetical interest might yield something like a stay, akin to Judge Calabresi's "constitutional remand,"[58] until that further evidence is provided.

pdf?la=en; Baltimore Police Department, "Use of Force" (2016), https://www.baltimorepolice.org/sites/default/files/Policies/1115_Use_Of_Force.pdf; Chicago Police Department, "Use of Force" (2017), https://home.chicagopolice.org/wp-content/uploads/2017/05/G03-02_Use-of-Force_TBD.pdf; Minneapolis Police Department, "Use of Force" (2016), http://www.minneapolismn.gov/police/policy/mpdpolicy_5-300_5-300; San Francisco Police Department, "General Order: Use of Force" (2016), http://sanfranciscopolice.org/sites/default/files/Documents/PoliceCommission/sfpd-dgo-5.01-101316-commission%202_0.pdf. See also the discussion in Ingrid V. Eagly and Joanna C. Schwartz, "Lexipol: The Privatization of Police Policymaking," *Texas Law Review* 96 (2018): 891–976.

58. See Judge Calabresi's concurring opinion in Quill v. Vacco, 80 F.3d 716, 738–43 (2d Cir. 1996). The concerns that propelled his advocacy of a constitutional remand are

Suppose a state, like Washington, were confronted with what appears to be an ambivalent stance toward its purported "unqualified" interest in the value of life, or suppose Pennsylvania's state interest in fetal life was questioned based on its failure to legislate comprehensively, to address in a coherent way embryos both inside and outside of a woman's body. A court sensitive to the question of whether a state *had* the relevant interest it asserts might stay the state regulation until the legislature did more to demonstrate its interest—such as legislating more comprehensively, repealing the laws that demonstrate a commitment to an interest to the contrary, evincing concrete plans to do so, or offering a reasoned account of the distinction it is making after holding hearings and inviting notice and comment.[59] In the alternative, where the state alleges

related to but distinct from mine. His worries are more exclusively temporal and concern the potential obsolescence of the ban on assisted suicide given the distance of contemporary legal circumstances from the circumstances that gave rise to the ban. Those worries seem valid, but I am less convinced they can be ameliorated solely by contemporary legislative validation should there be little else to demonstrate commitment to the relevant state interest. See also Guido Calabresi, *A Common Law for the Age of Statutes* (Cambridge, MA: Harvard University Press, rev. ed. 1985) (advocating judicial power to amend obsolete statutes with an eye to prompting a legislative response); Bickel and Wellington, *supra* Ch. 2 note 37, at 34–35 (defending the "remanding function" and advocating the denial of jurisdiction to effect a constitutional remand).

59. Compare Baker v. State, 744 A.2d 864, 886 (Vt. 1999) (holding that same-sex couples have a right under Vermont's constitution's common benefits clause to the benefits of marriage but remanding to the legislature to craft a remedy consistent with its holding) with Goodridge v. Dep't of Pub. Health, 798 N.E. 2d 941 (Mass. 2003) (staying entry of a declaratory judgment that the state's limitation of marriage to opposite-sex couples violated state constitutional guarantees of equal protection and construing marriage as the voluntary union of two persons while giving the legislature six months to take appropriate action). The technique of a legislative remand is interesting and worth using, whether or not its application in these cases was appropriate. Contrast *Baker*, 744 A.2d at 898–904 (Johnson, J., concurring in part and dissenting in part) (complaining that deferring the construction of a remedy to the legislature abdicates judicial responsibility to redress rights violations) with Tonja Jacobi, "Sharing the Love: The Political Power of Remedial Delay in Same-Sex Marriage Cases," *Law & Sexuality: A Review of Lesbian, Gay, Bisexual and Transgender Legal Issues* 15 (2006): 11–58 (articulating political advantages of wielding remedial delays to elicit legislative responsibility).

that it is engaged in gradualist experimentation and convincingly alleges that this route is the appropriate first pass at the interest in question, a court might suspend proceedings, permit its implementation on a temporary basis, but revisit the challenge in a few years to assess whether the state has made steps to evaluate and expand its experimentation or whether it offers a convincing reason why this first step alone should suffice.

In the alternative, a court might ask the state for further explanations. Even while upholding a law on the basis of the asserted interest, it could make clear its dissatisfaction with the flimsiness of the support for the state's asserted interest: such a recording might expose the inconsistency which could have later political ramifications or might work to set the bar higher with respect to the necessary showings by the state in the future. Whatever procedure and remedy are appropriate, the importance of the inquiry is my focus here. Whatever the appropriate venue, having to mount a pro tanto case that the state has an actual interest may prompt the sorts of public deliberation that yield greater collective self-understanding of the commitments we have undertaken, what their full prosecution and expression would involve, and where our demonstrated resolve is wanting.

These questions should not occur only to a court. In deliberating about whether and how to defend state action, the state's legal representatives may initiate inquiries of their own, attempting to ascertain whether, in good faith, they are in the position to represent a potential state interest as actual and to explain any apparent inconsistencies or hesitancies in the pursuit of the interest. Those inquiries, like those made by a court, need not conclude in a binary determination that the state either has or lacks the interest. Having to advance a justification might itself be salutary for a state office, forcing questions to be faced that have been avoided and generating greater levels of accountability via justification.

CONCLUSION

The two examples I have explored in this Part, one about common law and the other about constitutional reasoning, highlight a characteristic emphasis of the communicative approach to democratic law; namely, an interest in how legal actions structure, facilitate, or preclude other forms of collective communication and public moral reasoning through law. Both bodies of jurisprudence, as I have argued, currently exhibit a troubling indifference to disjointed bodies of law and should instead be more attentive to the importance of understanding, articulating, and communicating a coherent set of joint commitments. In the preemption case, the legal system seems to flirt excessively with the view that democratic law's main function is to resolve individual disputes—in which case the question would naturally be whether there are faster, cheaper substitutes that still preserve fairness toward the disputants. If dispute resolution is merely one important aim of a legal system, but democratic law also attempts to articulate our joint moral commitments, then displacing the articulation and development of common law should strike us as undemocratic, whether that displacement happens through unreflective forms of preemption to a market devoid of law or through active encouragement of mandatory arbitration clauses given that private arbiters do not represent *us* or generate public principles. A communicative, democratic approach would pay more heed to the consequences for the resultant legal landscape, including development of a collective and unified, if local, perspective about important areas of law.

Constitutional balancing should also be more responsive to whether state interests reflect a coherent public moral vision. When the boundaries of constitutional rights are being demarcated, state actors should demonstrate an articulate commitment to the interests they cite to defend their directives, rather than presupposing that their commitments may be read off of isolated actions, motivated assertions, and hypothetical justifications. The idea is not simply the rationalist one that checkerboard, scattered approaches to law are objectionable because no sensible justification could make them cohere. That defect is truly problematic, making it difficult to see the law as a rational system of directives.[60] My further, more positive point is that legal decisions should themselves be more sensitive to protecting, promoting, and pushing for the realization of the positive potential of democratic law; namely, its potential to communicate, through speech and action, our joint commitment to and a distinctive perspective on our collective moral ends. If democratic law is important, in part, because it affords *us*, as a collective body, the possibility of communicating with each other and pursuing our public moral ends in distinctive ways, then a more prominent factor in the jurisprudence in both areas should consider how a decision will affect the deliberative depth and unity of the resultant structure of law.

Our failures so to proceed may trace to a widespread preoccupation with outcomes and insufficient concern with the objective reasons and motives that produce them. These reasons and motives, however, are crucial elements of our moral communications and relations as well as essential components of what make our moral communities distinctive. Contemporary legal and moral theories may also be overinfluenced by pronounced anti-perfectionist allergies to governmental articulations of morality. These allergies may trace back to exaggerated sensitivities and interpretations of liberal commitments. The important and defining liberal tradition of preserving substantial room for individual judgment and control over the values and ends each citizen pursues should not be confused with collective indifference to the development of moral agency among citizens or

60. Ronald Dworkin, *Law's Empire* (Cambridge, MA: Harvard University Press, 1986), at 180–87.

with the idea that our only collective moral concerns are those that can be specified through completely determinate directives of justice. Communities depend on their members being moral agents, and the development of moral agency and moral character is partly, but not wholly, a filial affair. How we, as a community, develop and express our moral commitments is part of how we pursue justice and how we render our communities distinctive. Doing so deliberately and publicly is the mission of democratic law.

COMMENTS

Democratic Law as Medium and Message

NIKO KOLODNY

It's a staple of academic gossip that moral philosophers make little effort to live up to their own ideals. Whether or not the charge sticks to the rest of us, it misses Seana Shiffrin completely. In particular, she really does strive, even in the most everyday encounters, to treat people as autonomous, responsible equals, even when habit and convention conspire to make that impossible. She raises up timid voices, quiets overbearing ones, all the while trying to show to best advantage the views of her interlocutors even when she finds them wrongheaded or worse. So it couldn't be more fitting that she should take up the question of what we need to communicate with one another, and how we need to communicate it, in order to recognize one another as free, yet accountable, equals.

1.

I begin with an executive summary, with the usual virtues and vices of that genre. If you do not believe that I see you as an equal, Shiffrin

Niko Kolodny, *Democratic Law as Medium and Message* In: *Democratic Law*. Edited by: Hannah Ginsborg, Oxford University Press.
DOI: 10.1093/oso/9780190084486.003.0005

argues, this undermines your self-respect.[1] Since I have a duty to support your self-respect, I have a duty to get you to understand that I see you as an equal.[2] In order for you to understand that I see you as an equal, it is not enough that I merely comply with institutions that otherwise treat you as an equal (say, in the way they distribute "material resources" (p. 28).[3] For all you know, I might be complying from ulterior motives.[4] Moreover, even if you have other, "indirect" evidence that I see you as an equal, I sow doubt by not "directly" communicating this to you when I could. Consequently, I have a duty to *communicate* to you, when it's in my power, that I see you as an equal.

How do I communicate to you that I see you as an equal? I must communicate that I am undertaking an *enduring commitment*, proof against changing moods and weathers, to fulfill my duty to treat you as an equal in some specific way. And I must communicate this to you *publicly*, in two senses. First, it must be open to you to know what my commitment is. Second, I must communicate my commitment in a register that is somehow separate from my partial attachments to my

1. This need not be, as Shiffrin rightly observes, because you suffer from a weakness or vulnerability, at least not of a sort that you would better be rid of. On the contrary, it is part of your recognition of me as "a distinct individual, as a moral agent and as a moral equal capable of moral judgment whose life and thoughts matter" (pp. 28–29). However, it's not clear why the fact that my thoughts matter to you must imply that your self-respect depends on them. There are other ways my thoughts might matter.
2. Is it necessary to say anything about self-respect to establish this? Don't I have a duty to communicate to you that I see you as an equal (e.g., not to address you, even in a closed-door meeting, with racist epithets) even if you are unsinkably self-assured?
3. "Material resources" may suggest something narrower than Shiffrin means. It's still not enough that the institutions secure "intangible" procedural protections, rights of privacy, etc. in the way demanded by our equality.
4. However, some of the ulterior motives Shiffrin lists (e.g. "mutual indifference, grudging accommodation" (p. 27) are not, at least not at first glance, failures to regard you as an equal or, at any rate, attitudes that should compromise self-respect.

family, church, or other private association. Otherwise, you may misinterpret my partiality to them as a judgment that they are superior to you. Since these features of my communication just are marks of *law*, Shiffrin suggests, my communication to you must take the form of law.

Furthermore, it is not enough that the communication recognizes a duty to treat you as an equal: that it is democratic in its *content*. It must also issue from a democratic *process*. First, the communication must be *crafted*, not simply affirmed. Second, the communication must be *ours collectively*. Finally, each of us must play an *equal role* in the process.

In sum, because the self-respect of our fellows depends on our communicating to them that we see them as equals, we need, and we need to participate in and comply with, a *system of democratic law*.

2.

So much for summary. Now for (a lot of) questions. To begin with, the law often threatens to penalize me for violating it.[5] Isn't that a reason for you to wonder whether I am complying because I see you as an equal? Perhaps I'm complying instead because I fear the penalty. However, given that law sends such mixed messages, might it not be better, all things considered, to look for another

5. I don't mean to suggest that coercion is essential to law. Nor do I mean to be endorsing the common assumption (of, e.g., Rawls) that, even in the ideal case, coercion is necessary to assure otherwise well-intentioned cooperators. I'm just assuming that we are trying to identify a role that law would be well-suited to play even if it was (perhaps non-essentially, non-ideally) coercive.

channel of communication?[6] With so much interference on this line, maybe we should try transmitting on another.

3.

Next, why must we *craft* the message? Why can't we instead *affirm* a message that someone else crafted (so long as the message regards us)? As a general rule, affirming words that I did not craft doesn't make my affirmation insincere or unserious. Beckoning me to your bedside, you whisper, "Promise me this." Is my reply, "I promise," lacking because I didn't craft what the "this" was?

Indeed, that words aren't ours to craft, that they come with their own history, can give them power and resonance. "Passing the peace" before communion, when parishioners turn to one another and say, "Peace be with you," is about as close to an explicit, direct, reciprocal acknowledgment of equal regard among strangers as some of us will experience. I'm not sure it would be an improvement if congregants cast tradition aside and tried to freestyle.

In any event, as far as the law is concerned, affirming the message, rather than crafting it, is by and large what we do. Most of the law—for instance, much (although of course not all) of the First Amendment—was crafted without our input, by (some of) the ancestors (of some of us).

Shiffrin might reply that the relevant "we" *did* make this law: namely, a "we" that includes our forebears. But this reply would strain the idea that each of us must have an equal role in crafting the law. You and I simply weren't around at the time—setting aside the

6. Shiffrin might point out that we already knew that coercive penalties, even if necessary, are regrettable. This is just one more reason to regret them! But this doesn't reach the question of why, given that, we shouldn't find some other vehicle of communication.

point that many of the people who were around at the time weren't included in the "we" to begin with.

4.

Even supposing that the sender must craft the message, why must the sender be *the collective of all of us together*? Why not a Facebook page, say, where *each* of us *individually* posts that they recognize the equality of everyone else? One answer is that each of us individually simply *cannot* communicate in this way. Since senders cannot affirm, but must craft, a message, senders will (almost certainly) craft different messages. No mortal could scroll to the end of so many personalized posts. Moreover, since these messages are commitments to *act*, the attempt to fulfill those commitments would be disastrously uncoordinated. Grant, then, that *I as an individual cannot* send a message. Why should it follow that *we together*, as a collective, *should* send a message? If your self-respect needs to hear from me as an individual, how does it help to hear instead from this corporate agent, the collective? If *I* owe it to you to express my gratitude, what good it is for *our homeowner's association* to promise to water your garden?

Indeed, if I *can't* communicate, isn't the consequence simply that it shouldn't matter to you that I *don't* communicate, so that there's no need to recruit a corporate spokesperson in the first place? The argument, recall, is that my failure to communicate is normatively significant only when and because I *could* communicate but *choose* not to. Otherwise, "indirect" evidence of my motives should suffice.[7]

7. "Our important capacity to control what we reveal about our thoughts renders the distinction between what we intentionally convey, what we conceal, and what we leave to be indirectly inferred about our wills normatively meaningful" (p. 29).

Perhaps the crux is not that I *can't* communicate to you as an individual, but instead that your self-respect depends, at least in part, on how the *collective* itself sees you, independently of how individuals see you. And only the collective can communicate how *it* sees you. But it's harder to see why your self-respect should depend on the attitudes of the collective, understood as something genuinely distinct from the attitudes of other individuals.[8] At any rate, if this is the crux, Shiffrin says little about it. On the contrary, at what seem the crucial points, she instead stresses that you care how I as an individual see you.[9]

5.

Why must we each play an *equal* role in crafting the collective message? After all, our orchestra's performance, our team's victory, our unit's aid mission, and so on, are our collective successes, even if we did not elect our conductor, coach, or commander, and even if their management style was decidedly top-down. One case for equal roles runs as follows. If the *process* of crafting the collective message does

8. Among other things, I, as an individual, can communicate that I recognize you as my equal. But it seems like a category mistake for the collective to communicate that it recognizes you as *its* equal.

9. That is, "as a distinct *individual,* as a moral agent and as a moral equal capable of moral judgment whose life and thoughts matter" (pp. 28–29). "It is an aspect of our respect for each other as *individuals* that we afford special significance to agents' efforts to make their thoughts public and thereby to affirm and endorse those thoughts. Our important capacity to control what we reveal about our thoughts renders the distinction between what we intentionally convey, what we conceal, and what we leave to be indirectly inferred about our wills normatively meaningful. . . . [W]hen I make an intentional effort to convey my respect, other things equal, my action is more meaningful than my leaving my respect to be assumed or inferred by you because I do not leave it to you to infer my attitudes from my actions and omissions. Rather, I assume responsibility *as an individual* to affiliate myself with that respectful content, and I aim to ensure you know it matters enough *to me that I exert my agency* to convey it" (p. 29; emphasis added).

not itself treat people as equals, then that process compromises the *content* of the message. (It's like how the process of manufacturing the hat overseas compromises the content of the message, "Make America Great Again.") Next, make the key assumption that, in general, people are treated as equals by a process only if they have an equal say in that process. Then it follows that, in order for the collective message to have the right content, people need to have an equal say in the process of crafting it.

However, Shiffrin never argues for the key assumption: that people are treated as equals by a process only if they have an equal say in that process. Moreover, that assumption seems to short-circuit her larger argument. With it in hand, we can argue simply: since we must, in general, treat people as equals, we must, in the specific context of the process of political decision-making, treat people as equals. According to the key assumption, the process of political decision-making treats people as equals only if it gives them each an equal say. So, they must each have an equal say. No need to say anything about communication.

A different case for equal roles is that, otherwise, as Shiffrin writes, "the message will not be *each* of ours" (p. 39). Here, the trouble is that, again, Shiffrin elsewhere says that the collective message *cannot* be each of ours as individuals, period—*whether or not* we have an equal role.[10] Shiffrin must mean that, in one sense, the collective message is not the message of each of us, but that, in another sense, the collective message is the message of each of us—provided that we play an equal role in crafting it. And the self-respect of others

10. "[I]n a democratic structure, law has a communicative dimension whose content may be attributed to all of us together, even if not to each of us as individuals" (p. 53); "it certainly does not represent the convictions of many of us as individuals" (p. 55); "the collective message is not necessarily the individual message of each co-author" (p. 21, fn. 6).

depends on whether the collective message is the message of each of us, in that special sense.

What's the special sense? The only real clue I find is that each of us can be "responsible" for the message, in the sense of appropriately feeling or expressing pride, regret, etc. for it.[11] But I can be responsible, in this sense, for my collective's actions even without an equal role. It's appropriate for me to feel (to put it mildly) "apologetic" as an American visiting Hiroshima for events that took place before I was born.

In any event, why should your self-respect depend on whether I *can appropriately* feel apologetic for the collective message? That might say *nothing* about my attitudes toward you. If it was appropriate for Anthony Romero to feel apologetic greeting his Muslim neighbors the morning after Trump's election, then it was also appropriate for Jeff Sessions to feel. But that says nothing about their attitudes toward their Muslim neighbors, which are miles apart.[12]

11. "Still, each co-author has a reason to assume responsibility *as a member of the collective* for the joint message that was sent, even while she may disagree with it as an individual. Sometimes that responsibility may take the form of collective pride (e.g., for having participated in the process that led to successful legislation even if one was a dissenting voice about its exact contents). And, sometimes, that form of responsibility may take the form of collective regret. If the religious card offended the mourner, even the agnostic may owe an apology qua member of the collective and even though the agnostic pointed out, at the time, that the mourner might be offended by the card" (p. 21, fn. 6).

12. Shiffrin might propose an alternative explanation of how the collective message can both be and not be the message of each of us. The collective message is the message of each of us as citizen, but not of each of us as private individual. "I need to communicate as a *citizen,* not only as a private individual" (p. 32). But then I worry about equivocation. That I communicate "as a citizen" might just mean that I communicate "publicly," in the second sense above: that is, in a way that is somehow separate from my partial attachments to my family, church, or other private association. Although I decide what to say, as, say, the lone dissenter at the town hall, I nevertheless address the others in the hall as fellow citizens, not as cousins or congregants, and I offer grounds rooted in the public interest, not in my family's advantage or fear of God's wrath. But what I then say is not what we together—the town—say. Alternatively, communicating "as a citizen" might just mean being an equal part of a public collective that communicates. But then "as a citizen" seems more like relabeling than resolution of the present problem.

6.

Before Shiffrin's discussion, one might have observed that democratic law serves certain values. Its content treats people as equals, and the process by which it is made doesn't subordinate anyone to anyone else. Those values give me reasons, of a kind, to participate in democratic law-making and to comply with the laws so made. By participating and complying, I respect, or affiliate myself with, those values. Of course, the value of bolstering self-respect through communication might be yet another value that my participation and compliance might respect or affiliate me with. But Shiffrin seems to suggest that this communicative value supplies some more distinctive and direct reason to participate and comply.[13]

I struggle to see what this reason might be. On the one hand, my individual compliance or participation does not affect whether or what the *collective* communicates to you—let alone in a way that would touch your self-respect. On the other hand, my individual participation or compliance does not communicate something *as an individual* to you because, again, I can't communicate as an individual.[14] Nor can it be said that I am responsible for the communication only if I participate or comply. Setting aside why your self-respect should depend on whether I'm responsible, I'm responsible even if I spoil my ballot or break the law. That's what made the bumper sticker, "Don't blame me, I voted for Nader," so annoying.

13. "This account offers answers to puzzles that dog other democratic theories: it offers reasons why one has reason to participate in democratic processes even when, predictably, one's preferred position would win without one's support or lose even with one's support; it offers reasons to follow and respect laws; and it supplies a connection between the two endeavors" (p. 53).

14. And note that this would make too much turn on whether you *know* about my participation or compliance. For, unless you know about it, my participation or compliance can't communicate anything to you. But it's not as though I have less reason to comply when there's no way for you to come to know whether I complied.

7.

To sum up what I have said so far, there seems to be a basic tension. On the one hand, Shiffrin's problem—that you need to know that you are seen as a fellow equal by other equals—seems to press us toward saying that I, as an individual, say something to you. And there is much else that she says—about my reasons to participate and comply, about my need for an equal role, and so on—that suggests that you need to hear from me as an individual. On the other hand, Shiffrin's solution—that democratic law can communicate—seems to press us toward saying that we, as a collective, are speaking. And there are other themes in her lectures that seem to ask all of us together to say something.

Any friend of democracy has at times felt the temptation, which Shiffrin expressly resists, simply to identify what "I" say with what "we" say. Rousseau might be read as succumbing to this temptation when he writes that, in a properly constituted democracy, each obeys none but himself, that the general will is his, and suchlike. But surely, one wants to say, and Shiffrin seems to want to say, there's some difference between what "I" will and what "we" will.

Now, perhaps there is some *other* sense in which, at least in the right context, what "we" say is what "I" say. The challenge is to articulate what this sense is. It has to be enough what "I" say to address the basic problem—my need to communicate—but still enough what "we" say for the proposed solution—democratic law—to count as a solution.

8.

The leading idea of Shiffrin's lecture is not so much about law or democracy, but instead about the connection between the two: that some "distinctive, essential" "role" (or "function" or "virtue") of law is "uniquely display[ed]" by democracy (pp. 17–19). As far as I can tell, though, what she shows is instead that law has the role of *communicating public commitments*. And, as far as I can tell, that role might be just as fully realized in *non*-democratic systems. An aristocracy or theocracy can have its reasons to communicate public commitments. Of course, such public commitments would not be to equality. They would be instead to the immutable order of castes or to the one true faith that is taken to define the society in question. But that's the point. Law's capacity to make public commitments is one thing. The democratic or non-democratic character of those commitments is, it seems, another.

9.

As it happens, I agree, albeit for different reasons, with Shiffrin's broader thesis: that there is an aspiration of law that is realized only in democracy. This is the aspiration to a society in which, while every person's actions will be constrained or concerted by something of human invention, no person will be subordinated to the rule of any other person. This is the aspiration expressed by the call for "a government of laws, not of men."

But law alone cannot realize this aspiration. For if only one or a few make the law, then the law risks being a self-disciplined form of subordination of the rest. So, in order to live in a society where no one is subordinated to the rule of any other person, the law must be democratically made, at least in the weak sense that none of us has greater opportunity to influence it than any other. When this is so, there's no one I can point to and say, because he had greater opportunity to influence it, I am, in being subjected to that law, being subordinated to him. Of course, the *content* of law might be still subordinating, but at least the *process* of making it would not be.

Granted, democracy in this weak sense is achieved even when *none of us* makes the law—when, say, we merely receive it from our ancestors. But, provided that the content of the law is OK, inheriting it also seems to me OK. Jefferson's idea that democracy requires each generation to draw up its own constitution seems misplaced in theory and not just, as Madison gently pointed out, unworkable in practice.

10.

Shiffrin says that the "moral and expressive collective opportunities that democracies afford, not their status and function as lesser evils, are what make sense of the passion for democracy" (p. 60). Yet her communicative picture can lay claim to, as she puts it, "the virtue of befitting the urgency of democratic movements" (p. 59) only if that picture faithfully depicts what moves these movements. That is, only if democratic movements are moved by the desire to communicate to their fellows, so as to shore up their self-respect, but keep being frustrated by authoritarian forms of government, that, like a smiley face on a condolence note, can't help but garble the message.

But do democratic movements say any such thing? If Shiffrin is struck by "a puzzling mismatch between the . . . zeal people have for democracy and the resigned air of many . . . accounts of democracy" (p. 59), I'm struck by a puzzling mismatch between the motivations she imputes to democratic movements and the motivations the movements themselves express. Now, perhaps there are filed reports somewhere of democratic activists expressing this frustrated desire to communicate. Or perhaps there's some reason why, counterproductive though it seems, democratic activists refuse to communicate their desire to communicate.

But, at risk of being naïve or overly literal, I'd guess that if one tries to take democratic movements, yesterday and today, at their word—if one reads, say, Elizabeth Cady Stanton's address at Seneca Falls, or Frederick Douglass' "What the Black Man Wants"—one finds different aspirations. One finds, first, the aspiration that *the content of political decisions treat them as equals*—or at least with enough fairness and humanity as to let them carry on with a modicum of dignity. And one finds, second, the aspiration that they *enjoy the equal status that comes, in part, from having an equal say in making political decisions*. And those far-from-fulfilled aspirations, even without the imputation of others, seem urgent enough.

11.

Comments on philosophical lectures, of course, are never the last word. But these comments are even further from the last word than usual because of the nature of the lectures themselves. It's all well and good to analyze a proposed philosophical justification into simple component parts and then try to test what work each part does by imagining cases where one part is in play but not the other. But this approach has its limitations, especially when applied to Shiffrin's invitation to view democratic law as communication. For what communicates what is a question of meaning, and—although this is something that perhaps only an analytic philosopher like me needs to be reminded of—meaning depends on social context.

Should, for example, the fact that violations of the law are met with, for lack of a better word, "punishment" cast doubt on the sincerity of our commitment to it? Well, it depends on what punishment is in our social context. Is it a deterrent or moral education? Similarly, whether I meet my communicative responsibilities better by putting the message in my own words or someone else's will depend on the wider context. My replying at your deathbed, "Yes, I promise to do that," where I simply affirm your terms, is, as it were, a once-in-a-lifetime situation. We need to say something about it, but it's a special case.

Again, whether we simply receive the law from our ancestors depends, among other things, on what context guides the interpretation the law: how far the materials that determine what the law says were fixed by our ancestors and how far they are still being refashioned by us.

And so on.

All this makes Shiffrin's project hard work. It requires, at every step, interpretation. But, by the same token, all this makes it a conceit to think that one might refute her thesis with, say, stylized hypotheticals. On the contrary, we critics will have to be just as attentive to the social and legal fabric as she is. I am not sure where we are headed, but I'm game to follow as far as I can, especially so long as Shiffrin will be the one lighting the way.

Common Knowledge and Cheap Talk in Democratic Discourse and Law

RICHARD R. W. BROOKS

1. INTRODUCTION

Every democratic order committed to recognizing its members' status as equals, among other "mandatory moral ends" (p. 25), must overcome what Seana Shiffrin describes as "communicative challenges of a moral nature" (p. 26). These challenges, she argues, are uniquely addressed by law, and in particular "democratic law."[1] By communicating public commitments "the law gives specific shape and coordination to the direction of our actions and the content of our expectations" (p. 48). Law's public communication, however, must do more than simply facilitate coordination in complex

1. Shiffrin broadly characterizes "democratic law" throughout her lectures. Early on, for example, Shiffrin writes, "By 'democratic law,' I mean a legal system the content and generation of which justifies its characterization as democratic. . . . Democratic law is a constituent condition of the full realization of such conditions and hence of the full realization of justice" (pp. 25–26).

Richard R. W. Brooks, *Common Knowledge and Cheap Talk in Democratic Discourse and Law*
In: *Democratic Law*. Edited by: Hannah Ginsborg, Oxford University Press. © Regents of the University of California 2021. DOI: 10.1093/oso/9780190084486.003.0006

democratic societies. Democratic law demands, insists Shiffrin, "that we manifest our respect for one another and not merely that we co-exist" (p. 27), even if that existence is otherwise efficient, equal or fair. "A just allocation of material resources is compatible with mutual indifference, grudging accommodation, or even mutual contempt" (p. 28). So what? "Why, it might be asked, should this matter so long as the conditions of material (and intellectual) justice obtain, whether through coercion, grudging compliance, or barely registered automation?" (p. 28).

Shiffrin thoughtfully tackles this question, among others, in her Tanner Lectures. In the following pages I will attempt to characterize and comment on her basic insight, which I take to be that a robust democracy requires more than a commitment to materially just outcomes and more still than commitments of equal regard and respect of its members. Democratic legal commitments must be reflected in both high-order legal norms as well as basic "bread-and-butter laws" and, moreover, these commitments should be communicated through routine encounters among citizens. Were our democratic bonds the only source of commitments to manifest in our dealings with each other that would be demanding enough, but, Shiffrin observes, "[o]ur communicative challenge is compounded by the fact that, in our daily lives, it is nearly inevitable that we will send mixed signals" (p. 31), given competing "partial commitments—to family, to smaller communities and affiliations, and to associations with strong substantive commitments" (p. 31). Hence, as citizens, "we need to convey our mutual recognition of each other's moral status[,] to counteract any inadvertent suggestions to the contrary" (p. 31).

Democratic law is an essential instrument for communicating our commitments *as citizens*.[2] However, and this is key, it is not enough

2. "While each of us cannot *show* our recognition of each other's mutual equal status and belonging through our everyday interpersonal conduct, our legal system can do this. It can

to communicate the content of these commitments. In order to realize and maintain robust democratic commitments, they must be communicated routinely—which is to say, through routines—and publicly. Routines ought to reveal our commitments, and our public commitments should be observable in our routines. Another way of putting it, if somewhat arcanely, is to say that routines should support *common knowledge* of public commitments[3] and that publicly stated commitments absent actual investments and routines are little more than *cheap talk*.[4] These particular notions of "common knowledge" and "cheap talk" are used in the comments that follow to recharacterize Shiffrin's subtle yet forceful claims and thereby reveal in a slightly different light her compelling vision of democratic law. Allow me to clarify.

adopt explicit laws that declare and support our equal status and needs . . . [it] can . . . create environments in which individuals interact with one another on an equal basis . . . [it can] [through its procedural and enforcement mechanisms] reflect this fundamental recognition. The state [unlike families and other associations] is the crucial organizational structure to achieve these communicative aims" (p. 51).

3. Here I invoke "common knowledge" in the technical sense used by game-theorists. Something is common knowledge between or among persons if each person knows that thing and knows that others also know it, and they all know that they all know it, and they all know that they all know that they all know it, and so on ad infinitum. See, e.g., Robert Aumann, "Agreeing to Disagree," *Annals of Statistics* 4 (1976): 1236–39; Paul Milgrom, "An Axiomatic Characterization of Common Knowledge," *Econometrica* 49 (1981): 219–22; John Geanakoplos, "Common Knowledge," *Journal of Economic Perspectives* 6, no. 4 (1992): 53–82; Robin Cubitt and Robert Sugden, "Common Knowledge, Salience and Convention: A Reconstruction of David Lewis' Game Theory," *Economics and Philosophy* 19 (2003): 175–210.
4. Like "common knowledge," "cheap talk" is a term of art among game theorists. Cheap talk specifically refers to speech or other communication that does not directly affect the value or values (or, in the conventional economics parlance, the "utility") of the speaker. See, e.g., Joseph Farrell, "Communication, Coordination and Nash Equilibrium," *Economic Letters* 27 (1988): 209–14; Robert Aumann, "Nash-Equilibria Are Not Self-Enforcing," in J. Gabszewicz, J.-F. Richard, and L. Wolsey, eds., *Economic Decision Making: Games, Econometrics and Optimization* (Amsterdam, New York and Oxford: North-Holland 1990), 201–206; Joseph Farrell and Matthew Rabin, "Cheap Talk," *Journal of Economic Perspectives* 10, no. 3 (1996): 103–18.

One interpretation, or perhaps an emphasis, of Shiffrin's thesis in *Democratic Law* would stress the reciprocal role of law and democracy for their mutual achievement. On the one hand, law and legal institutions in their public and reason-granting channels (such as that observed in the common law, but also with respect to "notice and comment" in administrative rule-making, *inter alia*) may generate common knowledge about commitments that are necessary for her vision of democracy. On the other hand, democracy and democratic institutions, especially a free speech culture (but also referenda and open elections) may generate "common ground" of the social bases of self-respect and compromise that are required for our legal and constitutional order.[5] Together, law and democracy respond to the "communicative challenges of a moral nature" to which Shiffrin calls our attention.

Democratic law, she argues, has a unique capacity to communicate egalitarian commitments. It is important here, however, to distinguish between free speech and cheap talk. Free speech institutions, essential elements of our constitutional order, are far from costless. Cheap talk, by definition, is always costless. Moreover, in contrast to free speech, cheap talk (i.e., claims and assertions without costs or commitments) threatens the constitutional balance, warns Shiffrin, between citizens and the state. Constitutional courts ought to hear such claims and assertions with caution, she advises, and should certainly avoid uncritical deference to them, given the interests at stake. These arguments are elaborated later in the comments that follow. Next, however, an old tale is told to illustrate the

5. I take the expression "common ground," as Shiffrin uses it, to be quite close to, if not the same as, common knowledge. Hence, my interpretation or emphasis may be little more than a restatement of her thesis and a less eloquent one at that, but hopefully it will be of some use, if only for the examples.

link between common knowledge and, as Shiffrin describes it, the social bases of self-respect.

2. A FOLK TALE OF THREE FRIENDS

Arlie and Britt are in an admirable and avowedly exclusive relationship. They are the envy of their friends. There is no abuse, verbal or otherwise, in their relationship. Rarely is a voice raised, and anger is rarer still. They maintain an orderly home, wherein each provides for the other's every material need. They enjoy each other's company and consider themselves the best of friends. They share everything, except one very poorly kept secret. Each is having a romantic relationship with another person. They both feel guilty about their hidden relations, which each understands as contrary to their public commitments and the commitments they made to each other. Yet neither chooses to stop, perhaps because each suspects, to the point of knowing, that the other is also cheating. They are not open with each other about their beliefs and suspicions for, if they were, they would be forced to reevaluate the kinds of persons (their individual sense of self-respect) they are and the kind of relationship they have. Through their individual actions and silence, each is able to maintain the pretense of being in an avowedly exclusive relationship and not the type of person who would knowingly remain with a philandering partner.

One day, seemingly out of nowhere, Arlie confides to a mutual friend, Chris: "I am cheating on Britt, but I don't want to discuss it any further. I just had to tell someone." Chris is stunned and uncomfortable being made party to the deception, but respects Arlie's wishes and says nothing concerning the revelation. Several days later the three of them meet for a long-scheduled dinner. When Arlie steps away from the table for a moment, Britt leans over and whispers to Chris: "I have a new lover. It's not serious. Don't tell Arlie." Just then Arlie returns to the table, and Chris, now visibly befuddled and disgusted, stands up from the table and announces before abruptly departing: "What is wrong with the two of you? It's not enough that you are both cheating on each other, you have to drag me in on it, too. I will not be part of your duplicity."

Sitting together in silence at the table, reflecting on Chris' announcement, Arlie and Britt are confronted with a knowledge they did not possess before. While before, when each knew of the other's infidelity (as well as, of course, their own) they could pretend not to know about any disloyalty. But Chris' announcement made their mutual disloyalty "common knowledge" between them, which is to say, not only do they each know that the other is cheating, but they each *now* also knows that the other knows this fact, and, moreover, they have higher levels of knowledge about that subsidiary knowledge. In other words, there is no longer room for pretense, no plausible deniability, concerning the nature of their relationship. They are now forced to reevaluate their commitments, public and private, and align their actions if each is to maintain the sense of self-respect and mutual regard for the other and their collective endeavor, all to which they had previously vowed.[6]

Knowledge alone, or simply knowing the expectations and obligations of others and oneself, is often not enough to allow persons to fulfill *certain* commitments and realize *some* relationships. Nor might it be sufficient that each knows that others know of these expectations and obligations. Public communication of a duty, Shiffrin argues, is constitutive of some commitments and relationships. "Even if redundant, its articulation has distinctive communicative moral resonance

6. None of this is to suggest that persons in avowedly open relationships are unable to maintain a sense of self-respect and mutual regard—of course they may—in such a collective endeavor.

because it conveys to everyone that we, as a community, know we have this duty, we know it is relevant to our situation" (p. 48).[7] When public communication generates common knowledge, "moral resonance" often follows, as in the tale of Arlie, Britt, and Chris, exposing speaker and addressee to the actual nature of their relationships and commitments.[8]

In this way common knowledge is a useful lens through which to consider Shiffrin's insights, but it is important to stress that her claims are, ultimately, not epistemological. Shiffrin is concerned with the moral and dispositional resonance of knowledge and communication.[9] Common knowledge and cheap talk are helpful lenses through which to view her insights, but as these notions are essentially cognitive in character, these notions are insufficient to capture or fully restate her more subtle normative claims. Shiffrin elaborates these claims through the common law of contracts and other basic "bread-and-butter laws" in the second lecture and then, in third the lecture, turns her attention to higher order legal norms and constitutional balancing. I will now briefly consider each.

3. COMMON KNOWLEDGE AND THE COMMON LAW

Our democratic laws are not just determined through popular referenda and legislation promulgated by elected officials. Other legal

7. "[W]e aim to convey our knowledge of this duty to each other as fellow duty-holders and claimants" (p. 48).
8. Note that it is not only the truth of the relationship between Arlie and Britt that is revealed by common knowledge, but also their mutual and individual relationships with Chris.
9. Consider, for example, Shiffrin's comment on public communication of one's duties. "Public articulation forges a personal connection to the duty in a way that silent acknowledgment does not, reinforcing the duty's role as an organizing principle for the speaker" (p. 49).

institutions also promote democratic law, Shiffrin reminds us, including a culture of free speech and, I would add, an independent and transparent judiciary. It is also important to appreciate, she stresses, the common law's contribution to our democratic legal tradition. Common law did not originate in the rulings by appointed judges, as often suggested, but rather in the accepted norms and practices of communities.[10] Early common law courts were not the only places where parties went to settle their disputes. Feudal societies and ancient guilds had their own courts and, of course, the law merchant is well-known. Their rulings reflected, as John Commons wrote, "the approved common practices of business men, first enforced in their own courts and then enforced, with enlargements or restraints, in the common law courts."[11]

One of the most important rules articulated in these court—surviving today in most private law jurisdictions around the world, often as a mandatory rule of contract law—is the duty of good faith.[12] What constituted good faith was determined by the reasonable expectations of transacting parties and the standards and practices of the communities in which they transact, all of which to be sure were evolving with time. What the common law added was publicity of these reasonable expectations, standards, and

10. Edward Coke, Matthew Hale, and William Blackstone, among other early English lawyers, identified the common law with sets of customs and approved routines of local communities.

11. John R. Commons, "Law and Economics," *Yale Law Journal* 34 (1925). As Commons observed, the common law derives from "the Common Practices of feudal lords, of the early guilds, of agricultural communities, of merchants, manufacturers, business men, of workingmen, professional men and others, in their daily transactions with each other. . . . And the Common Law evolves in proportion as the courts decide disputes in accordance with the common practices of these several classes deemed to be good and proper" (371, 373).

12. Richard R. W. Brooks, "Good Faith in Contractual Exchanges," in Andrew S. Gold, John C.P. Goldberg, Daniel B. Kelly, Emily L. Sherwin, and Henry E. Smith, eds., *The Oxford Handbook of New Private Law* (New York: Oxford University Press, 2021).

practices, exhibiting them even as they evolved. Unlike arbiters in the feudal courts and private guilds, judges in common law courts do not merely resolve disputes. The common law provided them a mechanism for the *public* dissemination and resolution of disputes. In other words, the common law is a mechanism for generating common knowledge about disputes, including their "good and proper" disposition.

Consider, in contrast, modern consumer and commercial arbitration, which preserves strong norms of confidentiality with respect to disputes and their resolution. To be sure, confidentiality (as opposed to common knowledge) may often serve the interests of one or both parties to a dispute. However, as Shiffrin points out, that private benefit comes at a public cost, a cost borne by the community.

> As enforceable arbitration clauses proliferate, in addition to depriving individual litigants of due process, the common law may languish because substantive, important disputes over commonplace contracts may never reach court. (p. 69)

As disputes are sequestered to private arbitration, it becomes increasingly difficult to achieve common knowledge regarding, for instance, what constitutes "good faith and fair dealing" in contractual exchange relationships. And this inability to achieve common knowledge about what constitutes "good faith and fair dealing" can bear meaningfully on our disposition and dignity within these relationships, even if the same material outcomes are otherwise realized. Shiffrin explores this issue with the case of *Northwest v. Ginsberg*, concerning the Airline Deregulation Act preempting state (contract) common law. Her insightful analysis of the demands of good faith in contracts generally and in that case, particularly, should be required reading for students as well as the US Supreme Court.

Rather than restating Shiffrin's analysis of good faith through the *Ginsberg* case,[13] I will make use another airline case, one more personal and mundane, to illustrate how common knowledge, or its absence, may impact our dispositions, expectations, and dignity within ordinary contractual exchanges. Several years ago I called an airline carrier to book a flight across country. At the time, when I called, I was still not entirely sure of my travel dates, although I was somewhat confident. Still, I did not want to delay my purchase any longer, because the two-week departure window for booking was closing. I told the airline agent that I would like to buy the ticket now, then confer and confirm with counterparts at my destination later in the day and, if necessary, cancel the ticket (without a charge) that night or the next morning. There was a long pause. Then somewhat hesitantly, but politely, the agent said, "Well, ah, OK Mr. Brooks, yes, I think I can do that for you."

I was confused by her reply. I didn't know if she was thinking or suggesting (1) that it was within her power and discretion to grant a special dispensation to me or (2) that it was my special privilege as a medallion member of the airline's frequent flyer program that allowed me the option of cancelling the ticket without charge. I was, in any case, seeking neither to invoke a special privilege nor to ask for a special dispensation. I was rather seeking to clarify what I took to

13. Shiffrin offers her own effective restatement, observing that, "in this example, the doctrine of good faith plays an important role in publicizing and enforcing expectations about the significance of making a binding agreement. Through interpretation of the duty of good faith, courts contribute to the development of a public articulation of how to assess the spirit of a bargain and what it means to respect it in one's reasons when exercising discretion. How good faith is enforced and interpreted—whether they can expect that their agreements will be interpreted to have robust meaning or whether they should regard themselves more warily as at extended arms-length—in turn, has an influence on the scope of trust that it is safe for a contractual party to invest in her partner; the narrower that scope, the more anxious parties may be to attempt to devise explicit constraints to insert into their agreements. Indirectly and directly, the legal doctrine contributes to the nature of the local social-moral culture" (pp. 86–87).

be an entitlement belonging to all persons under the US Department of Transportation's implementation of the "Enhancing Airline Passenger Protection" rule, which then allowed for effective costless cancellation of all reservations made seven days or more prior to a flight's scheduled departure time.[14] All domestic airline customers were accorded this entitlement, provided by basic "bread-and-butter" law. It was neither a matter left to the discretionary authority of agents nor a question of privileges accruing to certain customers.[15]

Now, imagine that I did not know about this law, but that I am a savvy traveler, someone who knows that if I ask to cancel my flight in a very short period after initial booking, then the airline will grant me that option (maybe because I'm savvy or an effective bargainer, or because the airline has come to know that the goodwill and the associated expected future revenue it will generate will more than make up for the transaction costs related to rebooking flights). Let's also imagine that *all* travelers are savvy like me and equally ignorant about the law. Now in this imagined world, every passenger seeking to cancel or modify a reservation within 24 hours of booking will request a waiver of any change or cancellation fee, and the airline will always grant those requests. Here the material outcome is the same as if customers and airlines were knowingly acting under the provisions of the law, and they all knew that they were—and so on. But they act here under a different moral and dignitarian disposition.

14. 14 CFR 259.5(b)(4), 76 Fed. Reg. 23110, April 25, 2011; see also the USA Department of Transportation's "Guidance on the 24-Hour Reservation Requirement" prepared by Samuel Podberesky, Assistant General Counsel for Aviation Enforcement and Proceedings, May 31, 2013, available online at http://www.dot.gov/airconsumer.

15. Commercial airline travel today is, in my opinion, an often undignified experience where customers are subject to the most inegalitarian norms and practices over a sustained period in a given space. With competing (fare) classes sharing one vessel, all getting the same basic transportation service, airlines have perfected means of elevating and degrading their passengers in order to profitably (price) discriminate among them.

Absent the law *and* my knowledge of the law along with the agent's knowledge of the law *and* our common knowledge of these prior facts, we have the same material outcome but with a dignitarian and egalitarian shortfall. Important moral questions are left open. Am I to feel beholden to the agent? Am I to feel entitled and privileged above lower medallion passengers and infrequent flyers? The Department of Transportation created a rule, under the authority of the Federal Aviation Act, whereby all prospective passengers stand on equal footing with respect to this legal entitlement. We are all entitled to the privileges and immunities of the rule, and knowing that we are all equal before the law reinforces the democratic and egalitarian ethos of the law. And that, of course, matters.[16]

Now, the travel agent may derive some personal benefit from having me believe that she is doing a favor for me (granting a special dispensation to me), or I may like to believe that I am myself special, entitled, or otherwise superior to lesser flyers. These pretensions are, however, inconsistent with the actual state and democratic aim of the law. The Department of Transportation's rule-making was meant, among other things, to preempt such partial and private sources of dignity and regard. In a similar vein, in the aftermath of the September 11, 2001 (9/11) attacks, when the US Congress debated and eventually passed the Aviation and Transportation Security Act, creating the Transportation Security Administration (TSA), proposals for first-class passenger screening were raised and rejected as antithetical to the then national sentiment following the attacks that "we are all in this together."[17] Such legal expression of egalitarian sentiment (e.g.,

16. "Bread-and-butter" entitlements to enter and enforce contracts have, at least since the Civil Rights Acts of 1866, occupied a substantial core of the democratic and egalitarian ethos in the US constitutional law tradition.

17. Today, to be sure, most airports have established priority lines for certain customers. TSA, as a governmental (public) agency, insists that decisions regarding those special lines are made by private entities (the airlines and airports) on the private property of those entities. When passengers arrive at the point of inspection and screening, where state

"we are all in this together") is necessary but not sufficient, Shiffrin tells us, to satisfy the demands of democratic law. Our egalitarian commitments should also be routinely and publicly communicated by individuals, including, for instance, TSA and airline agents as well as, insists Shiffrin, fellow passengers, among others.

"Law plays a special role in fulfilling this communicative mission," Shiffrin informs us. For instance, when I raised the possibility of reserving my ticket and then canceling without a fee within 24 hours, the agent might have made it common knowledge between us that doing so was a legal privilege afforded to all airline consumers. She certainly should not have hedged, obfuscated, or otherwise concealed this fact surrounding the legal entailments of our interaction. Law required a candid reply to my inquiry.[18] Although I was then vaguely aware of the regulation, it wasn't the exact content of the rule that I was seeking so much as the connection that the communication would bring about. I wanted to be sure that we were on the same page before investing time in an extended exchange relation. When the agent hesitated, however, it became more than a matter of wasting time; in the pause, new and uncomfortable questions surfaced. Was this not an entitlement for all passengers? Was I dependent on the whim of the agent or my special association with her airline? My standing and disposition in the exchange at hand, if not more broadly, was in part determined by the answers to these questions,

agents exercise authority, all passengers then stand on equal footing, according to TSA, with access to the same rights and privileges.

18. "[C]arriers must fully and accurately disclose their cancellation policies, including the 24-hour reservation requirement, through reservation agents or customer service agents *upon receiving direct inquires from consumers by telephone* or in person at the ticket counter." Podberesky (2013) "Guidance on the 24-Hour Reservation Requirement" at 3, http://www.dot.gov/airconsumer (emphasis added). It is, of course, possible that the agent was herself unaware or unsure of the rule's requirements. I will presume she knew, for the sake of argument, and, in any event, her airline employer is legally, if not morally, chargeable with this knowledge since it should have known, as a matter of law.

which, Shiffrin might say, touch on, however subtly, the social bases of self-respect. As such, the agent had a communicative obligation of a moral nature, not merely some minor duty of cognitive conveyance.

No doubt, one may reasonably ask if it was incumbent on me to make my understanding of the rule common knowledge from the start. Perhaps it was senseless, or worse, for me to inquire about a rule I already knew, even if vaguely. Without addressing my own communicative culpability and obligations, I'll close this section by noting that Shiffrin would, I suspect, place the burden of articulating the rule on the agent as a further dispositional gain, but this one accruing to the duty-holder. "Public articulation forges a personal connection to the duty in a way that silent acknowledgment does not, reinforcing the duty's role as an organizing principle for the speaker." Whether the duty and its required articulation rest with the airline or *directly* with the agent is a matter that may be debated. Questions of agency and representation add further complication to the moral "communicative challenges" that concern Shiffrin. Some of these complications are revealed in her discussion of constitutional balancing, to which we now turn.

4. CHEAP TALK AND CONSTITUTIONAL BALANCING

States are rightly called to justify themselves when taking action—be it advancing some law, regulation, ordinance, ruling, or policy—that threatens to harm the constitutional interests of individuals. No doubt states have their own constitutional interests to protect, and doing so may require compromising the interests of individuals. To determine whose interests will prevail, courts use varying degrees of scrutiny in weighing or balancing competing considerations. A number of important cases and an extensive academic literature broadly outline the domain of illegitimate state interests, actual and pretextual interests, that carry no weight against the rights of individuals in constitutional balancing tests. However, when agents of the state assert interests falling outside of this forbidden domain, then, writes Shiffrin, "our jurisprudence does not typically dwell on whether the particular state agent is truly committed to an asserted interest in a way that would justify that interest's exerting weight in a balancing test" (p. 93). Why should this be this so? "If we are truly balancing," Shiffrin demands, "why don't we regularly investigate whether the state has real interests that merit compromise?" (p. 95).

To justify serious consideration of compromise to individuals' constitutional interests, state agents should offer more than mere assertions of interests, Shiffrin argues, particularly when it comes to advancing their own "discretionary interests"—that is, interests "that would be permissible for a state actor to entertain or promote, but are not required" (p. 97).[19] For claims concerning constitutional discretionary interests, she urges courts to hold state actors to the same standards of substantial incorporation and sincerity which they require of citizens.[20] After all, state actors are merely agents and sometimes agents do not faithfully or authentically reflect or represent the interests of their beneficiaries.[21] But the "agency problem" is

19. Discretionary interests stand in opposition to mandatory interests, which "may be defined more or less broadly. . . . A narrow textual approach would identify mandatory interests as those interests the Constitution, through its explicit language, requires state actors to have. . . . A wider textual approach might [include] what interests a particular state must have in light of its history, traditions, and culturally understood commitments" (p. 97).

20. "To 'ask' citizens to compromise constitutional interests for state interests seems reasonable only where the state actor has itself invested in those interests, thereby absorbing and reflecting the deliberative lessons such investments provoke" (pp. 118–119).

21. Elections and referenda provide democratic mechanisms of disciplining or correcting disloyal or unfaithful assertions by state officials. Shiffrin proposes another mechanism: examine the "deliberative credentials" of the (state actor) speaker. As she observes, "the question arises whether the *mere articulation* and in-principle defense of a discretionary interest could establish that a state *has* that interest for constitutional balancing purposes. . . . [C]ertain commitments and attitudes, such as respect or gratitude, *may require*

not the only concern here.[22] There is also, more fundamentally, the problem of cheap talk, which is to say, "[t]he problem is that we have no link between words and actions."[23]

Speech linked to prior sunk investments are described by economists as "costly signals." Costly signals (under some, not all, conditions) may be taken as credible or authentic or truthful representations. Otherwise, one might ask, why would someone send *that* signal given the costs associated with it? Costly signals are, in a sense, the opposite of cheap talk, which has no direct costs associated with its utterance or presentation.[24] As such, cheap talk is presumptively not credible, and this leads Shiffrin to question the existing regime of constitutional balancing with respect to discretionary interests.[25] Why should courts defer to cheap talk by state agents, particularly when constitutional entitlements of individuals rest in the balance. Why allow it, moreover, when individuals are called to put in evidence their own investments and commitments to their asserted interests?[26]

certain forms of explicit action as a condition of their sincere, apt conveyance" [emphasis added, except "*has*" which was italicized in the original] (p. 98).

22. Roughly speaking, the so-called agency problem results when one party (the agent) is enlisted to act on behalf of another party (the beneficiary) where the interests of the two parties are not fully aligned and the agent can effectively exercise discretion to promote her own interests above the beneficiary's.
23. Joseph Farrell, "Communication, Coordination and Nash Equilibrium," *Economic Letters* 27 (1988): 209–14.
24. Nor are there any direct benefits—value from merely saying or presenting—to cheap talk, although there may be indirect benefits and costs.
25. Shiffrin writes, "the reasonability of expecting citizens to compromise a fuller realization of their constitutional interests on the grounds that substantial community interests weigh in the counterbalance, should turn, at least for discretionary interests, on the actuality of the state's commitment to those community interests" (p. 118).
26. "I have been arguing for two principles that should inform our approach to these constitutional balancing questions: (A) Mere assertion of a legitimate state interest should not always suffice to establish that a state [actor] *has* that interest in the sense that should be relevant to constitutional balancing. (B) At least for discretionary interests, a demonstrable commitment (that shows more investment than the assertion of a mainly aspirational,

One answer may be that, as democratically elected representatives, state actors are presumed to speak authentically when representing or asserting the interests of the state. That presumption follows not from any intrinsic deference owed to the office or role of state actors, Shiffrin would claim, but rather from the sense of respect for self and others that justifies and encourages compliance with democratic law. I suspect that Shiffrin would be amenable to allowing this presumption. However, I am even more confident that she would insist that it be a rebuttable presumption. But then this raise the question of what standard is required to overcome this presumption. If it involves demonstration of tangible prior investments, then what kinds and degree of investments would be required by the standard?

Shiffrin recognizes these considerations and prudently hesitates to put forth any bright-line test or standard. Rather, she calls for greater sensitivity by the court in evaluating assertions of state officials when their actions would impinge on meaningful interests of citizens. To accommodate the standard, whatever it turns out to be, she suggests some useful interlocutory remedies—such as staying the proposed state action until it has a chance to demonstrate or clarify its purported interests, or suspending the citizen's action and allowing the state some room to demonstrate or clarify its purported interests. These suggestion are thoughtful and, like so much of her work, grounded while at the same time always deeply aspirational. Which brings me to two final points, in closing.

5. CONCLUDING COMMENT

A couple of points bearing on cheap talk and constitutional balancing are offered here in closing. First, there are a number of doctrinal

fledgling, or ambivalent interest) is necessary to establish that the state *has* that interest" (p. 109).

approaches in agency and organizational law that may be usefully incorporated in Shiffrin's more sensitive constitutional balancing analysis, such as duties of impartiality, disclosure, and candor. Agency problems in corporate bodies (not just corporations) are matters of long-held concerns for courts. Second, it is important to point out that cheap talk may sometimes be reasonably relied on. The cheap talk literature suggests that when the interest of speaker and addressee are sufficiently aligned, cheap talk could be credible. Hence, the problems associated with cheap talk may be addressed not only by making talk less cheap (through costly signals or prior tangible investments), but also through better alignment of the interests of the agent and their beneficiaries, which may be accomplished by focusing on the democratically representative institutions that promote the interests of agents.

Communication Through Law?

ANNA STILZ

I have long been an admirer of Seana Shiffrin's work, and it's an honor to have the opportunity to comment on her ideas. I'd like to start by recalling my first encounter with her. Shiffrin came to Harvard to give a lecture when I was a young graduate student. There was a large audience, and—impressed with the depth and richness of her argument—I asked a question following her talk. The next afternoon I happened to bump into her in Harvard Square. She stopped to elaborate on her response to my question and proceeded to inquire about my own work and discuss it with me at some length. Despite my lack of status, Shiffrin treated me and my thoughts with a level of seriousness and respect that one rarely encounters. I remember hoping that someday I would have the courage and grace to treat my own colleagues and students exactly the way she treated me.

Shiffrin argues in these lectures that democratic law-making is intrinsically valuable because it allows us to communicate morally important messages to one another. This requires that law be coherent and legible to citizens so that these messages may be properly received. Each individual citizen, on her view, has a moral duty to communicate to every other citizen a message of respect and

Anna Stilz, *Communication Through Law?* In: *Democratic Law*. Edited by: Hannah Ginsborg,
Oxford University Press.
DOI: 10.1093/oso/9780190084486.003.0007

recognition for the other's equal moral status. To discharge these communicative obligations, it is not sufficient to bring about a just distribution of goods in society or merely to endorse egalitarian institutions. As Shiffrin puts it, these actions are "compatible with mutual indifference . . . or . . . mutual contempt" (p. 27). Only by actively *participating* in creating and implementing democratic law can we fulfill our communicative duties to one another. On Shiffrin's vision, then, an ideal democracy is like a highly intricate switchboard in which each citizen is connected, via democratic law's moral circuitry, to every other citizen as a sender and a receiver of messages.

Shiffrin motivates this by analogy to an interpersonal case: by making and carrying out a promise to my neighbor to water her plants while she is away, I express my gratitude for her past good deeds. This is a demanding model of interpersonal communication. For the promise to water the plants to intentionally communicate a message of gratitude from one individual to another, a number of conditions must be satisfied. The promisor must sincerely have motives of gratitude, and she must make and carry out the promise from these motives. And the neighbor must be in circumstances where she could come to have knowledge of those motives and appreciate the act's communicative significance. So it seems that much in Shiffrin's communicative model of democracy depends on citizens' actually having the right motives and participating in democratic practices with the intention of communicating these motives.

Here I pose four critical questions about Shiffrin's view. First, why does our duty to communicate recognition for others as moral equals ground a special duty to our *fellow citizens* to cooperate together in a democracy? Second, *whose* messages exactly does democratic law communicate: Is it the messages of individual citizens, or the messages of the state as a corporate agent? Third, why does discharging our communicative duties require us to institute democratic procedures? And, finally, how does the state's pursuit of discretionary interests help us to send morally valuable messages to one another?

1. SELF-RESPECT

Shiffrin writes that our communicative duties are grounded in the fact that human beings' sense of self-respect is (appropriately) sensitive to the recognition they receive from others. Self-respect has certain social bases, and each of us has a duty to contribute to maintaining these bases by publicly manifesting our respect for others. Yet since this need for reinforcing regard is a quite general fact about human beings, it would seem that I have a duty to communicate my respect to all human agents. What, then, is special about my *fellow citizens,* such that my communicative duties ground a requirement to participate in democratic law-making alongside *them* in particular? Shiffrin briefly mentions that the "reinforcing regard I am due as a moral equal . . . is also due to visitors" (p. 30). But surely some reinforcing regard is also owed to foreigners outside our territory. How might I communicate my recognition of these foreigners' equal moral status since I don't share a system of democratic law with them?

This sets up a dilemma for Shiffrin's view. If there is some way that I can communicate my recognition of foreigners' equal moral status that doesn't require a democratic state, then why can't I communicate my recognition to fellow citizens in that same way? If instead I must be involved in a project of democratic law-making to appropriately and publicly communicate my recognition, then why doesn't our law-making project need to include all human agents since—plausibly—I owe them all recognition of their equal moral status?

My sense is that membership in the state is doing some under-acknowledged work in Shiffrin's account, helping to transform our general duty to recognize others' moral status into a more specific duty to engage in a project of democratic law-making. In this vein, Shiffrin speaks of a need to be "respected as an equal member of the community—one among her peers whose belonging is secure" (p. 30) and of our "legitimate need to have a home among others—a place to which we belong" (p. 52). But Shiffrin does not analyze the notions of "peers" or "home" in much depth or explain how they connect to our presumably universal duty to communicate recognition. Why is it necessary to grant others democratic citizenship and participate in law-making together with them and not just to manifest our reinforcing regard? And who exactly are the "peers" to whom we owe democratic membership? Do the current boundaries of the territorial state define those "peers," or is there some other criterion?

2. THE MESSAGE

Next I'd like to investigate the relation between our communicative duties as individuals and the messages sent by a collective political organization to which we belong, the democratic state. How does the interpersonal model of communication scale up to the state, where (1) individuals do not directly send messages to other individuals but instead rely on the law to communicate their joint commitments to one another; and (2) individuals are rarely in a position to have direct knowledge of their fellow citizens' motives? How do we communicate with one another via our participation in a complex, impersonal, hierarchical legal organization?

As I interpret Shiffrin's account, although communicative duties are duties that I, *qua* individual, have to you, *qua* individual, these duties must be carried out collectively, via democratic law. Why is such collectivization necessary? Partly this is because of law's practical advantages: as Shiffrin notes, it would impossible to communicate our respect by writing messages to all 324 million of our fellow citizens. She also suggests that our partial commitments to family and associations make it difficult for us to signal respect for others' equal moral status in our daily activities. Finally, she writes: "my words as a lone individual, absent a collective method of representation, will represent me as a private individual and not the collective . . . I need to communicate as a *citizen*, not only as a private individual" (p. 32).

I'd like to better understand what exactly is meant by communicating as a *citizen*, rather than as a private individual. Are the messages I communicate as a citizen still *my* messages? If so, in what sense is that the case? It seems to me that in order for democratic law to communicate sincere, morally important messages, these must be interpersonal messages. Communicating as a citizen should therefore mean communicating commitments that I and my fellow citizens jointly share. But another interpretation—sometimes suggested by Shiffrin's remarks—is that democratic law instead communicates messages about the *state's* commitments, where the state is a collective agent considered separately from its members. As she puts it, "democratic law is important . . . because it affords *us*, as a collective body, the possibility of communicating with each other" (p. 129). On this alternative view, communicating as a citizen means communicating the commitments of a corporate body to which I belong.

I do not think it would suffice to achieve Shiffrin's aims if the messages inscribed in democratic law were merely attributable to the state as a corporate agent. My objection here is not a metaphysical one: it is coherent to think that the state, as a group agent, could have commitments that depart from the attitudes and commitments of its members.[1] The state has an internal decision-making structure that gives its attitudes a certain independence from the attitudes of those individuals who make it up. Commitments will be attributable to

1. Christian List and Philip Pettit, *Group Agency* (Oxford: Oxford University Press, 2011).

the state whenever they are arrived at through the appropriate "constitutional" procedures. The state is similar in this respect to other incorporated groups like churches, universities, and business corporations. When the board of Exxon votes to acquire Texaco, the intention to acquire Texaco is attributable to the corporation-as-a-whole, even though only one person might actually sign the papers and some lower-level employees might not even be aware of the decision.

Yet I don't see how the state's articulation of *its own* corporate commitments would satisfy the interpersonal communicative duties from which Shiffrin's theory begins. It would remain unclear whether the attitudes expressed by the state bear any relation to *our* attitudes. Consider the statements of "core values" often produced by large corporations. These statements strike many as pure boilerplate because the words mean nothing to the people they are supposed to inspire. If the state's declaration of our joint moral commitments is analogous to Goldman Sachs' list of its core business principles—including, as Item Number One, "our clients always come first"—it will be hard to take them seriously. In order to publicly convey our respect for our fellow citizens, the moral commitments articulated in democratic law must—in some non-fictive way—be *our* shared moral commitments. By this, I mean that they are not simply the commitments of the state, as a collective agent (though they might also be that), but joint moral commitments shared by each and every citizen.

If this interpersonal reading of Shiffrin's project is correct, the question becomes: In what way are democratic law's commitments *our own* commitments? In what relation must we stand to a complex, impersonal, hierarchical legal organization in order for its commitments to count as *ours* in the requisite sense?

It seems to me that there must be some non-fictive relation of authorization between ordinary citizens and their legal system in order for obedience to democratic law to fulfill interpersonal communicative duties. In other examples of co-authorship that Shiffrin discusses, I have to *do* something in order for a joint message to count as mine. I have to sign my name to a joint condolence card, for example. Or I have to agree to allow my co-author to present our paper at a conference or "sign on" to a joint committee report. In order for the messages of democratic law to be *mine,* don't I also need to "sign on" in some way? Of course, the commitments articulated in the law might count as the *state's* commitments even if I don't sign on, but then it is not clear how articulating and implementing *the state's* commitments would count as me fulfilling my interpersonal communicative duties.

What might be the act of "signing on" to the state look like? Perhaps individuals recognize that they *ought* to come together in a democratic legal state to publicly recognize everyone's equal moral status. They therefore form a joint intention to cooperate. Suppose they further recognize that the execution of their joint intention will require the formulation of more concrete shared commitments. They may be aware that if each acts individually to specify those commitments, their interpretations and actions are likely to conflict. So they might delegate the task of specifying concrete commitments to a set of representative bodies that could fill in, unify, and integrate them, working out a specific plan about how they might all act together to publicly recognize everyone's moral equality. So long as the interpretations laid down by their representative agencies count as "reasonable" elaborations of the foundational commitment to recognize everyone's equal moral status, each individual might be willing to "go along" with it, allowing it to speak for him even though he would personally have chosen a slightly different message.

On this reading, democratic law will fulfill communicative duties so long as citizens "sign on" to their joint enterprise: if they are willing to allow the group venture to speak for them even when they don't endorse all aspects of its message.[2] Ordinary citizens "sign on"

2. Shiffrin stresses that co-authorship need not involve unanimity, and I do not mean to disagree. Still, I must be willing to "go along" with whatever compromises are made, allowing

if they participate with a certain sincere intention—to act together to publicly recognize everyone's moral equality, "playing their parts" in a concrete plan laid down by their law-making agencies. Citizens authorize their representative institutions, on this view, by sharing plans to act together to uphold these institutions, comply with their rules, and do their parts to carry them out and by acting publicly from these motives.

If these conditions were satisfied, then the moral commitments articulated by the state *really* would be shared, at an appropriately fundamental level, by ordinary citizens. Complying with democratic law under these idealized conditions would indeed communicate interpersonal commitments. The laws would express shared intentions that ordinary citizens actually hold, and ordinary citizens would view the decisions of their representative agencies as specifying their own fundamental moral commitments. But, on this reading, we cannot tell whether democratic law fulfills our communicative duties without making reference to the *actual attitudes* of ordinary citizens. Only in states where citizens participate with sincere intentions does obedience to democratic law fulfill interpersonal communicative duties. And, of course, this is a demanding ideal, of which every actual citizenry likely falls far short.

Occasionally Shiffrin suggests a view like this one. She argues that ordinary citizens have reason to vote and to adhere to the law because in so doing, "I . . . express my affiliation with the joint collective body that has the function of embodying our commitment to our equal status" (p. 53).

the group to speak for me even when I don't endorse every detail of the message. When my department sends a card to our bereaved colleague, I can endorse the joint message even when, as an atheist, I would have chosen a card did not include religious language. I don't necessarily agree with every aspect of the card, but I agree with the broad sentiment it expresses. In signing my name, I choose to affiliate myself with that sentiment, allowing it to stand for me.

But I am not sure the view I have sketched is ultimately Shiffrin's. At other times she suggests that law communicates the commitments of a collective body, which cannot be fully ascribed to its members, as when she says that law's "content may be attributed to all of us together, even if not to each of us as individuals" (p. 53). But if the commitments of democratic law cannot be imputed to individuals but only to the collective, then how does acting on these laws fulfill our interpersonal duties to communicate our respect for one another as moral equals?

3. EQUAL PARTICIPATION

I turn now to the role of equal participation rights in Shiffrin's view. Many theorists define democracy with reference to a procedure in which all subjects have an equal opportunity for influence. But why does fulfilling our communicative duties require formally equal votes? I am not sure that egalitarian procedures are actually essential to democracy on Shiffrin's communicative conception. It is clear that Shiffrin does not think the existence of such procedures is *sufficient* for democracy. She stresses that a free speech regime is arguably even more fundamental to democracy than are elections. And she holds that judicial, administrative, and custom-based authority are potentially democratic institutions, emphasizing, for example, that the judiciary plays a "special role" in a democracy, a role that is "neither secondary nor subordinate to the legislature's" (p. 63).

As I understand Shiffrin, however, she does see the existence of a procedure that offers all citizens equal opportunity for influence as *necessary*, somewhere in the system, in order for that legal system to count as democratic. She holds that "[t]he terms of . . . participation must . . . be equal, under some salient description, or else the message will not be *each* of ours and the participatory structure will belie at least part of the message of our mutual equality" (p. 39). But why, on her view, are formally equal votes necessary, especially given her willingness to accept judicial, administrative, and custom-based authority as in no sense "lesser" from a democratic point of view? Couldn't individuals choose to "affiliate" themselves with a non-democratic state, complying from sincere, communicatively resonant intentions and expressing their support for its legal institutions? If they did so—and if the substance of that state's laws expressed a commitment to citizens' reciprocal moral equality—wouldn't the commitments embodied in its laws count as discharging their communicative duties to one another?

Let me relate this concern to one of the central examples of Shiffrin's second lecture: federal preemption of state common law. Shiffrin defends the common law as a practice that is perhaps more democratic, in certain respects, than the statutory laws produced by an elected legislature. The common law involves explicit reasoning, practices of precedent, and conversation between a wide variety of social points of view (p. 84). Shiffrin also stresses that the common law affords relatively equal access to potential litigants, that cases "bubble up" from a local moral culture, and that the role of precedent involves pressure toward coherence and unity. All of this, in her view, makes the common law an especially good way to articulate our collective moral commitments.

But is the common law a distinctively *democratic* institution? I don't deny that the common law could form one part of a democratic legal system. But, on a charitable reading, modern democracy dates only to the revolutions of the eighteenth century (or, on a less charitable one, to the elimination of property, sex, and racial qualifications for voting in the twentieth). The common law, on the other hand, goes all the way back to the Middle Ages. So it seems perfectly possible to have a common law practice in a non-democratic regime (if we see an equal distribution of political power as fundamental to democracy). There seems to be no special connection, then, between the common law and egalitarian participation rights. Furthermore, the common law does not seem to satisfy an important criterion for democratic communication that Shiffrin outlined in the first lecture: that democratic law must be *produced* by us. There she suggests that to truly express our commitments to others' moral equality, we must jointly craft the state's commitments. But the common law is not (or at least not obviously) produced or crafted by us: it is produced and crafted by judges. So what makes the common law inherently democratic?

Shiffrin might respond here that "co-authorship" can involve a division of labor in which some parties speak in the name of others, crafting a joint message that can stand for them all. Because common law judicial institutions are an authorized part of our political system, the public commitments it articulates count as ours. At some appropriately fundamental level, we are co-authors of these commitments.

But if we accept that the common law counts as a form of democratic co-authorship, then why couldn't a "democratic" regime consist *entirely* of inegalitarian representative institutions so long as ordinary citizens were willing to "sign on" to these institutions and so long as the institutions gave equal weight to everyone's important interests and claims? Suppose again that a group of individuals recognizes that they ought to come together in a state that can publicly affirm everyone's equal moral status. And suppose everyone in the group simply agrees that a particular judge is wise, virtuous, and especially good at interpreting the fundamental commitment to recognize everyone's equal moral status. So instead of instituting a political procedure in which all have equal influence, members of this community simply defer to their judge. And indeed, the laws the judge lays down do reflect the demands of justice, and everyone in his society recognizes that fact and complies with these laws in a communicatively resonant way. What is lacking in this picture? Why would it matter here that citizens lacked the right to participate on equal terms so long as they accepted their representative agencies at a more fundamental level and saw their compliance with them as fulfilling their communicative duties? Why would this group further need formally equal votes in some appropriately fundamental legislative procedure?

4. DISCRETIONARY INTERESTS

I'd like to conclude my comments by asking why the communicative model of democracy should endorse discretionary state interests. Shiffrin emphasizes that democratic law not only enables us to achieve morally mandatory aims, but also serves as a system for pursuing ends that are purely discretionary. Discretionary interests are "those it would be permissible for a state actor to entertain or promote, but are not required" (p. 97). Shiffrin argues on this basis that her communicative view supports a new approach to constitutional balancing. Since our joint moral commitments must be sincerely conveyed, this licenses an inquiry into the state's record of action in order to ascertain whether it is genuinely committed to the discretionary interests it asserts.

In the case of individuals, the adoption of discretionary interests is part of a process of shaping one's own identity as a unique person by committing to dancing, gardening, and so on. Analogously, Shiffrin emphasizes that both the common law and the adoption of discretionary ends enable a democracy "to adopt a distinctive identity." These aspects of the law afford "opportunities for developing distinctive communities that elicit strong affiliations" (p. 67).

But why is it so important, on the communicative view, that states have a distinctive local identity? To enable individuals to express their respect for one another's equal moral status, must their state have a unique culture? Though I don't mean to push a strong anti-perfectionist stance here, I would like to know more about the rationale for the state's adoption of discretionary ends within Shiffrin's broader communicative view and also whether there are limits on the discretionary ends which a state might be permitted to pursue.

Consider an example somewhat removed from the cases Shiffrin discusses. Some people believe it is permissible for the state to take a discretionary interest in the protection and promotion of a particular national culture even if there are significant minorities in its territory who do not share that culture. The state is not required by prudence or morality to adopt this end, but it is not wrong for it to do so. On this view, it is acceptable for the state, at its discretion, to grant that national culture preferred status in its symbols, ceremonies, holidays, official language, public education system, and so on.

There is also a familiar objection to this view: organizing the state around the national culture of a particular group sends the message that this group is favored and that cultural minorities are second-class citizens—the state does not "belong" to them in quite the way it "belongs" to the members of the dominant culture. Furthermore, pursuing these discretionary ends empowers the dominant subgroup to use the state to impose its sectarian preferences on others.

Would it be permissible, on Shiffrin's view, for the state to adopt this sort of discretionary end? I am not sure. One might rule out promotion of a national culture in a diverse society as involving the "diminution of the status of equal citizens, or . . . interests that essentially are cover for state (or private) motives of animus and exclusion" (p. 93). Maybe the preceding example can be interpreted as running afoul of the constraints of justice, if those constraints are interpreted to include a sufficiently strong "status egalitarian" component. This would rule out any discretionary state interest that might be construed as expressing an invidious message. Perhaps, though, this still leaves some room for the state to pursue ends that, while not required by justice, are also not at odds with it.

Still, if justice is interpreted to include a strong status egalitarian constraint, then I worry that this constraint will render many of the other discretionary ends that Shiffrin discusses impermissible. Take, for example, the interest in the preservation of fetal life. Shiffrin seems to suggest that if a state were to require waiting periods and compulsory education *both* for the destruction of in vitro fertilization embryos *and* for women seeking abortion, this would evince a sincere and coherent commitment to a discretionary interest in fetal life (p. 107). The adoption of this discretionary state end would therefore seem to be permissible, on her view. But some might see an important parallel between the invidious message sent by state promotion of a national culture and the message sent by policies that protect fetal life. These policies place special burdens on women that are not equally faced by men and might be taken to send a message of second-class status. So if justice is interpreted in a robust status egalitarian way, this may mean ruling out many (though perhaps not all) discretionary state ends. One wonders how much room justice actually leaves open for the state to shape a unique identity?

Finally, what is the relationship, if any, between the discretionary ends of the state and the discretionary ends of its individual members? Are citizens meant to be jointly committed, in some sense, to their state's discretionary ends? And, if so, must the state's discretionary interests be generally "shareable" by those it represents? The discretionary ends that Shiffrin mentions—an interest in preserving life even against a patient's will or in facilitating patients' choices regarding the timing of their deaths—are of considerable controversy among citizens. Might the state pursue discretionary ends that were endorsed by very few of its citizens or, at the limit, by none of them? I can see how the state's adoption of discretionary interests might help to establish and convey a local identity even if those interests are not fully shared. But how does the existence of discretionary state interests help individual citizens to convey morally valuable messages to one another? If the content of these messages involves affirming that *we* are committed to discretionary purposes that many constituents deeply reject, then is this a morally valuable message to send?

Replies to Commentators

SEANA VALENTINE SHIFFRIN

I am so fortunate to have the opportunity to discuss these issues with Richard Brooks, Niko Kolodny, and Anna Stilz, three thinkers I admire and from whom I have learned a great deal. In addition to offering supportive interpretations and welcome parallel insights, their comments also raise many challenges and questions. Here, I can regrettably tackle only some of these challenges and must reserve the remainder for future work.

In what follows, I start by responding to some common themes in the commentators' remarks, namely by expanding on the duties of citizens to respect one another and communicate that respect—specifically, the moral imperative for collective, communicative action, carried out through active participation and on the basis of equality in a democratic legal environment. I then proceed to answer some more specific questions about this idea and to clarify the role of democratic law, generally, in meeting our communicative responsibilities. In Section II of these replies, I address some more specific questions about the communicative democratic perspective on common law and constitutional law.

Seana Valentine Shiffrin, *Replies to Commentators* In: *Democratic Law*. Edited by: Hannah Ginsborg, Oxford University Press.
DOI: 10.1093/oso/9780190084486.003.0008

Before proceeding, I should clarify that, for convenience, I use the term 'citizen' throughout to denote a full-fledged member of the collective, as distinguished from a mere visitor. In using this term, I do not mean to embrace the contemporary legal lines that police who may become a citizen nor do I countenance the contemporary treatment of refugees, undocumented persons, and asylum seekers. Quite the contrary. I affirm that many permanent resident-members of the collective, whether documented or not, should be understood and treated as citizens in this sense.[1]

COMMUNICATING RESPECT

Collectively and Individually, Through Law and Democratic Culture

Some forms of communication demand, in virtue of their subject matter, that they include both discursive and more concrete forms of overt action to convey their content appropriately and sincerely. As Kolodny correctly surmises, I believe that, for many of the moral stances we must occupy and convey, the communicative form must be collective and involve collective action, indeed systematic collective action, of a particular sort (pp. 135–138). Those communications or their omissions then, in turn, infuse our interpersonal

1. This characterization highlights the importance of issues about whether permanent expatriates should be treated as active and current members of a collective, both in terms of their rights and responsibilities and whether they may indefinitely occupy the position of permanent residents whose status falls short of full-fledged members. For the purposes of this reply, I acknowledge but largely bracket these questions, as well as the question of how to think about temporary residents who stay longer than short-term visitors. I note that my account gives some reason to think that, morally, permanent residents should become citizens of their place of residence and that permanent expatriates are outlier cases. It is, obviously, a further question whether permanent residents should be required to take on the responsibilities of citizens and whether permanent expatriates' rights should differ from those of resident citizens.

interactions and our interpersonal moral relations, as is most evident in cases of failure.

For instance, the encounters between the housed and the homeless are fraught with the wrongness of our relationship and the injustice of the disparities between us, even as those disparities are not the product of our individual actions toward each other. Similar things may be said about how the activities and pronouncements of the US government during the Trump Administration have further damaged, on racial lines, the already weak interpersonal bases of trust and goodwill between citizens. We do not stand in the right relations to one another. To say that is to say more than saying that there is an injustice in the world that happens to be at the same coordinates as my habitat and that I interact with some of its victims. Living amid each other—sharing the same space and culture over a prolonged period of time—generates more robust relational obligations toward each other in ways that do not hold of the temporary relations between groups of people passing each other in transit at an airport. Some of the most important aspects of these obligations require collective action for their fulfillment.

Saying hello, asking after their welfare, and offering money and blankets to the homeless are all partial but utterly incomplete gestures, as all parties realize. Doing even more might help with the material needs of a particular person but at the hazard of creating elements of a personal relationship of dependency and control. For *me* to be in the right relation with them and vice versa, we must both be situated in a collective system that recognizes our equal status, one part of which involves ensuring at least our mutual equal opportunities for autonomous welfare. That these conditions must be effected through collective action does not make the duty less mine; it just means the duty is shared by others and must be realized indirectly, through collective action.

Just as the problem is not one adequately described by observing there is an injustice at 37.8 degrees longitude and 122.2 degrees latitude for which I happen to be a witness and an outraged denizen of humanity, so an adequate *relational* solution is not achieved simply through the installation of conditions in which all, including the homeless, are ensured shelter as well as equal access to other resources, welfare, opportunities, or what have you— preventing domination—and that's all. That solution, as described, is compatible with our being equally subjugated to a benevolent dictator or through the anonymous beneficence of a group of obscenely wealthy donors. That outcome would not reflect anything about how we felt about allowing or repairing these conditions. That outcome is compatible with our occupying a stance of separate, grudging subjugation to equality, however comfortably, rather than reflecting a stance of mutual affirmation. It thus, on its own, will not achieve the recognitional component of our obligation.

To achieve that recognitional component—for each of us to be in good relations with each other, as a part of a community of people who live together and compose a joint social environment—our equal flourishing must be an intentional product of our joint activity, chosen and committed to for the right reasons[2] *and* publicly conveyed as such. My contention is that a system of democratic law is a

2. I take issue with Kolodny's remark that ("at first glance") indifference and grudging accommodation are not failures to regard others as equals (p. 134, fn. 4). If I respect you as a free and equal person in virtue of your needs, interests, and rights that morally require attention and fulfillment, I cannot at the same time be indifferent to your needs and interests. If your needs, rights, and interests are important and I appreciate that, I cannot also be grudging about their accommodation. An absence of appreciation and attention of another's status, needs, interests, and rights is one manifestation of a lack of respect. Or, in other words, contempt and animus are not the only forms of salient disrespect. These claims are connected to larger issues about the moral wrong of negligence that I discuss in "The Moral Neglect of Negligence," *Oxford Studies in Political Philosophy* 3 (2017): 197–228, at 225.

necessary but not sufficient condition of achieving that recognitional component.

We need a structure, the operation of which can produce articulate, sincere, co-authored commitments—democratic law—to enable our mutual communication. The mere existence of the system's structure, absent our active, informed participation in and around it, however, is insufficient to fulfill them. Furthermore, the right sort of complementary culture and minimal convergence on foundational commitments may need to emerge for the system to succeed.

To elaborate: the success of an institutional system of democratic law's efforts to underwrite the social bases of self-respect will require citizen activity and engagement—including the maintenance of political literacy and alertness, voting, legal compliance, jury service, other forms of community service, commentary through official mechanisms and in the culture, and litigation to spur interpretation. That engagement can serve as evidence that citizens act as co-authors. Its absence, whether by disengagement or outsourcing to Hercules, may reasonably generate skepticism about whether the system does communicate for its citizens. Too much outsourcing, whether expressly through delegation to experts or private entities or implicitly through non-participation, can reasonably cast doubt on citizens' endorsement. Failures to participate may also undercut the underdiscussed function of democracy to help orient citizens to their impartial duties. These hazards hold true in the Hercules case and, in more realistic cases, may be a reason for concern about overreliance on the judiciary to articulate and enforce collective norms.

How Could Law *Perform Recognitional Work?*

Kolodny also wonders how a system of democratic law could perform the collective recognitional work that I claim must be done to achieve mutual respect (pp. 135–136). Where penalties figure as an important mechanism of compliance, it is unclear to him that either the law or legal compliance convey *respect*. It may rather seem that enacting penalties conveys uncertainty of compliance by the legislature, which in turn might seem to reflect a more ambivalent posture toward the law's substantive content on the part of the citizenry. To the extent that penalties are necessary to enact the law's substantive aims, then a version of the skepticism we mean to keep at bay may resurface: perhaps citizens comply not from respect but for fear of being penalized for violating the law.

My answers are multiple. Most are familiar and not especially original, but my articulating them will situate my position. To start: when we think of law, our first thought should not be about penalties, punishments, or other remedies for non-compliant behavior. A great deal of the law is not associated with penalties at all. Much of the law is fruitfully devoted to articulating norms, standards, directives, and programs to direct and coordinate *compliant* behavior by government agents, government institutions, non-governmental institutions, and individuals. Other aspects of law generate opportunities and confer status, as when the law directs that all people born in the United States or to parents who are citizens are themselves citizens.

Moreover, even among the arsenal of remedies used to address non-compliance, *penalties* are just one of many mechanisms that legal systems use to implement legal directives. In addition to sheer articulation, other methods of implementation may include compensatory damages, restitution, education, decrees, positive incentives, oversight, public–private partnerships, and nationalization, among others. Indeed, the use of penalties and punishments to respond to (or perhaps to deter) non-compliant behavior is not, in my view, an essential aspect of a democratic legal system.[3] Moreover, I am not

3. See Tom Tyler for an argument that successful legal systems cannot (and do not) primarily rely on instrumental methods of eliciting compliance and must draw on residents'

persuaded that coercion, whether direct or indirect, is an essential feature of government or of democratic law. If the law's primary function is communicative (keeping in mind that some forms of communication require action), then whether coercion is necessary to achieve that function is a contingent matter.

Still, Kolodny might respond, unless we engage in hyper-ideal theory, it is likely that many democratic systems will use penalties, punishments, and coercive measures to implement other remedies to respond to and deter non-compliance. Furthermore, he may think the issue has less to do with the *fear* of penalties or punishment, and more to do with the direct or indirect use of coercion. Even should legal implementation take a more gentle form, if the government is sufficiently powerful to ensure that its will be done and it is empowered to use coercive means to do so, then the objection resurfaces. Kolodny may worry that we cannot infer a communicative message from democratic law. A functioning democratic legal system may simply reflect fear, a sense of futility, or a savvy cost-benefit analysis of the comparative cost of resistance compared to compliance.

So, assuming that a democratic legal system, in fact, if not by necessity, deploys (some) coercive methods to encourage compliance or to respond to non-compliance, should this cast doubt on the communicative message? Perhaps, but I don't think it's the obvious interpretation for a few reasons.

On its face, I do not think it is plausible to conclude from the existence of some coercive measures that they are what motivate citizen

perceived sense of the system's legitimacy and their own internalized norms of justice and obligation. Tom R. Tyler, *Why People Obey the Law* (Princeton: Princeton University Press, 2006), 22–27. Reviewing the conclusions of his study of legal compliance in Chicago, Tyler reports that people "evaluate laws and the decisions of legal authorities in normative terms, obeying the law if it is legitimate and moral and accepting decisions if they are fairly arrived at." *Id.* at 178.

compliance.[4] Keeping in mind that legal remedies are the product of citizen authorship provides further support for interpreting many remedial measures as messages of mutual assurance about compliance, rather than as sheer threats.[5] To be sure, others' reciprocation should not be a condition on one's compliance with many laws, including most criminal laws. But sufficiently widespread reciprocity may be a more understandable expectation for other laws that presuppose collective and widespread participation. Even for criminal laws, the mutual assurance offered by a coercive backstop may give citizens reasons not to pursue alternative protective or remedial measures (or to make investments in them). In these cases, assurance does not act as a primary motive for compliance even if it does defuse possible defeaters to compliance. I may contribute to the tax scheme willingly as part of my sense that justice requires contributing to the joint social mission executed by government, even while thinking that I would be less willing to do so if there were a chance of sufficiently widespread evasion or of large-scale corruption and embezzlement.

Of course, I concur with a premise underlying Kolodny's worry: namely, that it matters what remedial measures are used to communicate mutual assurance. The wrong sorts of remedies and the wrong framing can send the wrong message. While well-crafted remedies may communicate our mutual commitment to a rule and our stance that non-compliance is regarded as a form of disrespect, draconian penalties may convey mutual distrust and preclude effective

4. This issue and the ensuing discussion have certain parallels with the issue and literature about whether the background operation of the impartial motive of duty necessarily precludes or crowds out the operation of other, partial motives and the realization of their virtues. See, e.g., Barbara Herman, "Integrity and Impartiality," in her *The Practice of Moral Judgment* (Cambridge: Harvard University Press, 1993), 23–44; Barbara Herman, "Agency Attachment and Difference," in *id.*, 184–207; and Julie Tannenbaum "Acting with Feeling from Duty," *Ethical Theory and Moral Practice* 5, no. 3 (2002): 321–37.

5. John Rawls, *A Theory of Justice* (Cambridge, MA: Harvard University Press, 1971), 240–41.

communication of willing compliance. Similarly, a dominant framing (and design) of penalties and other remedial measures as disincentives or deterrents rather than as forms of rehabilitatively motivated moral education may ambiguate a message of mutual respect. This, in turn, may loosen some of the motivations for compliance that are conditional on mutual respect and reciprocal performance. So, although I resist the idea that legal enforcement measures, whether prospective or retrospective, *intrinsically* undermine the moral messages conveyed by democratic structure, the aims of democratic law do offer substantive guidance and limits about how enforcement measures and remedies should be framed and structured.

From the perspective of interpreting compliance, it should also be registered that, in well-functioning states, enforcement is rarely comprehensive. Many infractions are likely to go unperceived and others will not be the target of police and prosecutorial discretion. This suggests that in a well-functioning state, much compliance is not rationally motivated by any strong sense of fear of detection and enforcement. Were infractions more plentiful, either the state could not function well or the state would have to spend extraordinary resources to pursue comprehensive surveillance and enforcement. The latter involves expenditures and actions that are inconsistent with other democratic commitments. To the extent that a state must rely on comprehensive surveillance and enforcement efforts, coupled with draconian penalties, I would be inclined to agree more with Kolodny; that need would suggest a rampant form of citizen resistance or indifference to the content of law. When high levels of voluntary compliance render such efforts unnecessary, I find it less plausible to interpret the use of penalties as offering a substantial explanation of citizen compliance or attitudes toward the content of law.

My skepticism that legal remedies necessarily drive legal compliance is buttressed by my belief that there are important, alternate reasons for compliance: namely, that compliance with a just law communicates one's own commitment to justice. To the extent that the law conveys equal respect and facilitates or demands patterns of equal respect, to comply consciously and openly rather than to ignore, resist, or comply passive-aggressively as in Brooks' airline story, is to express one's own commitment to that equality (pp. 156–160).

Although Kolodny expresses doubts that one's participation can make a difference to the communicative message, I am less sure that we should think of the communicative message of law and its distribution as the sort of thing modeled by standard Sorites problems (p. 141). The conscious compliance of each of us plays a rôle in forming and maintaining a national culture, with multiple local branches, that renders the endorsement of the law's message clearer. With respect to many laws, my compliance and my attitude toward compliance express and reinforce the social message directly to others by observation and through my interactions with them. So would my indifference and my lack of compliance. Furthermore, my conscious compliance plays a role in reinforcing my own commitment to the content of the relevant social message.

Finally, it is worth emphasizing that my claim is that a democratic legal system is a necessary but not sufficient condition of our mandatory communication. Its success will depend on a complementary ethos emerging in the culture. Because my understanding of what a democratic legal system is includes a free speech culture, the line between culture and the democratic legal system is not a stark one. Our understanding of why people follow the law, whether from fear, endorsement, or some intermediate form of affiliation, will not follow just from the structure and rate of enforcement actions. It will also be informed by such things as how, in the culture, we speak about compliance, our common enterprise, and about each other, as well as the level of participation in elections and in other fora including editorials, what books are published and read, and attendance at citizen meetings and protests, as well as private conversations.

Why an Equal Role?

As part of interrogating the case for *democratic* law, Kolodny and Stilz both ask how my argument supports the conviction that we must have an *equal say* in the production and execution of law (pp. 138–140, 173–176). Kolodny further contends that there is an independent argument for equality in decision-making, one that short circuits my argument because it does not make reference to communication. This further point sounds more damaging than it is. My claim is not that such arguments are inherently flawed, but that they fail to supply a complete account of democracy's value and that an account of its full value will recognize its communicative function. A communicative account need not reject these arguments and indeed may draw on them.

Nonetheless, it may be useful for me to clarify the role of equality in democratic structure *qua* communicative enterprise. Kolodny speaks of my advocating our playing an "equal role" in producing the message, but that idea can be ambiguous. As in any workable form of co-authorship, I do not think it makes sense to imagine that each of us contributes a letter (I've always been partial to the letter "s") and *we* see what words, if any, emerge. Because communication requires coherence, its production will frequently involve delegations to smaller groups to coordinate the production of our messages and to represent us in much the way that Stilz describes (pp. 173–176).

On the other hand, egalitarian co-authorship does involve a myriad other components of equal participation that complement mechanisms of representation, including that each of us has an *equal right* to deliberate, an *equal right* to have access to the materials necessary to do so, an *equal right* to weigh in through reasonably regular formal and informal channels, and an *equal right* to responsive consideration from those taking the (temporary, nonentrenched) oar to craft the message (Brooks, pp. 150, 158–160). As suggested by what I said earlier, these rights are not mere liberties but also represent responsibilities. Those delegates who take the oar must see themselves as attempting to pursue our joint end, responsible to each of us as co-authors to take our thoughts and concerns seriously, and as eligible to act as our representative, not from entitlement or assertion, but because of our selection and delegation. When the process operates this way, the output represents each of us *as citizens*, citizens engaged in a joint enterprise, even if *as individuals* some of us wish we had chosen a different content. Depending on the size of the polity and, thus, the relevant constraints set by the aim of producing joint coherent commitments, the shape that an equal say takes may vary. But it is important that whatever the details, it must be a real say and an equal say.

One might interpret Kolodny as asking why the process must involve equal inputs of some sort and why it isn't sufficient that the output be a substantive message of equality. After all, other non-democratically structured organizations seem capable of communicating for us and can generate responsibilities of us (pp. 138–140). To reply, if we understand ourselves as equals in virtue of our normative capacities and interests, including our capacity and responsibility for justice,[6] then it would seem to follow that we have equal interests in and, importantly, equal responsibilities for discharging our duties of justice. The idea that we need not have an equal say in

6. Here, I signal my endorsement of a Rawlsian conception of our moral equality, with some modifications. See Rawls, *A Theory of Justice*, at 504–13; Seana Valentine Shiffrin, *Speech Matters: On Lying, Morality, and the Law* (Princeton: Princeton University Press, 2014), at 167–75.

order for our interests to be communicated and given equal weight does not have a particularly esteemed track record despite its once-frequent invocation for the disenfranchisement of women, to take just one example. But one can see its *theoretical* appeal: assuming we can understand each others' interests and could be trusted to convey them accurately and respond to them fairly, their content *could* be conveyed by others. Perhaps if one were focused only on our equality *qua* interest-bearers and, contestably, we thought that our relevant interests could be entirely satisfied through what we *receive* from government, rather than also *how* we receive it and what we contribute to the process, then an equal say would not be required under very ideal circumstances for our collective's message to convey a commitment to equality. Concomitantly, the argument for democracy would rest on solely non-ideal premises, imagining the likely betrayal of the trust and accuracy that the ideal argument presupposes.

But our equality and our need for recognition as such is not solely interest-based. In these lectures, I have stressed the duty-based foundations of equality and democratic law. It is a less simple matter to imagine that, from the outset and apart from our agency, others could assume our *responsibilities* to act and communicate. Duties are things we must see to ourselves. Others cannot just decide to assume them for us. Depending on their content, *some* duties are delegable, but their susceptibility to delegation is a delicate matter, not a given. Furthermore, there are limits on the identity of the delegate and the scope of delegation. One must have reason to think one's delegate is qualified, and one cannot delegate a duty to someone who would have a conflict of interest. Assuming one has the means and capacity to care, one can be a good parent and delegate *some* childcare responsibilities but far from most of them. One can send a taxi to the airport for a friend, but one cannot outsource the more intimate responsibilities of friendship to another and remain a friend. Without good reason, one cannot be on terms of equality with another if there is a substantial asymmetry of delegation behavior with respect to reciprocal duties.[7]

Where the responsibility or the circumstances require delegation, that delegation must be our own doing. Notably, we will still retain some measure of responsibility if our delegates fail to discharge these responsibilities appropriately. If we start with a conception of equality that stresses our equal moral agency and responsibility for justice, then, at the foundations, we must start with equal opportunities to participate and have a say in the joint communicative enterprise (and its delegated subprocesses) that both serves our interests and is the object of our duties. If our equality, in part, rests on our equal responsibility toward each other, responsibilities that include communicative dimensions, then a system designed to satisfy our responsibilities that did not give each of us an equal say, suitably construed, would be inadequate and in tension with the affirmation of our equality. It is similarly perverse to imagine that one's needs for *recognition* as a moral equal capable of and responsible for articulating her interests, responsibilities, and recognition of others as her peers could be satisfied through a process that excluded her from engaging in that articulation or that relegated her to an unequal status.

An equal role in authorship, suitably construed as just described, allows each of us to discharge our equal responsibility to communicate and consider the message we produce to be just as much mine as anyone else's. Whereas to be excluded from having an equal say would require a justification for this inequality that was at the same time consistent with a conception of equality as involving equal responsibility as well as equal interests. I strain to understand what its content could be.

7. There is more to be said about the scope and conditions on delegation of duties, but I'll have to defer that task to another occasion.

Of course, as Kolodny points out, there are non-democratically structured organizations in which we participate and in which we may feel ownership, achievement, and responsibility for their products and actions. That's true and important. At the same time, these examples of "our orchestra's performance, our team's victory, [and] our unit's aid mission" (p. 138) do not seem like plausible cases in which these non-democratically structured organizations communicate for us *qua* equals; nor do their actions convey messages of our equality. We might regard that as a shortcoming in some cases. Indeed, as I mention briefly in the text, I take it to be a virtue of my account that it can say more about why there is some imperative to structure voluntary associations democratically (p. 56, fn. 44). Accounts of democracy that stress a particular form of political status are more hamstrung in that dimension.

Of course, the impetus for democratic structure is not limited to the state and voluntary associations. The anti-democratic organization of most corporations (and other sorts of workplaces)—including their denial of the *entitlement* of many stakeholders such as employees and consumers to a say in their organizational decisions—is not anodyne. Corporations form a substantial component of the basic structure in our society, controlling an immense amount of capital and exerting an outsize influence on the life prospects and experiences of their employees.[8] As a complement to Brooks' observations on the inventiveness of airlines in generating hierarchy within a shared experience, one might reflect on the role of employers and particularly large corporations in inculcating expectations of hierarchy in

8. So, while I share much of Anderson's outrage about the hierarchical and often inhumane conditions within which many Americans work, I was disappointed and puzzled that she conceives of workplaces as "private governments" but evinces an efficiency-driven, "pragmatic" resistance to workplace democracy. Elizabeth Anderson, *Private Government: How Employers Rule Our Lives and Why We Don't Talk About It* (Princeton: Princeton University Press: 2017), 69, 130–31.

the workplace and of insensitivity to voice and accountability in their use of unreadable standardized contracts and mandatory arbitration agreements (p. 155). The standard workplace is not a uniform site of self-affirmation and mutual respect. Concomitantly, when the organization is not democratically structured, it seems more natural for participants to adopt a stance of diminished responsibility and cynicism in the face of their disempowerment not only with respect to expressing their needs and interests, but also with respect to ensuring that our productive activities are environmentally and socially responsible.

HOW DOES THE COLLECTIVE COMMUNICATE FOR EACH OF US?

Kolodny and Stilz both raise the question of how the collective may communicate for us if, at the same time, some of us dissent from the particularity of its message. I want to consider this question from two angles, from the standpoint of citizens as speakers and from the standpoint of citizens as listeners or recipients of messages.

The Citizen as Speaker

Each person may have an identity, or at least a perspective, as both a private individual and as a member of a collective, in this case as citizen. The two perspectives may come apart when the collective acts or speaks in ways the private individual does not endorse even when she is thinking from a public-spirited point of view. Nonetheless, it may still make sense for that person to think the collective in some sense speaks for her, on her behalf, and in ways she bears responsibility for—at least should she bear the right relation to the collective and should its fundamental operating structure be sound.

The intelligibility of retaining both perspectives at once depends on the idea that the collective may speak for me. I think it may do so when I have the equal rights to participation I just wrote of and when the governing, communicative system functions as it ought, in the sense that the system and its components embody and make good faith efforts to discharge some fundamental commitments. The fundamental commitments I have in mind include a commitment to equal regard and concern for the rights, needs, and interests of all members and a commitment to eliciting and working out, in good faith, through deep, responsive engagement with its members' interpretations of these commitments, how they should be made concrete.

When the system functions as it ought, I think it sensible for me, as a citizen, to regard the collective's message as speaking for me in the sense that it transmits commitments to these fundamental values and the significance of making them concrete. Where I may part ways, as a private individual, is with the collective's particular method of concretization. In that way, it may not speak for me, but that divide seems inevitable in any multiparty joint endeavor.

It is, as Stilz and Kolodny note, important that the two perspectives be on coherent terms with each other. Otherwise, it becomes difficult for the private individual to recognize herself as a citizen or to see the citizen as speaking in some way for the private individual.

Notably, the tension between these perspectives is minimized on the democratic communicative view, at least relative to some other democratic theories. For example, on theories of democracy that imagine democracy providing a fair resolution to conflicting preferences, when one is the loser in that fairly fought battle, the outcome may bear no substantive relation whatsoever to one's preferences. They were simply inputs to an algorithm that did not gain enough adherents to make a difference. Here, the divide may become untenable when the collective's choices land systematically very far down on one's list of preferences and are, perhaps, entirely antithetical to what one believes justice requires.

By contrast, on a democratic communicative view, we imagine that the aim of the community is to pursue justice and other collective moral ends within a framework dedicated to our mutual equality. That framework, in turn, is designed to be responsive to and communicative of our understandings of those commitments. This conception requires a certain substantive framework that, in turn, is dedicated to interpreting a variety of substantive requirements to instantiate our mutual equality as free citizens. Unlike exclusively procedural conceptions of democracy where everything but the procedure is up for grabs, on a democratic communicative account, the collective's decisions must conform to reasonable interpretations of various substantive standards of equal treatment. Such substantive constraints offer greater assurance that the divide between my convictions and the decisions of the collective will not be as yawning as may be possible on more purely procedural conceptions.

What is more important is the role our input plays in the process that generates decisions. As opposed to models that portray democratic procedures as methods of calibrating competing preferences, our input is not well understood as encapsulated under the label of "preference," whether self-interested or with a broader scope. Rather, each of us is attempting to interpret our mutual commitments (and responsibilities) and *judge*, for reasons, what would implement or further those commitments. Furthermore, our various judgments and reasons are not to be considered as merely inputs to be tallied. Instead, where the system is responsive to reasons, other citizens and our delegates in particular will have considered the reasons for our various interpretations. Hence, my interpretation's lack of success will not be merely a matter of the numbers. My view may not prevail but I can still regard it as a path substantively considered in the process of executing a joint project. Its rejection will rest, at least partly, on reasons. By contrast with purely algorithmic models of tallying, weighing, and outweighing, my perspective may have been potentially influential in virtue of its content and its good faith consideration by my fellows. Participation in a process with this sort of substantive engagement and the possibility of having influence, not just exerting pull, facilitates a sense of being a joint author and not a mere input.

It also matters that the ability to offer one's perspective and reasons and have them considered is a matter of *right* and civic obligation because I am a constitutive, equal participant in the system. This posture of entitlement, and its rationale, is what distinguishes my relation to my democratic government from my relation to Coca-Cola, for instance. Coca-Cola may be very responsive to its workers' or its consumers' desires, but not because it regards its workers or its consumers as having any right to that responsiveness. Rather, Coca-Cola views such responsiveness as more likely to conduce to its profitability. For those reasons, never mind when I disagree, even when Coca-Cola does what I wish and its action is related to the fact of my preferences, I will not regard myself as a co-author of that decision or as though Coca-Cola has represented me. (Similar things may be said even in cases where I am treated less instrumentally, when my opinion is valued in itself, as when my advice is solicited as a consultant.)

So, I've argued that the collective may speak for me when its decisions may be reasonably understood as good faith efforts to express our shared fundamental commitments (e.g., to equality, belonging, and freedom) and when my contributions to the decisions about their expression are treated not merely as a preference to be tallied and weighed, but as a judgment to be considered, as a matter of right, by virtue of my membership in the collective. So long as the underlying commitment may shine through and be recognizable even in the guise of what I take to be flawed conception, I may still reasonably regard the community as speaking for me. For any co-author relationship that takes place in an environment in which there may be significant differences in judgment, I'm not sure what more one could *expect*. These two features, it seems to me, render it coherent to think that the perspective of the private individual and the citizen bear a legible relation to one another.

It will make sense that I have to explain how the community arrived at the policy to critics or to the confused, not as an outside observer, but as a participant in the process. Such explanations are consistent with simultaneously voicing that one thinks the community took a wrong turn. Furthermore, I may feel I have to apologize for it when it is seriously misguided or worse.

The Citizen as Listener-Recipient

From the perspective of citizen *qua* recipient of the message, the lion's share of the work is done by the fact that laws represent commitments that grow out of a collective process of co-authorship and not just cheap talk. Stilz mentions the way in which Goldman Sachs' communiqués "our clients always come first" are hard to take seriously (p. 170). I agree, but that's partly because they are not products of a co-authorship process reflecting thoughtful engagement with contributions by entitlement of clients, employees, or even shareholders. The incredibility of their statements is also partly due to the fact that such communiqués are protected puffery, a regrettable legal doctrine that permits businesses to make general claims about their goods and services without accountability to evidence or sincerity. In other words, they do not reflect true commitments, and we've come to sense that when we step back and reflect on their content and the process and impetuses behind their production.[9]

9. At the same time, we may be taken in by puffery—whether because of wishful thinking or because consumers lack the time for careful reflection on commercial advertisements (and it is unreasonable to expect that attention from them). For these reasons, it is worth

Democratic law, by design, differs. It is the product of a co-authorship process in which all citizens are entitled contributors. Even if the co-authors' input was not homogenous and contained disagreements, the product—the law—both articulates a substantive message and takes the form of a commitment to which it may be held accountable, rather than an empty statement or a trap for the unaware.

The Limits of Unification

So far, I've sketched some conditions under which citizens' dual standpoints may be rendered coherent, if not fully unified. It may be worth acknowledging how these conditions may break down. Of course, some decisions made by a collective cannot be reasonably understood by certain citizens as an expression of their shared commitments. The nature of the values to which we are committed will place limits, often rigorous ones, on what may be decided. There may be room for disagreement about whether to implement universal private insurance, national health care, or a public option as well as whether public insurance may be topped up with private supplements or not.[10] But a shared commitment to equality is inconsistent, for instance, with relations like coverture, indentured servitude, poll taxes, and debtor's prisons. There may be room for disagreement about how to regulate commercial speech and whether and how to recognize intellectual property. But a shared commitment to our equality as free citizens is inconsistent with punishments for disloyal speech or denouncements of dissent as "treasonous."[11]

revisiting this legal protection of insincerity. See my discussion in *Speech Matters: On Lying, Morality, and the Law*, 188–91.

10. See discussion by Robert C. Hughes in "Egalitarian Provision of Necessary Medical Treatment," *Journal of Ethics* 24 (2020): 55–78.

11. Donald Trump often accused dissenters of treason for speaking out against him during his presidency. In one instance he tweeted, "I think what the Democrats are doing

In addition to the objective dimension of interpreting our shared commitments reasonably, a successful system of communicative democratic law will also depend on the achievement of some minimal convergence around our actual understanding of our shared commitments. One might think of this as the collective subjective dimension to meaningful shared commitments. Any recognizable democratic system should expect disagreement about particular policies and decisions that, like most communication, will require interpretation. Some level of disagreement confirms there is a healthy level of engagement aimed at working out what our commitments mean. But deep and persistent disagreement by the citizenry (or a substantial component thereof) with the collective's decisions may underwrite concerns about whether the citizenry's conception bears a sufficiently tenable relation to the fundamental concept or whether the collective's conception is so far afield of the citizenry that there is a flaw in the responsiveness of the co-authorship scheme. In such cases, even if the collective's conception is not objectively flawed, the division between it and (portions of) the citizenry may render the relation of communicative representation strained.

The most troubling sort of disagreement may be when a significant subset of the population regards the enacted conception of our fundamental commitments as not merely wrongheaded-but-recognizable but rather as a *betrayal* of our fundamental commitments, one that is incompatible with regarding the system as still expressing the fundamental concept. Such disagreement drives skepticism that we could

with the Border is TREASONOUS. Their Open Border mindset is putting our Country at risk. Will not let this happen!" Trump, Donald. Twitter Post. April 10, 2019, 7:33 PM. President Trump also called for a treason investigation into Representative Adam Schiff in response to Schiff's speech to Congress about President Trump's phone call with his Ukrainian counterpart. Trump, Donald. Twitter Post. September 30, 2019, 5:12 AM.

be or could continue forward as one community, unified in our commitment to equality and other fundamental values.

I am palpably aware that evidence is accumulating that we may be approaching that sort of crisis in the United States. It may be some comfort that such crises may often, at least initially, be due to flaws in the implementation of the institutional architecture of co-authorship. As Brooks observes, well-operating institutions may inspire and feed a thriving social culture (p. 158). Conversely, breakdowns in the democratic public culture may often have their origins in inadequacies in the institutional structure. In our own case, our burgeoning rifts seem to trace back to massive economic disparities, racial segregation and subordination, and disenfranchisement and other mechanisms that render some populations' voice inaudible, as well as an inequitable campaign system that allows the wealthy a disproportionate voice. Such flaws may drive or exacerbate fissures in the complementary democratic (social) culture, depleting citizens' willingness to participate, cooperate with one another, and compromise in ways appropriate to co-authorship in circumstances of diversity— including listening closely to each other, reading each other charitably, and tempering one's pursuit of personal self-interest with efforts to contribute to and fortify endeavors of mutual interest.

I do not want to place too much weight on the institutional causes of cultural fissures. Furthermore, even if the causes of many cultural fissures that stymie political collaboration trace to institutional failures, that does not mean that institutional reforms will, alone, effect the necessary forms of cultural repair to allow a group to function as a unified community after serious, prolonged lapses in justice and mutual understanding. I agree with Stilz that proper institutional architecture alone cannot always prevent or repair the ruptures that drive secession and other forms of political separation. But, to be plausible, a theory of democracy need not provide the ingredients to guarantee success under all cultural circumstances. Nonetheless, as is probably obvious, I think the ingredients it does provide are powerful and inspirational candidates for building common ground, both with respect to the future and with respect to the responses necessary to past injustice.

Why Must We Craft Respect for Ourselves?

Kolodny correctly surmises that my model of democratic participation involves more than a simple, one-time affirmation of a structure crafted by others (p. 136). One way to put this is that we need to be involved enough and frequently enough so that the metaphor of authors, rather than mere signatories, resonates. Why? Kolodny seems skeptical, insofar as I advocate authorship rather than mere affirmation as necessary for conveying (substantive) mutual respect.

The main argument I offer in the text is one of sincerity, about which I elaborate and supplement here. Our claims to sincerity are more credible to the extent that we craft our sentiments for ourselves, about ourselves, as relevant circumstances arise, rather than relying entirely on mouthing sentiments crafted by others, inspired as responses to the conditions and qualities of other people, at different times, rather than of our own comrades. Crafting our responses for ourselves, innovating for our own time and culture, demonstrates active thought and responsiveness to the complex circumstances that we and our contemporaries face. Brooks aptly notes that "cheap talk may sometimes be reasonably relied upon . . . [W]hen the interest of speaker and addressee are sufficiently aligned, cheap talk could be credible" (p. 164). In this case, however, as I discussed in Chapter 1, the moral interests (and duties) of speaker and addressee are only partially aligned given the competing pulls of our personal moral relations and our moral relations *qua* citizens. Furthermore, our history and our contemporary moral failures offer many addressees reason to be anxious and suspicious. Taking measures to demonstrate sincerity is all the more imperative in contexts such as ours in which our history and the behaviors of some of our contemporaries belie a substantial commitment to equality and freedom and must be repudiated.

Whereas, *mere* adoption or affirmation of the sentiments and commitments drafted by and for others risks an ill-fitted and insufficient response to our own circumstances. Legal transplantation or borrowing, rather than self-crafting, also risks non-transparent, surprising alterations of interpretation as the transplanted law meets a distinct political context.[12] Even if the verbatim commitments that others drafted represent a good fit for our own situation at a particular moment, and even if they are faithfully followed as such, the risk of adopting a prefabricated system of law rather than playing an active role in authoring our own is that the commitments we adopt and the sentiments we voice may have or take on a rote and superficial feel.[13] This in turn undermines their purpose both in the moment and over time. Because these are commitments and institutions that require vigilant maintenance, we will have to engage in active forms

12. Matthew J. Nelson, Aslı Bâli, Hanna Lerner, and David Mednicoff, "From Foreign Text to Local Meaning: The Politics of Religious Exclusion in Transnational Constitutional Borrowing," *Law and Social Inquiry* 45 (2020): 935–964 (discussing India's constitutional provisions protecting religious freedom and their transformation in Pakistan and Malaysia into narrower protections for majority religious groups, as well as the borrowing of France's secular presidential structure and its transformation in Morocco and Iran into support for religious, anti-republican structures).

13. "Passing the peace" in the traditional way may partly convey the relevant sentiment. Perhaps, in many contexts, it is better than congregant "freestyling" (Kolodny, p. 136). Using the traditional words is also a way to collaborate and commune with ancestors and other temporally and spatially dispersed members of one's community. See Samuel Scheffler, "The Normativity of Tradition," ch. 11 of his *Equality and Tradition* (Oxford: Oxford University Press, 2010), 287–311. Yet, these few words are a small part of a larger communicative context. For the exchange to have the meaning it is supposed to, congregants need, in words and actions, to generate a climate and culture in which they enact this mutual regard, or at least enact that it is their true aspiration. I doubt that just these words coupled with adherence to scripted rituals, without any self-generated annotation of one's own connection to them, would suffice.

of interpretation, implementation, and revision to ensure that our understandings of what equality, freedom, and respect require are correct, appropriately tailored to our changing circumstances, and implemented. Much of this work happens directly within overtly political institutions like courts, legislatures, and agencies, but much of it happens on the streets, in the shops, in the schools, and in other facets of the daily lives of citizens. As Brooks observes, many day-to-day, routine interactions generate a culture of common knowledge of our commitments and our relation to them—whether affirming, merely acknowledging, ambivalent, or resistant (p. 149). The vibrancy of this culture and the clarity of our attachment to our core commitments play an integral role in achieving our communicative duties of conveying mutual respect.

In Brooks' terms, more active participation than simple affirmation of others' speech is often necessary to avoid producing mere cheap talk (pp. 149, 160–63). That said, I resist Kolodny's implicit casting of me as a Jeffersonian advocating generationally scheduled revolutions, in contrast with Madison's appreciation for the necessity of building on tradition (p. 144). Indeed, I resist the dichotomy. Crafting and authoring for ourselves need not and could not mean starting from scratch every time. Much of the project of justice is a multigenerational collaboration. Especially for a large-scale society with a corrupt moral history, the sorts of institutions necessary to achieve, maintain, and mutually affirm our status as free equals do not spring up overnight, nor do the changes in culture and ethos necessary to sustain them. We can fulfill our participatory communicative responsibilities and transmit sincerity both through some original drafting tailored to our present circumstances and also through active forms of interpretation and selective curation of the achievements of past generations, including those parts of the Constitution that do encapsulate just commitments, including many elements of the Bill of Rights. Justice Marshall was surely correct that the founders' Constitution was "defective from the start" and also that our Constitution's partial virtue has been in its ability to sustain moral growth and evolution away from its original form toward a more inclusive, egalitarian structure.[14] Not every element of the original Constitution is the enemy of democratic law, but an originalist approach to interpretation surely is, all the more so given the highly imperfect and impartial fealty to equality and inclusion shown by the founders.

Democratic Movements

At the conclusion of Chapter 1, I noted that because a communicative conception of democracy and democratic law is grounded in an inspirational, substantive moral vision, it is better placed to make sense of the fervor of democratic movements than are "desultory," lesser-evil theories of democracy that question democracy's intrinsic value or portray democracy merely as a procedural mechanism of conflict management.

Kolodny registers skepticism—perhaps about whether there is an explanatory gap here at all—but certainly whether a communicative conception could fill it (pp. 144–145). To put it bluntly, Kolodny thinks the rights and benefits associated with democratic constitutions and elections are what motivate people to clamor for democracy, not the ability to form a communicating collective of equals.

I am unsure how large the disagreement is between us. I was certainly not offering a sociological account of how members of

14. Thurgood Marshall, Commentary, "Reflections on the Bicentennial of the United States Constitution," *Harvard Law Review* 101 (1987): 1–5 at 2, 5. Within another speech of Justice Marshall about the ongoing obstacles African Americans encounter, he tells an amusing story about the hazards of having someone else author one's speech that I will not spoil for the reader by summarizing. http://thurgoodmarshall.com/the-equality-speech/.

democratic movements describe or understand their motivations. Certainly, there are a variety of concerns and motivations that propel different participants. Rather, my brief remarks were intended more as a sympathetic theoretical account that could rationalize the urgency, energy, and moral force of these movements. A moral cause, rather than a posture of resignation, seems better suited to that task.

Kolodny's rival explanation, which is also framed in terms of moral values, need not be understood as a competitor. To seek democratic rights is to seek the status and treatment of living in community, together, on an equal basis that operates according to mechanisms of joint, communicative action within a free speech environment that enables joint action to be meaningful, articulate, free, and sincere. In other words, the rights and benefits associated with democratic institutions are not separable from the ability to communicate with one another individually and as a group to affirm, forge, and implement our political, moral commitments to each other.

To be fair, I suspect Kolodny's point is that a fully adequate rationalization may be found by appealing only to the aspect of democratic rights and benefits that contribute to or secure *individual* dignity, status, and welfare, without appealing to the aspect of democratic rights and benefits that I emphasize: namely, those that also enable and express our commitments to morally important relations between us. Plumbing that difference returns us to other, previously explored points of controversy between us about how and whether opportunities for co-authorship and co-determination matter above and beyond their instrumental value in achieving other moral ends. I have little more to add here to that discussion, except perhaps to add that the communicative conception may resonate more with themes of moral solidarity and group identity, whereas more individualist rights and benefits conceptions would seem to support a more pragmatic conception of solidarity.

COMMON LAW AND CONSTITUTIONAL LAW

How Does Common Law Contribute to These Ends?

Among my themes is that the realized value of law differs depending on whether it operates inside or outside democratic settings and whether it is actualizing its function to serve and express our mandatory moral ends. Likewise, we miss something about democracy and democratic relations when we consider them apart from law and, specifically, the contribution that law, whether constitutional, statutory, or common, may make to our interactions with each other, whether on election day, at the workplace, in school, or even in mundane commercial settings that can impact our dignity and standing, such as those determining when and how we will interact in the confined, intimate space of a jet (p. 157, fn. 15).

As Brooks' discussion vividly brings out, one contribution that law may make to democratic relations is to render each of us entitled, in a public way, as part of the common ground, to respectful treatment without regard to any other feature about us. Those specific entitlements in concrete settings and their invocation both manifest democratic values but also instill them into our daily repertoire of habits, expectations, and self-conceptions. The articulate development of many such specific entitlements arises from grappling over how our joint commitments apply in a variety of local controversies. Common law methods and adjudication, I've argued, offer an important forum for the reasoned and articulate resolution of such controversies that, in turn, produce public understandings of these entitlements.

Stilz expresses some surprise that I characterize the common law as a (potentially) democratic institution (pp. 174–175). As she says, the common law harks back to the Middle Ages,[15]

15. See Roscoe Pound, "What Is the Common Law?" *University of Chicago Law Review* 4, no. 2 (1937): 176–89, at 180.

a period many centuries before the emergence of egalitarian or proto-egalitarian participation rights. It isn't produced by the people but by judges. She suggests a dilemma. Either my endorsement of (some) common law decision-making represents a limit on or a mystery about my democratic commitments, or, to the extent that I regard the output of judges as performing communicative labor on our behalf that elaborates upon and implements our values, then it becomes unclear why I stress the importance of equal participation rights within a democratic scheme at all. As she asks, " . . . why couldn't a 'democratic' regime consist *entirely* of inegalitarian representative institutions, so long as ordinary citizens were willing to 'sign on' to these institutions . . . [and they] gave equal weight to everyone's important interests and claims?" (p. 175).

I'll begin to answer this challenge by addressing my defense of the common law and my resistance to Stilz's implicit characterization of the judiciary as an inegalitarian institution in light of its origins and, presumably, in light of its non-electoral decision-making process. In some sense, common law processes predate more democratic settings, but I don't think their value is the same as when they are situated and integrated inside a larger system of democratic law. When the correct components of equal status and co-authorship are in place, the common law may take a democratic form even as it may fail outside that context to achieve its full potential. Similar points may be made about elections, which can be profoundly undemocratic in contexts that fail to treat citizens as equals or that fail to afford them the civil rights necessary for elections to convey their will.

Our common law institutions are more situated in a democratic context than in the Middle Ages, in part because there is a more complete franchise and a greater recognition of the scope of our egalitarian commitments and, in part, because the common law has come to incorporate equity and its more explicitly morally infused concepts.[16] The latter affects the content of the law as well as who has formal standing and other forms of access to courts.[17] Still, the context remains only aspirational given the many shortcomings of our current scheme, including the unjust and undemocratic property regime we still retain.

Nonetheless, as Brooks details, there are a variety of historical and inherent features of the common law that have democratic elements within them, many of which predate the modern, proto-democratic era. The common law aims for a sort of justificatory coherence, which lends itself to progressive forms of immanent critique. As Brooks notes, it has always attended closely to and been responsive to facts on the ground, including the customs and practices developed by discrete groups to regulate their internal conduct (p. 154). This resistance to top-down approaches represents what I consider a democratic attention to input from those most knowledgeable as well as those most affected by decisions. It reflects a *prima facie* stance of trust in their experience. I regard that as a profoundly democratic impulse.

The democratic contribution of the common law within a democratic legal scheme is skewed, I'll remark again, by our defective

16. Procedural codes in the middle of the nineteenth century merged law and equity in most American state courts while the federal court system began recognizing only one merged form of action under the Federal Rules of Civil Procedure in 1938. Thomas O. Main, "Traditional Equity and Contemporary Procedure," *Washington Law Review* 78, no. 2 (2003): 429–514, at 431.

17. The denial of women's voting rights prior to the Nineteenth Amendment was long based on traditional coverture concepts from property law that imagined a woman's interests as being represented through the vote of her husband or father who spoke for the family as one unit. The women's suffrage movement was in essence a challenge to coverture and pushed for the ability for women to have a direct relation with the state. "Just as state courts—and the Unites States Supreme Court—thought it reasonable to prevent wives from bringing tort claims against their husbands . . . so too did members of Congress think it reasonable to deny women the vote in order to preserve marital harmony"; Reva Siegel, "She the People: The Nineteenth Amendment, Sex Equality, Federalism, and the Family," *Harvard Law Review* 115 (2002): 947–1046, at 996.

property relations as well as by other failures to achieve and facilitate equality, access, and inclusion. The fault here does not lie with the basic methodology of the common law. As Brooks notes, common law starts with 'common ground,' refracts it through an independent judiciary's judgment (charged to represent the larger public's perspective), and disseminates the output to interested parties in ways that enrich the common ground of mutual expectations and help it evolve (p. 155). Whether through the rise of arbitration or particular mechanisms of preemption, the undervaluation and abridgment of common law processes represent a loss to *this* aspect of our democratic process. (That said, I agree entirely with Brooks' intimation [p. 158] that the problem is not with preemption per se but with an approach to preemption that is not sensitive to its effect on common law and that is not dictated by the nature of the problem and a demonstrated need for a national solution.)

I resist Stilz's worry that this appreciation of the democratic nature of common law courts is in tension with an insistence on rights of equal participation. To clarify, the defense I am offering is not one that stresses the wisdom of particularly virtuous interpreters of our joint commitments (p. 175). Rather, my stress is on the institution as the forum for an evolving, bottom-up reasoned articulation of the implications of (some of) our joint commitments. There are at least two aspects to its characterization as a bottom-up institution. First, the topics it tackles emerge from taking seriously the claims and arguments of those most affected by issues as they arise, whether or not the affected have the resources or the power to gain the attention of a large population capable of exerting electoral leverage.[18] Tackling small(er) bore issues, one by one, rather than through omnibus legislation, is a way to take individual encounters and the

18. See also Robert C. Hughes, "Responsive Government and Duties of Conscience," *Jurisprudence* 5 (2014): 244–64, at 261.

routines they follow seriously and establish public common ground about them that renders these routines meaningful as representing and enacting public commitments. I mean here to be wholeheartedly endorsing Brooks' observations about the significance of our structured daily encounters (p. 149).

Second, as Brooks emphasizes, significant portions of the common law scrutinize and then incorporate customs developed over time by a larger community. These parts of the common law originate on the ground, in our mutual informal practices and informally developed expectations, which then become public and 'common knowledge' through judicial recognition and articulation (p. 155). I might add that this process also adds a layer of deliberateness. By scrutinizing and then explicitly ratifying (some) of our customary practices, the judiciary draws from the experiences and practices of a popular base and then endorses them as expressions of our joint moral values and commitments—turning customary practices into an articulate, explicit public norm backed by reasons that serve as the public analog of a moral motivation.

Perhaps the more central pillar of my resistance to Stilz's worry is my sense that we should not think that any single democratic institution is a microcosmic model of the whole. Our duty, overall, is to manifest a collective, articulate commitment to certain ends that reflects our sincere endorsement of the appropriate reasons and values. Different parts of the system may contribute to the satisfaction of that duty in different ways, with some parts complementing the contributions of others; in some cases, we might say that some parts temper and check the potential excesses and shortcomings of other parts. Elections offer opportunities for each citizen to participate as an equal, with equal power, simultaneously with others and so for the entire collective (in theory, to have the opportunity) to experience itself in action as each of its co-authors act together, at once. But elections, especially of candidates, are not structured to articulate reasons. (Referenda are more articulate about what the commitment is, should it be made, but not of the reasons for it.) Furthermore, many electoral structures of resolution are prone systematically to be insensitive to persistent needs and perspectives of minorities, particularly entrenched minorities.[19]

Judicial institutions and some other democratic but non-electoral and non-legislative institutions (including Brooks' apt example of notice and comment procedures in administrative law)[20] permit participation by citizens that is dramatically more articulate and, as just argued, produce results that are dramatically more articulate than elections (p. 150). Thus, we might think these institutions complement each other fairly well. It is further worth remembering that their relationship is interactive. Legal recognition of and reasoning about emerging problems may percolate through courts and eventually inform, and often guide, legislative action. Where the issues are quite new, judicial attention may help to flesh out the complexity of the matters and offer a variety of articulate reasoned opinions on their resolution by impartial agents. This may enrich the legislative process. And, of course, judicial missteps on non-constitutional matters may be corrected by legislatures.

If our collective moral ends require the achievement of some outcomes through an articulate and public rendering of our sincere commitment to them, the judiciary plays a unique and necessary role, both in providing a model form of articulate, deliberate voicing of our commitments and by offering a distinctive avenue of access

19. Geographic representation through winner-take-all, single-member districting, for example, can serve to exclude minority groups from adequate representation. See Lani Guinier, "No Two Seats" and "Groups, Representation, and Race Conscious Districting" in her *The Tyranny of the Majority: Fundamental Fairness in Representative Democracy* (New York: The Free Press, 1994), 71–156.

20. See also Blake Emerson, *The Public's Law: Origins and Architecture of Progressive Democracy* (New York: Oxford University Press, 2019), chapter 4, section VII.

to citizens to force some parts of our commitments to be publicly recognized and made concrete.

Balancing and Discretionary State Interests

In Chapter 3, I argued that a democratic legal approach suggests a specific methodology for how states should approach their assertion and pursuit of discretionary interests when they threaten to impinge on important constitutional interests. Where that pursuit compromises liberty interests and demands sacrifices with respect to other mandatory ends, I think it is reasonable to ask that the state agent have shown some commitment to that path such that it can be said, credibly, that the path represents a true interest of the state.

Stilz does not question my claim about the conditions under which a state's asserted interest should be afforded respect. She presses a more fundamental question: Namely, why should we presuppose that states *may* have discretionary interests at all (pp. 176–179)?

ARE THE REQUIREMENTS OF JUSTICE TOO EXPANSIVE TO ADMIT OF DISCRETIONARY INTERESTS?

Working with a specific example from my text, Stilz wonders whether, in application, there is much room for discretionary interests given the expansive requirements of our mandatory commitments. Specifically, as she notes, I criticize the invocation of a state interest in fetal life as a part of the justification of compulsory "education" requirements levied on women seeking abortions. Where it has been invoked, there has been little effort to demonstrate that the state appealing to that interest has any track record of devotion to that interest. In fact, there are many cases in which the state fails to show any sensitivity to this concern outside of the context of coercing women and pressuring them to carry unwanted pregnancies to term.

Where there is no coherent and persistent track record of investment in a discretionary state interest and no strong reason explaining its absence, I argue against reflexively deferring to the state's sudden assertion of it as a reason to curtail an individual's constitutional liberty interest.

Stilz does not question this methodological point. She worries that my criticism suggests that if the state were more consistent in its pursuit of the protection of fetal life, I would have to acknowledge that the state may entertain an interest in protecting fetal life. That recognition and its pursuit would curtail women's reproductive choices and, in turn, their status as equals (p. 178). In effect, the implementation of this discretionary interest would be tantamount to the sorts of nationalist projects that sacrifice the status and autonomous aims of some portions of the population for the sake of achieving larger national goals. But, should I resist this consequence, citing women's equality, it raises the concern that there is little room for a state to develop and pursue discretionary interests.

I reject the dilemma. Granting that there are some conditions under which the state could plausibly assert an interest in embryonic and/or fetal life is not tantamount to imagining that there are circumstances under which these abortion regulations could be constitutional. The constitutional case against waiting periods and the forced, unnecessary education of women seeking timely medical care is overdetermined (even if currently unrecognized by the Supreme Court).[21] Still, one of the many infirmities of the judicial decisions to the contrary has been the reliance on an asserted state interest in embryonic and/or fetal life that is belied by other aspects of state

21. Seana Valentine Shiffrin, "Inducing Moral Deliberation: On the Occasional Virtues of Fog," *Harvard Law Review* 123, no. 5 (2010): 1214–46 at 1235–36; Seana V. Shiffrin, "Advance Directives, Beneficence, and the Permanently Demented," in J. Burley ed., *Dworkin and His Critics with Replies by Dworkin*, (Oxford: Blackwell: 2004), 195–217, at 214, n. 5.

practice and seems pretextual at best. Were this infirmity remedied, however, it would not cure the other lethal defects that beset these regulations.

In other words, I share Stilz's evaluation of these measures and their effect on women. Our agreement on this point, however, would not render a discretionary state interest in the protection of embryonic and/or fetal life empty. Its plausible (and constrained) assertion could, for example, undergird a variety of state policies concerning the use and disposal of fetal remains or the creation, storage, and disposal of frozen embryos that would not impinge on the bodily autonomy of women or their status as equals or insult their deliberative capacities. To be sure, I do not advocate the adoption of this interest, but it isn't obvious that justice precludes its adoption nor that it precludes its rejection.

Stilz may still suspect that its adoption could foster a climate that might be hostile to women's reproductive rights even while grudgingly and formally respecting them. This is a concern worth taking seriously. I think much depends on how the interest is articulated, especially in relation to other state interests. Were it articulated and understood as part of or growing out of a larger interest in protecting a range of forms of biological life, including that of non-human animals and plants, or as a larger interest in the disposition of human remains, I am less sure its expressive force would feel like an indirect targeting of women. Whether these more anodyne framings are available to us in the current political climate, I am less sure, but I do not deny the theoretical permissibility of adopting this interest should circumstances permit it to be articulated without connoting any indirect coercive message.

DOES LIBERALISM *PERMIT THE STATE TO PURSUE DISCRETIONARY INTERESTS*?

Another way (though perhaps not Stilz's) to press the question challenges why the state may pursue interests that are not themselves required by justice. For, it may be thought, the state's remit is both constituted and limited by the demands of justice. Even if no specific requirement of justice is undermined by the pursuit of some discretionary interest, it might be thought that principles of limited government or of inclusivity should limit the state's portfolio to realizing the demands of justice (perhaps expansively understood) and no more.

As I signaled in Chapter 3 (pp. 119–120), I am not tempted by the idea that state action is suspect unless it is *required* by justice. Such a presumption often depends on a crypto-libertarianism that all resources that are not devoted to implementing the demands of justice must belong to individuals. I see no reason to affirm this idea and to judge that liberalism is inconsistent with public, collective projects. It seems convoluted to claim that every public park or museum the state may create and protect is in fact required by some specific requirement of justice, whether for health reasons or minimal education. Principles of limited government and inclusivity do not demand these restrictions or this convolution. State action and inaction must respect individual rights, must generate an environment that makes generous room for the pursuit of a wide range of meaningful autonomous individual and collective projects, must be consistent with the core commitments of egalitarianism (including its message of inclusivity), and must be supported by coherent reasons. Those constraints substantially limit which discretionary moral projects may be undertaken by the state, but they do not make the case for a complete prohibition on discretionary interests.

Furthermore, the crypto-libertarian framing skips over some intermediate ground by assuming that the institutional dichotomy between constitutional interests and state interests maps cleanly onto an exclusive dichotomy between ends mandated by justice and discretionary state interests. In a federal system, an interest may be discretionary *for a particular branch of government* even if pursuit of that interest is itself required by justice and must be pursued by some branch of the system.[22] For instance, it isn't obvious whether criminal law or consumer protection should be state or federal projects or both. Such issues are connected to my earlier discussion of preemption in Chapter 2. One implication of the argument made in Chapter 2 is that we might answer those questions in part by looking to what resources and approaches each agent might take and whether some modalities of legal recognition (e.g., that offered by common law jurisprudence) are best suited to the interest or issue at hand.

Apart from the institutional options presented by divided government, there is also reason to think that some discretionary interests may serve mandatory ends of justice. That is, there may be a plurality of measures that could serve and express our commitment to the demands of justice (or may reasonably be thought to do so). Which ones we pursue may also reflect other interests and commitments we have.

These qualifications aside, I do suggest that it is reasonable for states (whether in the federal sense or in the nation-state sense) to pursue some moral projects that are not clearly demanded by justice, although they often cluster around the periphery of what is demanded by justice. (Notice that if we do not insist that the state's remit is limited to that required by justice, then it becomes less urgent to contest and resolve difficult boundary questions [e.g., whether securing the welfare of non-human animals falls within the demands of *justice* or not?]) Standard examples cite deep investment in the arts beyond what educational justice and

22. In *The Moral Habitat,* Barbara Herman argues that discretion and variation about who bears certain moral loads is often a feature of mandatory, imperfect duties. See Barbara Herman, *The Moral Habitat,* forthcoming (Oxford: Oxford University Press, 2021). Related points concerning imperfect duties and "political questions" in the legal domain are discussed in Lawrence Sager, "Imperfect Constitutional Duties," manuscript on file with author.

cultural preservation require or the establishment of state parks and access to nature that go beyond what health care and environmental justice demand. None of the moral projects I have in mind would defensibly take the shape of the development or endorsement of a national culture that, in content, is a subnational culture that singles out the traditions or beliefs of some specific group as representing the nation or as in some way being the standard. Projects of those sorts are incompatible with what I take to be a mandatory interest of the state: to provide a collective and a place in which its members belong without qualification, are equals, and are treated and communicated to as equals.

Although the sorts of discretionary projects I have in mind are not exclusionary or nationalist in nature, they may indeed ground the collective analog to individuality or individual expression that personal projects ground; that collective analog, in turn, may facilitate the sort of identification with the collective that encourages individuals' investment and participation in their communities. The identification and pursuit of such discretionary interests is an important method by which aspects of the public environment become deliberately chosen and structured, rather than the mere side-product of a variety of uncoordinated activities. Where the pursuit of discretionary interests advances or complements the fulfillment of the demands of justice, their pursuit—because discretionary in some aspect—also conveys deliberation about those demands and sincerity about the collective's endorsement of their importance.

Furthermore, the pursuit of discretionary moral projects provides an opportunity for collectives to develop distinctive identities that in turn provide a focal point for devoted but healthy forms of affiliation, engagement, and investment by the individuals who compose them as well as the development of a sense of responsibility for the collective's decisions. These ties in turn undergird the commitments necessary to participate actively in the project of collective authorship. Some speculative thoughts with both theoretical and empirical underpinnings may underlie my ideas here. They take something like the following shape. Successful forms of democratic participation are sufficiently demanding that they require connection to a particular community and polity. That is, they require partiality of attention. Homogeneity does not inspire attachment, nor is the prospect of achieving homogeneity together, whether at the individual or collective level, an aspiration that distinctive individuals who rightly value their own individuality are likely to achieve or be motivated to achieve. The particularity and individuality of collectives, including governments, thus plays an understandable role in inspiring the sort of partiality that makes collective endeavors thrive.

To be clear, such engagement and investment should not take the form of reflex, patriotic, positive endorsement of each and all of the state's projects, or even any of them. Dissent, criticism, and reflective efforts to improve are healthy forms of engagement. Any expectation to the contrary feeds the sorts of perversions of attachment that Stilz worries about. But, although unanimous endorsement is not a precondition for a state's pursuing a discretionary interest, it is hard to imagine how Stilz's hypothetical of the state adopting a discretionary interest that no one endorses could arise within a democratically responsive state of the sort I am defending.

The arts and nature examples could be used for further illustration, but, rather than developing them further, I'll elaborate on the ones discussed in Chapter 3. There may be a demand of justice that we are permitted to end our own lives and receive assistance if necessary, as when a disability precludes administering life-ending medication to oneself. I think it less obvious that we have a broad right of justice that we be entitled to receive help where that help isn't necessary but where assistance would serve patients' interests in convenience or comfort. A broad right to assistance would facilitate individual autonomy but some may worry that it also raises larger risks of coercion and a culture that encourages death as a solution to infirmity, discourages medical expenditures on the elderly, or otherwise undervalues resistance to the disabilities posed by old age. At least within an environment in which economic and cultural pressures render those concerns colorable, it seems permissible for a state to adopt a posture of facilitating patient autonomy by enacting the broad right or, instead, to adopt the opposite posture involving a risk-averse approach to coercion and to potential corporate pressures to minimize eldercare.

Or, to revisit the general theme behind the lawyer licensing example (pp. 108–109), justice may require a fair amount of regulation to ensure fairness and safety in the provision of services, goods, food, and drugs. But, beyond what is required, there are choices to make. A more permissive regulatory scheme may reflect an interest in cultivating a culture that tilts toward experimentation, even in the realm of expertise, and in encouraging consumer education and self-reliance. A more expansive regulatory scheme may reflect and express an interest in safety and in freeing citizens' time and attention for other pursuits. I think either path, so motivated, may be permissible from the standpoint of justice. At the same time, as I argued in Chapter 3, when their pursuit abuts against individual constitutional interests, mutual adjustment and accommodation between discretionary interests and constitutional interests make sense only where the state has a demonstrable commitment to this interest. That requirement represents a commitment to limited government but it takes a more nuanced form than a more full-blown skepticism toward discretionary interests.

None of these discretionary interests seems especially prone to blossom into proto-nationalism or other forms of exclusion. On the other hand, they may not seem like the most promising candidates for inspiring citizen affiliation and action. Licensing requirements may seem more like wonk territory than the gateway to citizen activism. Perhaps arts and parks can do so, but perhaps they are also rare cases. These concerns are fair enough, but I don't mean to rest much on the idea that *any specific* discretionary interests activate engagement. Rather, their pursuit in a coherent, reasoned fashion can contribute to a structured, deliberate culture that gives a polity a distinctive feel which in turn grounds the familiar feelings of belonging and affiliation.

We cannot always describe exactly what features compel these feelings of attachment, and we do not always endorse each of the features of those cultures to which we are attached. Nonetheless, their grounding seems to me connected to their distinctiveness, and the justification for acting on that attachment seems stronger when the factors giving rise to that distinctiveness grow out of coherently pursued, deliberate ends.

Given Stilz's important underlying caution about the structures and dynamics of attachment and affiliation harboring the potential to transform into virulent forms of nationalism, these ends must be carefully restricted to ensure their capability with lexically prior commitments of equality, freedom, and inclusion.

Stilz's reminders are unfortunately timely. Our political system is both under threat and being abused to achieve evil ends, including the vilification of refugees as a misguided technique of stoking attachment and the caging of children as a deliberate tactic of terror. Hence, it is admittedly fraught at this juncture to write about the benefits of discretionary state interests and the distinctive identity of particular polities, much less the promise of democracy and the structures that lend to achieving its potential. Persisting in the articulation of abstract ideals, the realization of which seems more than distant, can feel precious. Yet resistance can proceed at many different levels, just as authoritarians use force, fraud, and rhetoric in tandem. In that vein, it still seems important to remind ourselves of the richness of democracy's ambitions and requirements as against more pallid conceptions, if only to counter the arguments that would-be populist dictators' actions are democratically sanctioned, whether such arguments are offered in justification or as a cautionary tale about the paradox of democracy.

INDEX

For the benefit of digital users, indexed terms that span two pages (e.g., 52–53) may, on occasion, appear on only one of those pages.